MORE PRAISE FOR
COUNTDOWN 1945

"A compelling and highly readable account of one of the most fateful decisions in American history."

—**Gregg Herken,** *The Washington Post*

"Brisk, naturally propulsive . . . But *Countdown 1945* also reflects the rigor and fealty to facts that have distinguished Wallace."

—*Time*

"Everyone knows the outcome, yet Wallace manages to make this carefully researched account of the months before Hiroshima read like a tense thriller."

—**Bethanne Patrick,** *The Washington Post*

"Gripping . . . *Countdown 1945* is such a good read, crammed with information, fleshed out with vivid anecdotes, and told in a narrative that never flags."

—*The Washington Times*

"There is no finer journalist in America today than Chris Wallace and no more dramatic story in American history than Truman's decision to drop the atomic bomb. *Countdown 1945* moves at a breakneck pace and even though you know the ending, you can't put it down. This is the most exciting book I've read all year."

—**Admiral William H. McRaven (U.S. Navy Retired),**
#1 *New York Times* **bestselling author of**
Make Your Bed **and** *Sea Stories*

"As a reporter and a news anchor, Chris has been at the center of the biggest news stories of the last four decades. He's given perspective and insight when we've needed it most. Now, his same attention to detail fills the pages of *Countdown 1945*, the story of arguably the most consequential event in the U.S. since the Civil War. It's a stunning piece of work."

—**George Clooney**

"*Countdown 1945* goes beyond our history lessons. It tells moving, personal stories of Americans who played pivotal roles in one of our most important moments as a nation. From scientists at the top of their field, to heroic members of our military, to everyday Americans, it's an incredible story of how our country came together with a determined spirit to end a war and save countless lives."

—**Ambassador Nikki Haley,** *New York Times*
bestselling author of *With All Due Respect:*
Defending America with Grit and Grace

"*Countdown 1945* is a real-life thriller about one of the most important events of the twentieth century. Veteran journalist Chris Wallace takes readers behind the scenes and brings to life the compelling story of the 116 days leading up to Hiroshima. Written like a spy novel, this is a must-read history that will educate and keep you turning the pages. Not to be missed!"

—**Daniel Silva, #1** *New York Times* **bestselling**
author of *The New Girl*

"Vivid, fast-paced, and wide-ranging, *Countdown 1945* is a fine telling of one of the twentieth century's most remarkable tales—how the United States designed, built, delivered, and detonated the first two atomic bombs over Japan."

—**Rick Atkinson, #1** *New York Times* **bestselling author**
of *An Army at Dawn* **and** *The British Are Coming*

COUNTDOWN 1945

THE EXTRAORDINARY STORY
OF THE ATOMIC BOMB AND THE 116 DAYS
THAT CHANGED THE WORLD

CHRIS WALLACE

WITH MITCH WEISS

AVID READER PRESS

NEW YORK   LONDON   TORONTO   SYDNEY   NEW DELHI

AVID READER PRESS
An Imprint of Simon & Schuster, Inc.
1230 Avenue of the Americas
New York, NY 10020

First Avid Reader Press trade paperback edition May 2021

AVID READER PRESS and colophon are trademarks of Simon & Schuster, Inc.

For information about special discounts for bulk purchases, please contact Simon &
Schuster Special Sales at 1-866-506-1949 or business@simonandschuster.com.

The Simon & Schuster Speakers Bureau can bring authors to your live event. For
more information or to book an event, contact the Simon & Schuster Speakers
Bureau at 1-866-248-3049 or visit our website at www.simonspeakers.com.

Interior design by Ruth Lee-Mui

Manufactured in the United States of America

1   3   5   7   9   10   8   6   4   2

Library of Congress Cataloging-in-Publication Data has been applied for.

ISBN 978-1-9821-4334-3
ISBN 978-1-9821-4335-0 (pbk)
ISBN 978-1-9821-4336-7 (ebook)

To Lorraine
You are the best part of any adventure

COUNTDOWN:

116 DAYS

April 12, 1945
Washington, D.C.

Harry Truman needed a drink. It was his eighty-second day as vice president. And as usual, he spent the afternoon in the Senate chamber, this time overseeing a debate about a water treaty with Mexico. As senators droned on, his mind wandered to his mother and sister, who still lived near the old Truman family farm back in Grandview, Missouri. Truman pulled out some paper and a pen, even though he was seated at his elevated desk on the rostrum in the Senate chamber.

"Dear Mamma and Mary," he wrote, "a windy Senator from Wisconsin" was going on and on about "a subject with which he is in no way familiar." It was part of Truman's job as president of the Senate to officiate over sessions like this. But he couldn't wait for it to end. There was someplace else he wanted to be. He had no idea his life was about to change forever.

Now, just before 5:00 p.m., the Senate mercifully recessed for the day. Truman started walking across the Capitol by himself, without his Secret Service detail—through the Senate side, across the Capitol Rotunda, then Statuary Hall, and onto the House side. Dressed smartly as usual, in a double-breasted gray suit, with a white handkerchief and a dark polka-dot bow tie, Truman was always in a hurry. And part of that was he walked fast.

He headed from the main public floor of the Capitol down to the ground floor, downstairs to House Speaker Sam Rayburn's private hideaway, Room 9, which was known as the "Board of Education." It was the most exclusive room in the Capitol—entry by Rayburn's personal invitation only. Most afternoons, members of Congress met here after official business hours to discuss strategy, exchange gossip, and "strike one for liberty," enjoying a drink, or two. Truman was a regular. And his drink of choice was bourbon and branch water.

The Board of Education was a classic Capitol refuge, some twenty feet in length and filled with big leather chairs, a couch, and a long mahogany desk that doubled as a liquor cabinet. The only dissonant note was an ornate painted ceiling, festooned with birds and animals and plants. Rayburn had a mural with a Texas "lone star" added at one end of the room.

When Truman arrived, Rayburn—"Mr. Sam"—told him that the White House was looking for him. "Steve Early wants you to call him right away," Rayburn said, referring to President Roosevelt's longtime secretary. Truman fixed himself a drink, then sat down and dialed the White House switchboard, National 1414.

"This is the VP," Truman said.

When Early got on the line, he was brief and direct. His voice was tense. He told Truman to get to the White House "as quickly and quietly" as he could, and to come through the main Pennsylvania Avenue entrance. Rayburn was watching Truman, who he always thought was kind of pale. Now he "got a little paler."

"Jesus Christ and General Jackson," Truman exclaimed as he hung up the phone, too shocked to even hide it. He tried to remain calm. He told the others in the room he had to go to the White House on "a special call." He immediately stood up, walked to the door, and put his hand on the knob, then stopped and turned. "Boys, this is in this room. Something must have happened."

Truman closed the door firmly behind him, then broke into a full run, this time through the now almost-empty Capitol. His footsteps echoed around the marble corridors as he dashed past statues of generals and politicians, past the Senate barbershop, and up the stairs to his vice presidential office. He was out of breath. He grabbed his hat and told his staff he was headed to the White House, but to say nothing about it. He didn't have time to explain. And anyway, he really didn't know much more than that.

Outside, it was raining. Truman got into his official black Mercury car and gave instructions to his driver, Tom Harty. Once again, he left his Secret Service detail behind. Between the weather and traffic, it took Truman more than ten minutes to get to the White House. And all that time, he wondered what was going on.

President Roosevelt was supposed to be in Warm Springs, Georgia, where he had spent the past two weeks recovering from exhaustion after a wartime summit in Yalta with British prime minister Winston Churchill and Soviet premier Joseph Stalin.

Maybe FDR had returned to Washington. His old friend Julius Atwood, a retired Episcopal bishop, had been buried in Washington earlier in the day. Had the president attended the ceremony and now wanted to see Truman? But since becoming vice president almost three months ago, he had met privately with Roosevelt only twice. Why now?

At 5:25, Truman's car turned off Pennsylvania Avenue, passed through the Northwest Gate, and drove up under the North Portico of the White House. At the front door Truman was met by ushers, who took his hat and directed him to the president's small oak-paneled elevator.

First Lady Eleanor Roosevelt was waiting for him in her private study on the second floor, along with her daughter and son-in-law, Anna and Lieutenant Colonel John Boettiger, and Steve Early. The two women were dressed in black.

The first lady walked up to Truman, put her arm on his shoulder, and said, "Harry, the president is dead."

Truman was too stunned to speak. He had hurried to the White House to see the president. Now, here he was, suddenly finding out he was the president.

It took him a moment to steady himself. He asked Mrs. Roosevelt, "Is there anything I can do for you?"

"Is there anything we can do for you?" she replied. "For you are the one in trouble now."

Minutes later, at 5:47, the news bulletin flashed across the country and the world: FDR, the man who led the nation over the past twelve years, through the Depression and Pearl Harbor and now to the verge of victory in Europe in the Second World War, had died of a cerebral hemorrhage at the age of sixty-three.

The White House, mostly deserted with Roosevelt away, suddenly sprang into motion. A meeting of the Cabinet was called for 6:15. Truman directed that congressional leaders be asked to attend. And Harlan Stone, chief justice of the United States, was summoned to the White House to administer the oath of office. There was one more thing Truman needed to do.

At 6:00, he called his wife, Bess, at their modest two-bedroom apartment up Connecticut Avenue. His daughter, Margaret, answered the phone. She hadn't heard the news yet, and she started kidding around with him as usual. He cut her off and told her to put her mother on the line.

Truman normally shared everything with Bess. But there was no time for that now. He told her President Roosevelt was dead, and he was sending a car for her, Margaret, and his mother-in-law, Madge Wallace, who lived with the family. He wanted them by his side when he took the oath of office.

Truman hung up the phone. He could tell that the conversation had shaken his wife. Ever since he'd accepted the nomination for vice president the previous summer, he knew this was her greatest fear—that FDR would not live out his fourth term. Now he and his family had been thrust into the position she dreaded.

When Truman arrived at the Cabinet Room, he was the first one there. He sat at the big table. Soon the room filled around him. One Roosevelt staffer later described Truman looking "like a little man as he sat waiting in a huge leather chair." But when all the Cabinet officials who were in Washington arrived, Truman stood. "I want every one of you to stay and carry on," he told them, "and I want to do everything just the way President Roosevelt wanted it."

There was a delay as they waited for the chief justice to arrive. And Truman's family had to get through a large crowd that had gathered outside their apartment building. Staffers also scurried to locate a Bible, finally finding a Gideon in the desk of the White House chief usher.

At 7:09, Truman and Chief Justice Stone stood in front of the mantel at the end of the Cabinet Room, with Truman's family and top officials forming a semicircle behind them. The chief justice started the oath. "I, Harry Shipp Truman," he said, assuming Truman's middle initial *S* came from his father's family, when in fact it stood for nothing.

"I, Harry S Truman," he responded, correcting the chief justice.

That wasn't the only glitch. After Truman completed the oath, the chief justice told him that he'd held the Bible in his left hand, but placed his right hand on top of it. So they had to do it again, this time with the new president raising his right hand. When the swearing-in was finally over, Truman kissed the Bible, then turned to kiss his wife and daughter.

After the oath, Truman talked briefly to his Cabinet. He repeated his intention to pursue Roosevelt's agenda. He said he always wanted their

Harry Truman being sworn in as president on April 12, 1945.

candid advice, but made it clear he would make the final decisions. And once he made them, he expected their full support.

As the meeting broke up and the other officials went home for the night, one man stayed behind: Henry Stimson, the secretary of war. He asked to speak to the new president alone "about a most urgent matter."

At age seventy-seven, Stimson was a legendary figure who had served five presidents. Truman would be his sixth. Sitting with the new president, Stimson said he'd keep it short. The subject was complicated, and he'd provide more detail later. But he wanted Truman to know about "an immense project that was underway" to develop "a new explosive of almost unbelievable destructive power." The project was so secret—and so potentially dangerous—only a handful of people knew about it. Stimson said he would brief Truman about it fully after the president had a few days to settle in.

That was all. Stimson's short, mysterious briefing left Truman puzzled. But he was trying to process so much: FDR's death, the nation's reaction, his sudden responsibility for leading the war effort in both Europe and the Pacific. Stimson's "project" was one more job that was now his. And he had no idea what it really amounted to. It was a day, he later said, when "the world fell in on me."

"I decided the best thing to do was to go home and get as much rest as possible and face the music," he wrote in his diary.

COUNTDOWN:
113 DAYS

April 15, 1945
Los Alamos, New Mexico

It was supposed to be spring. But fresh snow crunched underfoot as J. Robert Oppenheimer trotted across the top-secret Army compound in the New Mexico mesa. He headed straight across the snow to the makeshift movie theater.

Oppenheimer was the scientific director of the Manhattan Project, America's massive secret effort to develop an atomic bomb. On any other morning, he'd be juggling a thousand different papers in his office: reading progress reports, writing memos, or returning urgent telephone calls from Washington. While the country outside fought World War II, Oppenheimer and his corps of scientists inside the fenced-off installation focused all their energy and expertise on "the gadget," a terrifying new weapon of mass destruction.

But not this Sunday morning. Today, he'd gathered the grief-stricken scientists, military men, support staff, and families living in the secret city of Los Alamos for a memorial service for President Roosevelt. He had never delivered a eulogy before.

A brilliant theoretical physicist, Oppenheimer had no trouble telling his peers or graduate students at the nation's top universities about complicated scientific theories that explained how the universe worked. He was fluent in six languages and well versed in classical literature and Eastern philosophy. He learned Sanskrit just so he could read the *Bhagavad Gita*, a Hindu devotional poem, in its original language.

Three days had passed since President Roosevelt died at a spa in Georgia. Oppenheimer had spent most of that time struggling to find the right words to memorialize him.

He felt the loss in a deeply personal way. The president guided the United States through some of its darkest hours. He'd been in the White House since 1933, stepping into the job in the depths of the Great Depression. He worked hard to restore the faith and confidence of the American people with ambitious programs designed to turn around the economy.

The nation turned to Roosevelt again when Japanese forces attacked the U.S. naval base at Pearl Harbor, Hawaii, on December 7, 1941. Most of America learned of the strike when a news bulletin interrupted their Sunday afternoon radio programs. "Japan?" People shook their heads in disbelief and adjusted their radios. Was it true? Could it be possible? The following day, Roosevelt addressed Congress and the nation via radio in a speech that would resonate through the years. The attack was "unprovoked" and "dastardly," he said. December 7, 1941, was "a date which will live in infamy."

The president made a promise to the American people. "No matter how long it may take us to overcome this premeditated invasion," he thundered, "the American people in their righteous might will win through to absolute victory."

Congress declared war on Japan. Four days later, Germany declared war on the United States. The nation mobilized. For many Americans, FDR was the only commander in chief they had ever known. He was elected president four times, and almost three and a half years into World War II, just as the Allies neared victory in Europe—and the war in the Pacific reached a bloody climax—Roosevelt had suddenly died.

Now a gust of uncertainty rattled the ranks of the Manhattan Project. Years earlier, it was Roosevelt who authorized the atomic bomb research and development project, bringing together the brightest scientific minds for an operation he hoped would one day end the war. FDR was instrumental in getting major corporations—DuPont, Standard Oil, Monsanto, and Union Carbide—to design, manufacture, and operate revolutionary new equipment and plants to help build the weapon. Academic and industrial laboratories offered up their best, most creative scientists. It was costly, chancy, and cloaked in total secrecy.

No one knew for sure where, or whether, Harry Truman would take the project. As physicist Philip Morrison recalled, "Now, there was no one we knew at the top."

The team at Los Alamos turned to Oppenheimer for answers. He was a genius of theoretical physics, but his gifts were not limited to science. His sharp mind could penetrate to the heart of any problem and deliver clear, concise solutions. His colleagues described him as the fastest thinker they'd ever met. At this moment, that clarity was needed more than ever.

Oppenheimer was six feet tall and weighed about 135 pounds, slender to the point of emaciation. But he dressed like a dandy in stylishly cut gray suits, blue shirts and ties, brightly shined shoes, and porkpie hats. With a cigarette dangling from his lower lip, bright blue eyes, and piercing gaze, he attracted women and intimidated men. "Oppie" was a rakish and self-assured character, as comfortable at a cocktail reception as he was in the lecture hall.

The son of a German immigrant who had made a fortune importing textiles in New York City, Oppenheimer was expected to succeed, and he didn't disappoint. He graduated summa cum laude from Harvard University in just three years. At age twenty-two, he was awarded a PhD in physics from the University of Göttingen in Germany, where he studied under the acclaimed physicist Max Born. Within a few years, Oppenheimer landed prestigious teaching jobs at both the University of California, Berkeley, and the California Institute of Technology in Pasadena. He split his time between schools; one semester at Berkeley, the next in Pasadena. Unlike most professors of that time, he was flamboyant, a bohemian Method actor who lectured with infectious enthusiasm. Without notes, he weaved poetry and literature through lofty mathematical concepts. He made it clear that the most important scientific questions were still unanswered and challenged his students to plumb the mysteries. As one colleague recalled, Oppenheimer brought a "degree of sophistication in physics previously unknown in the United States."

Students were fascinated and inspired. They followed the professor back and forth from Berkeley to Pasadena, captivated by his eccentricities and zest for life, his appetite for rare steaks, stiff martinis, spicy foods, and cigarettes. An accomplished horseback rider and sailor, he seemed to have a friend around every corner.

But Oppenheimer had a dark side, too. His brilliance could be clouded by melancholy and peevishness. He didn't tolerate small talk. He'd interrupt friends in midsentence, especially if he thought the subject wasn't intellectually stimulating. Students who asked mundane questions were subjected to public humiliation. A longtime colleague described Oppenheimer as "dismissive to the point of rudeness."

In 1942, when Oppenheimer was appointed to lead the Manhattan Project, some of his colleagues questioned his temperament and lack of executive experience, saying he couldn't "manage a hamburger stand." He'd have to bridge the gap between innovative, independent academia and the rigid structure of the military.

Oppenheimer charged into the job, which he viewed as the most efficient means of ending the war. He persuaded world-renowned scientists to uproot their families and join him at the secret atomic weapons laboratory in Los Alamos, a remote area surrounded by deep canyons and high peaks at the southernmost tip of the Rocky Mountains. Oppenheimer worked well with military leaders, including his counterpart, General Leslie R. Groves.

Over time, Oppenheimer morphed into a marvelously efficient and charismatic administrator, his friends and colleagues said. Some of the greatest physicists in the world were assembled at Los Alamos, including six Nobel Prize winners. Their egos were immense, but somehow, Oppie made it all work. One colleague said Oppenheimer was very close to being indispensable.

By April 1945, Oppenheimer thoroughly embodied his role as the project's scientific director. He was just forty years old. He lived with his wife, Kitty, and two small children in a little cabin in a secluded part of Los Alamos. The once-eccentric professor now threw dinner parties for visiting scientists and colleagues at his cabin. The fun started with dry martinis and spilled out onto the front yard as the sun went down.

Los Alamos had grown from a few hundred people to eight thousand scientists and military personnel and their families. The perimeter of the 54,000-acre site—"the Hill"—was surrounded by a ten-foot fence topped with barbed wire. Inside, another fence cordoned off the technical area, where only those with the highest security clearance could go. Oppenheimer's office was there, as well as the vast laboratories used for bomb research. Like a mayor, Oppenheimer often waved and greeted people as he strolled the treeless streets of Los Alamos. He was always poised and gracious, never at a loss for words.

A party at Los Alamos in 1944 (from left to right): Dorothy McKibbin, who was responsible for welcoming new recruits at the secret city; J. Robert Oppenheimer, the Manhattan Project's scientific director; and Victor Weisskopf, a nuclear physicist.

But on April 12, the news of the president's death was a terrible shock. Thomas O. Jones saw a more subdued Oppenheimer that day, a man grappling with profound loss.

An intelligence officer, Jones had his office in a building connected to Oppenheimer's by an enclosed walkway. He was getting ready to leave when his telephone rang. Roosevelt was dead, the caller said. Jones didn't believe it at first.

"Are you sure?" he asked.

The caller repeated the message. Jones sat in stunned silence. He knew he had to tell the others. The base was shut off from the world. There were no outside radio stations or newspapers. The nearest town was Santa Fe, some thirty-five miles away. Los Alamos, according to maps, didn't exist. So most people here would have to get the bad news over a tech area loudspeaker.

Jones decided to tell Oppenheimer. He bolted from his office to the walkway between the buildings. Halfway across, he glimpsed a familiar figure heading toward him.

Oppenheimer already knew, but couldn't believe it. "Is it true?" Oppenheimer asked.

"Yes, Oppie," Jones said softly.

It only confirmed what Oppenheimer expected to hear.

The workers in the tech area learned about the president's death simultaneously. Everything stopped. Scientists turned to each other. Did you hear that? they asked. Some were shocked into silence. Others cried. They spilled out of the laboratories into the hallways and the steps outside. No one wanted to be alone.

In the walkway, Jones could see that Oppenheimer was visibly shaken, his face pale and grim. They talked about the president, how he'd saved the nation. Oppenheimer praised the good Roosevelt had done, his intelligence and "magnetic personality."

In reality, Oppenheimer and Roosevelt never talked much. They kept a respectful distance, and mostly communicated through intermediaries.

Whenever FDR had the chance, he praised Oppie for the "highly important" work he was overseeing at the Los Alamos Weapons Research and Design Lab.

In a June 29, 1943, letter to Oppenheimer, Roosevelt tried to smooth over the growing antagonism between scientists and General Groves, the project's hard-driving military leader. Roosevelt had learned that some scientists were starting to snap under the pressure of what they considered impossible deadlines. They resented living under heavy guard. Some doubted the bomb could ever be built and questioned the wisdom of working with such dangerous material.

Roosevelt's letter acknowledged Oppenheimer as the leader of an elite group of scientists operating under strict security and under "very special restrictions." The president appealed to Oppenheimer to convince his team the restrictions were necessary. He asked him to convey FDR's appreciation for their hard work and "personal sacrifices."

"I am sure we can rely on their continued wholehearted and unselfish labors. Whatever the enemy may be planning, American science will be equal to the challenge," Roosevelt wrote.

Now, as Oppenheimer prepared for the memorial service, he knew some of his scientists still harbored doubts about the project to develop an atomic bomb. Lately, influential physicists like Leo Szilard were expressing moral opposition to using it in war. Szilard started a petition drive, collecting the names of fellow scientists who felt the same.

But for just this one day, Oppenheimer wanted to put those concerns aside. He stayed up late the night before to finish his eulogy. In the morning he saw the snow blanketing his garden, the streets, the entire town. Morrison, the physicist, remembered the snow as a "gesture of consolation."

The normally busy streets were quiet. Like most of America, Los Alamos was in mourning. The pavement outside the theater was bare, the snow trampled by the feet of hundreds waiting inside. Jones met Oppie at the door and ushered him in. The boss left behind his trademark porkpie hat.

THE WHITE HOUSE
WASHINGTON

June 29, 1943

Secret

My dear Dr. Oppenheimer:

       I have recently reviewed with Dr. Bush the highly important and secret program of research, development and manufacture with which you are familiar. I was very glad to hear of the excellent work which is being done in a number of places in this country under the immediate supervision of General L. R. Groves and the general direction of the Committee of which Dr. Bush is Chairman. The successful solution of the problem is of the utmost importance to the national safety, and I am confident that the work will be completed in as short a time as possible as the result of the wholehearted cooperation of all concerned.

       I am writing to you as the leader of one group which is to play a vital role in the months ahead. I know that you and your colleagues are working on a hazardous matter under unusual circumstances. The fact that the outcome of your labors is of such great significance to the nation requires that this program be even more drastically guarded than other highly secret war developments. I have therefore given directions that every precaution be taken to insure the security of your project and feel sure that those in charge will see that these orders are carried out. You are fully aware of the reasons why your own endeavors and those of your associates must be circumscribed by very special restrictions. Nevertheless, I wish you would express to the scientists assembled with you my deep appreciation of their willingness to undertake the tasks which lie before them in spite of the dangers and the personal sacrifices. I am sure we can rely on their continued wholehearted and unselfish labors. Whatever the enemy may be planning, American science will be equal to the challenge. With this thought in mind, I send this note of confidence and appreciation.

President Franklin D. Roosevelt's letter to J. Robert Oppenheimer, June 29, 1943.

Oppenheimer walked slowly to the stage, and the people, crowded into rows of wooden benches, fell silent. For some who had known Oppie for years, he looked a little older than the brash young physicist who had been such a star in California. Many of the people inside, like Jones and Morrison, wondered if this meant the end of the entire project.

Oppenheimer stood onstage against the backdrop of a lowered American flag and waited a moment. Then, in a voice no louder than a whisper, he began, delivering a eulogy designed to reassure the thousands working at Los Alamos.

"When, three days ago, the world had word of the death of President Roosevelt, many wept who are unaccustomed to tears, many men and women little enough accustomed to prayer, prayed to God. Many of us looked with deep trouble to the future; many of us felt less certain that our works would be a good end; all of us were reminded how precious a thing human greatness is.

"We have been living through years of great evil, and of great terror. Roosevelt has been our president, our commander in chief and, in an old, unperverted sense, our leader. All over the world men have looked to him for guidance, and have seen symbolized in him their hope that the evils of this time would not be repeated; that the terrible sacrifices which have been made, and those that are still to be made, would lead to a world more fit for human habitation. It is in such times of evil that men recognize their helplessness and their profound dependence. One is reminded of medieval days when the death of a good and wise and just king plunged his country into despair and mourning."

Then Oppenheimer turned to the text that brought him so much comfort over the years.

"In the Hindu scripture, in the *Bhagavad Gita*, it says 'Man is a creature whose substance is faith. What his faith is, he is.' The faith of Roosevelt is one that is shared by millions of men and women in every country of the world. For this reason it is possible to maintain the hope, for this reason it is right that we should dedicate ourselves to the hope that his good works will not have ended with his death."

Afterward, the scientists and their families stood, heads bowed and silent, too saddened to talk.

While it was unclear how Truman would handle the Manhattan Project, Oppenheimer tried to remain optimistic. After the service, he turned to a friend, David Hawkins, a physicist.

"Roosevelt was a great architect," Oppenheimer said. "Perhaps Truman will be a good carpenter."

But Oppenheimer was not sure. He only knew that after spending years of intense research and billions in taxpayer dollars, the scientists of Los Alamos had better deliver the goods, and soon.

COUNTDOWN:
105 DAYS

April 23, 1945
Wendover, Utah

Colonel Paul Tibbets Jr. grimaced and held the telephone handset away from his ear while a Salt Lake City policeman bellowed down the line. Over the weekend, some of the colonel's airmen had blown into the city like cowboys at the end of a cattle drive, and the policeman rattled off a long list of trouble. Speeding, running red lights, whooping it up at the Hotel Utah with whiskey and wild women, brawling with the local roughnecks.

Tibbets sighed. He and his men had been bottled up at this desert airstrip for way too long. It was time for the 509th Composite Group to leave Wendover Airfield and start making some real trouble for real enemies.

He told the policeman it wouldn't be long before they were out of his hair and out of town. Jailing his highly trained men over a weekend's mischief would solve nothing, and it would waste the nation's investment.

The policeman had to agree. After a few more soothing words, Tibbets hung up the phone.

For months, the colonel had driven his men relentlessly. They didn't know the details. His men only knew they had been training for a secret bombing mission that could end the war. Now they were ready, but what about the bomb? That was his only question. He'd been back and forth to Los Alamos, and was told that the scientists were still "tinkering" with it.

They were more concerned with producing the perfect weapon, instead of being satisfied with the one they had. It seemed they were forever improving the design, running more tests, making endless changes before they'd let Tibbets actually drop the damn thing. And of course, there were still questions about whether the weapon would work.

Tibbets wasn't only dealing with the cops, or the scientists at Los Alamos. He was running a complex secret military operation of his own here in Utah, involving hundreds of pilots, navigators, bombardiers, and support personnel. Only he and a handful of people knew what it was all about. And every problem in the 509th ended up on his desk.

His wife, Lucy, and two young children lived in a little house near the airfield, but he rarely spent time there. He was so consumed with the mission that playing with his kids and talking into the night with his wife had become sweet memories. That diligence was one reason why his commanders picked him for the job. He was organized, tough, and had joined the Army Air Corps years before the war started. But most important, he was "the best damn pilot" in the Army, as one general put it. His cockpit expertise was vital to the dangerous assignment. The pilot who ultimately flew the mission would not only have to drop the atomic bomb accurately. He'd then need to execute perfect turns and dives to avoid the bomb's blast. Otherwise, the aftershocks could blow the plane to pieces.

If anyone could do it, Tibbets could. He was a confident, handsome guy with a slight cleft in his chin. But Tibbets was no Hollywood character. He was a seasoned bomber pilot who thrived under pressure. Tibbets shepherded generals Dwight Eisenhower and Mark Clark on missions in North Africa in 1942 and 1943. Once, while he was flying Clark to Algiers, he landed flawlessly while under fire from antiaircraft shells and machine guns.

Tibbets flew dozens of combat bombing missions over North Africa and Germany, then was deployed to the United States to take charge of the B-29 Superfortress flight-testing program. The B-29 was designed by Boeing to operate faster, at higher altitudes, and with heavier bomb loads than its predecessor, the B-17 Flying Fortress. The B-29 was able to fly more than 3,000 miles—just what the U.S. military needed as it moved closer to Japan. But the new bomber killed its first test pilot and was thought by some to be too dangerous to fly.

Tibbets proved fearless, and he expected the same from his fellow pilots. A decisive commander, Tibbets was a perfectionist, which irritated some of his colleagues. But Tibbets didn't care. He was in charge, so they were doing things his way—"the right way."

He was born in Quincy, Illinois, the son of a former World War I infantry captain who afterward ran a wholesale candy business. That would lead, indirectly, to Paul's passion. He took his first flight in a biplane at age twelve, part of a promotion for the new Baby Ruth candy bar. His father was the area distributor for the product, and a local pilot was hired to drop Baby Ruths over a large gathering of people.

When the boy heard about the stunt, he begged the pilot to let him tag along. The pilot didn't say yes right away; he didn't want anything to happen to the boss's son. Once permission was granted, the pilot put the boy to work helping a corps of warehouse workers attach a tiny paper parachute to each candy bar, so they would fall gently to the ground.

When the plane was loaded with candy, Tibbets jumped in the cockpit and strapped himself in next to the pilot. The engine roared to life, the pilot pushed the throttle forward, and soon the airplane lifted free. With the wind in his face, Tibbets couldn't help grinning. It didn't take long for them to reach a race track, where the pilot circled low, letting the crowd get a good look at the biplane. As the pilot steered, Tibbets tossed candy bars overboard to the people below. For years after, Tibbets joked it was his first bombing mission. From the moment the plane was in the air, he was hooked. As he would later tell his friends, "Nothing else would satisfy me, once I was given an exhilarating sample of the life of an airman."

But his father wanted him to become a doctor. Tibbets attended the Western Military Academy in North Alton, Illinois, and in 1933 he enrolled at the University of Florida. After class, he'd often stop at Gainesville Airport to look at the planes. One day he decided it was time to learn how to fly. He took lessons, seven dollars for thirty minutes. He was a natural. He quickly outgrew his instructor.

After his sophomore year, Tibbets transferred to the University of Cincinnati to complete his pre-med studies. He lived with his father's friend, Dr. Alfred Harry Crum, a surgeon. Tibbets spent most of his weekends working as an orderly at the doctor's hospital, but in his spare time, he sneaked away to Lunken Airport to hang around with the pilots.

Dr. Crum noticed young Tibbets's interest in flying and encouraged him to follow his dream. Perhaps he could make a career of commercial aviation. But Tibbets knew his father wouldn't approve.

Then, toward the end of 1936, everything became clear. An ad in a *Popular Mechanics* magazine almost shouted out to him, "Do you want to learn to fly?" Tibbets already knew how, but it was the next line that really captured his attention: the Army Air Corps was looking for pilots. Tibbets, who was now twenty-one, sent an application in the next day's mail, and just before he headed home for the holidays, the letter came: Tibbets was accepted in the program. He would become a flying cadet.

Now he had to tell his parents he was dropping out of college to join the military. His father didn't take it well. "I've sent you through school," he said. "Bought you automobiles, given you money to run around with the girls, but from here on, you're on your own. If you want to go kill yourself, go ahead, I don't give a damn."

His mother, Enola Tibbets, sat quietly through her husband's rant. When he stopped to catch his breath, she let silence settle over the room before she spoke.

"Paul, if you want to go fly airplanes, you're going to be all right," she said in almost a whisper. Tibbets felt reassured. He was making the right decision. Nothing bad would happen to him.

Tibbets carried those words with him every time he got into a jam during combat. The day he left for basic training in February 1937 his mother told him: "Son, someday we're going to be really proud of you." And so far, in his eight years in the military, he had done everything right.

Colonel Paul W. Tibbets.

After basic flight training at Randolph Field in San Antonio, Texas, he was assigned to Fort Benning, Georgia. That's where he met Lucy Wingate, a petite southern belle. They fell in love and married in 1938.

Tibbets rose quickly through the ranks of the Air Corps, which was renamed the U.S. Army Air Forces in 1941. Shortly after his deployment to Europe in June 1942, he was named commanding officer of an entire squadron of the 97th Bombardment Group.

Tibbets led the first American daylight heavy bomber mission over occupied France in August 1942. All told, Tibbets piloted twenty-five combat missions in the B-17 Flying Fortress plane he named the *Red Gremlin*.

He flew Major General Clark from London to Gibraltar in preparation for Operation Torch, the Allied invasion of North Africa. A few weeks later, Tibbets flew Lieutenant General Eisenhower, the supreme Allied commander, to Gibraltar.

Tibbets's skills were praised by his commander, Major General Jimmy Doolittle, who was already a military legend. He had led a daring bombing raid over Tokyo in 1942, the first American attack on the Japanese mainland. The mission was later depicted in the film *Thirty Seconds Over Tokyo*. Doolittle was played by actor Spencer Tracy.

So when Tibbets was called into Doolittle's office in February 1943, he thought he'd likely be ferrying another high-ranking general somewhere. But Doolittle told him instead about a request from General Henry "Hap" Arnold, the Air Forces chief of staff. "General Arnold wants my best field-grade officer with the most experience in B-17s to come back to the United States," Doolittle said. "They're building an airplane called the B-29, and they're having a lot of trouble with it. It's yours."

A month later, Tibbets was stateside, doing flight test work with engineers at the Boeing factory. He went to Alamogordo, New Mexico, to help a professor calculate the B-29's vulnerability to fighter attack. Tibbets's job was testing out the theories in simulated combat runs. The B-29 assigned for the tests was fully equipped with weapons and armor plating, but when Tibbets arrived to work, he learned his plane was out of commission for at least ten days. He decided to try flying a "skeleton" B-29, a plane without any guns or armament. With the aircraft seven thousand pounds lighter, Tibbets was amazed at how easily it handled and how high it could climb. He filed that data in the back of his head.

The Army opened a B-29 training school in Grand Island, Nebraska, in March 1944, with Tibbets as director of operations. It made sense. He had spent more flying time in the Superfortress than any other pilot. The assignment didn't last long. In September, Tibbets was summoned to a secret meeting at the U.S. Army Second Air Force headquarters in Colorado Springs.

Tibbets knew nothing about the meeting, not even who would be there. He settled his nerves and stepped into the conference room. There were three people inside: Colonel John Lansdale, a U.S. Army intelligence officer; Navy captain William "Deak" Parsons, an "explosives expert"; and Professor Norman Ramsey, a Harvard physicist.

Lansdale said he wanted to ask Tibbets a few questions about his military career. But they quickly crossed into Tibbets's civilian life. Some questions were highly personal. This is an interrogation, Tibbets thought. Eventually, Lansdale said he had one last query: "Have you ever been arrested?"

Tibbets took a deep breath. Yes, he said. When he was a nineteen-year-old college student "a nosy policeman with a flashlight" caught Tibbets and a girl "during a love-making episode" in the backseat of his parked car in North Miami Beach, Florida. The charges were later dropped, he said. Everyone in the room already knew about his indiscretion. They had done their background research. They just wanted to see if Tibbets would come clean. When he did, they knew they had the right man. Then General Uzal G. Ent, commander of the Second Air Force, took over the conversation—and he got right to the point.

He told Tibbets about the Manhattan Project, a plan for a bomb so powerful it would explode with the force of "twenty thousand tons of conventional high explosive." Tibbets had been chosen to develop a method to deliver the atomic bomb over the skies of Germany or Japan. His mission was code-named "Operation Silverplate." Ent warned Tibbets he would be court-martialed if he spoke of it to anyone.

Tibbets could have anything he needed, they told him, from men to supplies. If anyone gave him trouble, all he had to do was say the request was for Operation Silverplate. He had a blank check.

Tibbets chose Wendover Airfield, a remote base along the Utah–Nevada state line, for the training program. He started assembling the right men for his new group. He combed his memory for outstanding members of flight crews who served with him in Europe and North Africa, as well as in the B-29 training program.

At the top of his list were Captain Theodore "Dutch" Van Kirk, a navigator, and Major Thomas Ferebee, a bombardier, his crewmates in the old *Red Gremlin* days. Off duty, Van Kirk and Ferebee, both young and single, had loved to drink, gamble, and carouse their way around London. Every now and then, Tibbets joined in.

Ferebee was the first to arrive at Wendover, and Van Kirk came soon after. On a mission, the bombardier was responsible for hitting enemy

Captain Theodore J. Van Kirk, Colonel Paul Tibbets, and Major Thomas Ferebee standing in front of a B-29 Superfortress.

targets. For Tibbets, no one did it better than Ferebee. From a small town in North Carolina, Ferebee was tall and handsome, a former high school baseball star who got a tryout with the Boston Red Sox.

With his mustache, smooth southern drawl, and his penchant for gambling and womanizing, he was like the fictional character Rhett Butler from *Gone with the Wind*.

Unlike Ferebee, Van Kirk had just settled down. The boyish-looking airman married a girl from his hometown in Northumberland, Pennsylvania. At twenty-four, Van Kirk was a little quieter than Ferebee, but both were perfectionists—like their commander. The trio worked together to assemble Tibbets's staffing wish list. That included Jacob Beser, a wiry, sarcastic Jewish kid from Baltimore who had been an engineering major at Johns Hopkins University.

Beser jumped at the opportunity. When Germany invaded Poland in September 1939, igniting World War II, Beser had lobbied his parents to let him join the Royal Air Force. He hated the Nazis. He knew his relatives in France and Germany were natural targets for Hitler's rabid anti-Semitism. His parents were angry, too, but they insisted he complete his degree. When the Japanese attacked Pearl Harbor, Beser had had enough. He enlisted in the Army Air Forces the next day.

But more than three years later, Beser still hadn't seen any action. After basic training, he was sent to Harvard to learn about radar. The technology was new and growing in importance, and he became one of the service's highest-rated radar specialists.

Beser kept asking to serve in a combat unit, to "avenge his relatives in Europe," but he was turned down every time. He was stuck teaching radar to recruits. He had just put in another request when Tibbets picked him for his team.

Tibbets did the same with Staff Sergeant George "Bob" Caron, a tail gunner. When Caron blew into Wendover—a dusty expanse of desert about 125 miles west of Salt Lake City—his uniform was dirty and his collar unbuttoned, violations of military rules. As an MP lit into him, Caron heard a familiar voice.

"Is that you, Bob?"

He turned, and Tibbets shook his hand. Caron grinned and the MP stood down. The commander took Caron to his office and got right down to business.

"Bob, I need a man who knows what he's doing and can teach others to do a similar job. And keep their mouths shut," Tibbets said.

"Colonel, I won't even mention I'm here," Caron said.

Another choice was Captain Robert A. Lewis, a cocky, Brooklyn-born aviator. In the B-29 program, Tibbets became a mentor to Lewis. If Tibbets was the Joe DiMaggio of pilots, then Lewis was Ted Williams. Lewis believed *he* was the best pilot in the military, and a lot of other folks thought so, too.

By the time Tibbets recruited enough men to make up a dozen crews, he had assembled some of the top pilots, navigators, and flight engineers in the U.S. military. For Tibbets, loyalty and secrecy were the most important qualities. He tolerated raucous behavior among his men so long as he knew they would not tell anyone what they were doing.

He summed it all up for them at his first briefing with the 509th in September 1944: "You don't discuss with anyone where you are, who you are, what you're doing. With your wife, your mother, your sister, your girlfriend or anything."

And to show how serious he was, the few men who spoke too freely were suddenly transferred to an air base in Alaska.

Tibbets's crews worked for months, studying, discussing, practicing. They worked hard and played hard, looking for ways to fill their time during the long wait to deployment. Now spring was here, and things were getting squirrely in Wendover. It was time to move on.

In the meantime, commanders had been busy preparing a new home for the 509th on the tiny, strategic Pacific island of Tinian, 1,600 miles south of Tokyo. Captured by U.S. forces in July 1944, Tinian had become a key air base, easy to supply by sea and perfect for launching B-29 air attacks against Japanese cities.

Tibbets was done with waiting around. He picked up the phone and dialed the Air Forces command headquarters in Washington. He invoked the name Silverplate. The 509th was ready to roll, he said. And so the process began. He knew it would take a few weeks for everyone to get there.

They'd start moving west on April 26, via the Western Pacific Railroad, eventually ending up in Seattle, where most of the ground crews would take a ship to Tinian. The B-29 crews would fly out later.

Tibbets set the plan in motion. It didn't take long for the phone to ring—an aide to General Groves said Tibbets must come to Washington for an urgent meeting. The general was unhappy, the aide said. He wouldn't give details. Tibbets went.

He wasn't even through the office door before Groves lit into him.

Who the hell did the colonel think he was, ordering the 509th overseas? Groves was the commander overseeing the project, wasn't that clear? This was tantamount to insubordination.

Tibbets stood quietly during Groves's profanity-filled rant. He knew why the general was chewing him out. Groves wanted to put him in his place. Tibbets should have cleared the move with him first. But when Groves finished, he did something that surprised Tibbets. He broke into a wide grin and slapped Tibbets on the shoulder. "Dammit, you've got us moving," he said. "Now they can't stop us."

Tibbets only hoped the general was right. He was sick of waiting around while the rest of the world was fighting.

COUNTDOWN:
104 DAYS

April 24, 1945

Okinawa, Japan

High up on the deck of a U.S. Navy destroyer, Commander Draper Kauffman peered through binoculars at the sea, the island, and the sky beyond. Closer in, zipping toward him, was a thirty-foot plywood boat, an oddly humble craft for an elite U.S. Underwater Demolition Team. The "frogmen" were returning from another reconnaissance mission.

The air shivered and boomed with artillery fire as shells streaked toward Okinawa and exploded in great clouds of dust.

Something else was moving out there. Kauffman shifted his gaze from sea to sky and saw what looked like a flock of birds on the horizon. Waves of Japanese planes flowed toward the U.S. fleet.

"Kamikazes," he muttered.

Kauffman had been in combat before. He'd seen some of the deadliest U.S. military action in the war in the Pacific: Saipan, Guam, Iwo Jima. He'd plunged into the ocean alongside his frogmen, blowing up underwater obstacles set to kill American troops landing on remote, Japanese-held islands.

They'd been here at Okinawa for almost a month, fighting endlessly. Kauffman had come to a stark conclusion: the earlier campaigns were just a warm-up for this one. Okinawa was a slog, a son of a bitch.

Covered in dense foliage, hills, and trees and honeycombed with caves and bunkers, Okinawa bristled with tens of thousands of Japanese determined to fight to the death. The enemy, even raw conscripts, did not believe in surrender.

How long would it take the Allies to overrun this godforsaken place? And once that was achieved, Kauffman didn't expect a victory celebration. Not anytime soon.

The next step after Okinawa was the invasion of Japan itself. No date had been set, but military leaders back home were already talking about it in the newspapers, preparing the public for the inevitable horror and loss of life.

A week earlier, General Joseph Stilwell, commander of U.S. forces in China, Burma, and India, said despite all the Japanese deaths in the Pacific, the "enemy is stronger than when the war started," and a "desperate struggle" awaited U.S. troops.

More Americans were being drafted and trained for the invasion. A month before he died, FDR declared the mobilization of the "largest armed force" in U.S. history would be completed by the end of June. Older men were being drafted, and "previously occupation-deferred" draftees— academics and farmers, monks and veterans—were being called up to replace massive U.S. casualties.

Kauffman loved the Navy and was committed to serving his nation. He was a problem solver, an optimist. But that day on the deck of the USS *Gilmer*, watching the kamikaze suicide pilots roll in, he had to dig deep to remain positive.

He headed down to meet the frogmen.

Almost drowned out by the din of exploding shells and pounding machine-gun fire, Kauffman greeted his men with smiles as they boarded the destroyer. "Great job!" he shouted. "Wish I could've been out having a swim, instead of stuck on the bridge." His men knew he meant it. He was a hands-on officer. He'd been right alongside them on missions in other hot spots.

Kauffman led by example, something he learned from his father, also a longtime Navy officer. The old man, James Kauffman, was an admiral now. Draper was determined to follow his path.

Even though he was an admiral's son, it hadn't been an easy journey. Kauffman was accepted to the U.S. Naval Academy, but was denied an officer's commission when he graduated in 1933, because of his poor eyesight. Instead, he worked for a steamship company in New York. In early 1940, he quit his job and joined the American Volunteer Motor Ambulance Corps in France. The move shocked his family. They worried about his safety. Europe had been engulfed in war since Germany invaded Poland in September 1939. And by the spring of 1940, France and England were desperately trying to stop the Nazi blitzkrieg. Kauffman just wanted to do his part. He explained his decision in a letter home: "I think there are times when things are worth fighting for, even if it's not in your best self-interest at the moment." But shortly after he arrived in France, Kauffman was captured by the Germans. A few weeks later, France fell.

Kauffman was an American. So the Germans decided to release him. But they gave him a warning: go home. If they caught him again, he wouldn't be so lucky. Kauffman crossed the Spanish border and made his way to England, where waves of Luftwaffe planes were dropping bombs every night on London. Buildings crumbled; fires consumed entire neighborhoods. Great Britain was the only country still standing against Hitler. He listened with thousands of Britons as Prime Minister Winston Churchill delivered passionate radio speeches, giving his people hope in a time of despair.

Draper Kauffman wasn't about to go home. He enlisted in the Royal Naval Volunteer Reserve and learned how to disable bombs. He got so good at it that he became a chief ordnance disposal officer. In November 1941, Admiral Chester Nimitz asked Kauffman to start a bomb disposal school for the U.S. Navy. Almost a decade after graduating from the Naval Academy, Kauffman finally got his commission.

Kauffman heard about the attack on Pearl Harbor just as he was choosing recruits for the bomb disposal school. He had to hurry the process. He

U.S. Naval Reserve   Nov. 1941
Lieut.-Lt. Comd.- Comdr.

Draper Kauffman after he received a commission from the U.S. Navy in November 1941 to set up a bomb disposal school. He had been a bomb disposal officer in Great Britain in 1940 and 1941.

quickly began staffing, organizing, and running the school outside Washington, D.C. It was a hectic time. He spent long hours in offices and classrooms. In off hours, he spent time with Peggy Tuckerman, his little sister's best friend. He'd known her for years, so it only made sense for them to get married before he moved his training group to a base in Fort Pierce, Florida, on the Atlantic Ocean. There his men could train in the water.

That's where the Underwater Demolition Teams were born. Kauffman first taught them to disable bombs and mines on land, then he moved them into the sea. This was the Navy, after all, and underwater mines and man-made obstacles were destroying ships and landing crafts transporting troops into combat.

Kauffman's expertise caught the attention of Admiral Richmond

Turner, commander of amphibious forces in the Pacific. Assaults from the sea had become a critical part of U.S. military strategy in the war against Japan. American commanders devised an "island hopping" strategy, capturing and fortifying key islands, one after another, until Japan itself came within range of American bombers. The Americans bypassed strongly held islands and struck the enemy's weak points.

They encountered problems along the way. Even though invasions were planned down to the last detail, amphibious warfare was risky. After a long bombardment by battleships and aircraft carriers, landing crafts, some transporting troops, others carrying equipment, moved in from a few thousand yards offshore in carefully timed waves to designated points on the beach. As they neared the shore, especially in shallow water, the crafts not only had to pass through enemy fire, they had to navigate natural and man-made obstacles lurking beneath the surface: reefs, wooden stakes, mines, and bombs.

Early amphibious operations cost thousands of American lives, as officers could only guess how deep the water was or whether the shallows were laced with obstructions. U.S. commanders learned they needed better reconnaissance. Somehow they had to scope out the underwater terrain between the line of departure and the beach so obstacles could be removed or avoided.

That's where Kauffman's elite underwater bomb squad came into play.

Frogman recruits had to undergo a grueling training program, six weeks of physical challenges. "Hell Week," at the very start, was the worst, seven days of nonstop physical training with only a few breaks for sleep and food. And their uniforms were barely clothes at all. On missions, the frogmen looked like they were headed to a swim meet instead of a war zone. They wore swim trunks, goggles, and fins to protect their feet against poisonous coral. Their limbs were strapped with knives, demolition kits, fuses, and marking slates with waterproof pencils to create detailed maps. They slicked their bodies with aluminum-based greasepaint tinted bluish-gray to camouflage and protect them from the cold water. "To be a frog, we had to be physically, mentally, and emotionally fit or we did not survive the course," recalled Electrician's Mate Harold Ledien. "We became naked warriors."

Each of their wooden landing craft carried an inflatable rubber boat to move supplies to shore and scoop up swimmers after the mission. By the time they deployed to Okinawa, the teams had already proved their worth. Invasion commanders came to depend on them.

Kauffman directed twelve teams at Okinawa, the largest of the Ryukyu Islands, which included Kerama Retto and Ie Shima. Each team had one hundred men and a small staff. They did a world of work before the battle commenced. A poor, densely populated farming community, Okinawa was targeted for one reason: its proximity to the enemy. It was only 350 miles from the southernmost Japanese home island, Kyushu. Simply put, it was the perfect spot to launch an invasion of Japan.

Kauffman's team prepared the way.

The frogmen blasted shipping channels through coral reefs. At one point, they used 16 tons of explosives to create a 50-foot-wide, 300-foot-long channel to allow wheeled vehicles to reach beachhead at low tide. The explosion was so massive, men on some of the U.S. ships thought they were under attack.

At another landing site, a frog team discovered 3,100 pointed wooden stakes laced with barbed wire and mines, driven into the coral floor six feet underwater. While U.S. gunboats fired over their heads to distract the enemy, Kauffman's men attached explosives to the stakes and blew them all up at once.

Another reconnaissance mission led to the discovery of 260 small vessels hidden inside a cave. These were "suicide boats," meant to be loaded with explosives and driven by Japanese soldiers into American ships, like waterborne kamikazes. Kauffman ordered his men to blow them up.

Besides the demolition work, Kauffman's men marked the water depths at reefs as well as the best places to land on the beach. Okinawa was sixty miles long and ten miles at its widest and had ten thousand yards of beach. Every time the Army or Marines plotted a landing on a new spot, they called in Kauffman.

Finally, on April 1, 180,000 Army and Marine troops descended on Okinawa.

Kauffman's frogmen were essential during the landing on Ie Shima on April 16. Everything went as planned for his men, but every time Kauffman heard the name of the island, he couldn't help thinking about his friend Ernie.

Ernie Pyle, a legendary war correspondent, was killed by a sniper on April 18 on Ie Shima. Pyle had slogged out the war in Europe alongside the GIs and had only recently arrived in the Pacific. Pyle wanted to write a feature story on Kauffman's teams. They were "half fish and half nuts," Pyle said, but Kauffman asked him to hold the story; the Japanese read newspapers, too. His frogmen might become easy prey in the open water if Japanese gunners knew to watch for them.

"Let me put it this way," Kauffman explained to Pyle. "I'm probably like a baseball manager who's won ten games wearing the same dirty shirt, and he's not going to take that shirt off no matter how much it smells, until he loses."

Pyle shook his head. "That's as poor a reason for the suppression of the press in the United States as I've ever heard."

Kauffman knew why Pyle wanted to write a story about his frogmen. It wasn't that the reporter was looking for a big scoop. Pyle wanted to make sure the frogmen got the "credit with the American people that they deserved."

News of Pyle's death left Kauffman and many of his men shaken. First FDR, then Ernie, not to mention the daily casualties that surrounded them.

Kauffman made sure his team members were back on board the destroyer. He ordered them below for chow, then some rest. The fighting was picking up and they had more recon missions scheduled. More enemy fire. More kamikazes. Years of war, fore and aft. They were surrounded by death. There was no end in sight.

Kauffman knew nothing of Los Alamos or the powerful bomb being developed there. He only knew the Japanese would fight to the last man, and after Okinawa, there was only one target left. The biggest, bloodiest one of all.

If they thought Okinawa was hell, they were in for much worse.

COUNTDOWN:
103 DAYS

April 25, 1945

Washington, D.C.

Harry Truman had now been president for just twelve full days. But he was already putting his mark on the office. FDR used to hold Cabinet meetings that dragged on and on, as he regaled his team with long stories. Truman was all business, moving from one item to the next, quickly disposing of them.

"Everything he said was decisive," noted one Cabinet member, Henry Wallace, who preceded Truman as vice president and stayed on as Roosevelt's commerce secretary. Then he added a backhanded compliment: "It almost seemed as though he was eager to decide in advance of thinking."

But this meeting was different. And the decision that would flow from it would be the toughest Truman—or any president—would ever have to make. The day before, Truman received a message from Secretary of War Stimson, who wrote: "I think it is very important that I should have a talk with you as soon as possible on a highly secret matter." Stimson reminded him of the brief conversation they had the night he was sworn in as president. Now he wanted to brief Truman in depth. "I think you ought to know about it without much further delay."

At the bottom of the message, Truman directed his staff: "Put on list tomorrow, Wed. 25. HST."

Less than a year before, it was almost unthinkable Truman would ever be vice president, much less succeed Franklin Delano Roosevelt as commander in chief. As FDR prepared to run for a fourth term in the summer of 1944, Democratic Party leaders were looking to push Vice President Henry Wallace off the ticket. He was too intellectual, too far to the left. And with Roosevelt's health declining, they worried he might end up serving out FDR's term as president. But who should replace Wallace? In spite of his poor health, Roosevelt never imagined anyone else leading the country.

While the president let the issue drift, party leaders argued about possible candidates. There was James Byrnes, the former senator and then Supreme Court justice, whom Roosevelt persuaded to leave the Court to run the Office of War Mobilization. Truman had agreed to give a speech at the Democratic convention nominating Byrnes for vice president. Senate majority leader Alben Barkley was also running. And Wallace thought he still had the job. A Gallup poll in July 1944 found only 2 percent of voters backed Truman.

The junior senator from Missouri was likable—a smart, hardworking, gregarious sort. At five feet nine inches tall, Truman was decisive, blunt, used salty language, and thrived on the rough and tumble of politics. His career had been, to put it charitably, circuitous. Farmer, bank teller, salesman, haberdasher. (That last business ended up saddling him with serious debt.) As a young man, he was an Army artillery officer and a decorated combat veteran of World War I.

In 1922, Truman was broke and out of work. But he had served in the Army with a fellow named Jim Pendergast. And Jim's uncle was Kansas City political boss Tom Pendergast, who needed someone to run for Jackson County judge, essentially a county commissioner.

Pendergast was widely thought to be corrupt, and Truman was good "window dressing." He ran on a platform of honesty—he wouldn't steal any money—and he would pave local dirt roads. He won by fewer than three hundred votes. At age thirty-eight, he started a new career in politics.

His next step up the ladder was just as unlikely. In 1934, a U.S. Senate seat in Missouri came open. Boss Pendergast approached three candidates, and was turned down by all of them. Time was running out. And there was another consideration: St. Louis already had a man in the Senate. Pendergast needed a local senator to protect his Kansas City machine in the western part of the state.

When Pendergast's boys approached Truman, he immediately noted all the reasons it didn't make sense. "Nobody knows me and I haven't got any money," he said. The Pendergast team countered that they would back him—with financing and a strong organization. Truman knew that gave him a chance.

He ran on his record, mostly of paving roads. "He pulled Jackson County out of the mud," one of his teachers said. His platform was just as simple—"Back Roosevelt"—which counted for a lot, two years into the New Deal. Most of all, he had the backing of the Kansas City political machine. When he won the primary, which ensured his election in heavily Democratic Missouri, the *St. Louis Post-Dispatch* dismissed him as "Boss Pendergast's Errand Boy."

But he achieved some measure of attention as chairman of the Senate Special Committee to Investigate the National Defense program, known almost immediately as the Truman Committee, whose job was to look into the awarding of defense contracts.

In July 1944, he had absolutely no thought of running alongside Roosevelt. And apparently neither did FDR. The president said that month, "I hardly know Truman. He has been over here a few times, but he made no particular impression on me." Party power brokers were making a different calculation. As they surveyed the field of potential candidates, each one had a problem. Truman's strength? To put it bluntly, Democratic leaders thought he would hurt the national ticket the least.

But Truman resisted repeated attempts to join the race. He finally explained why: his wife, Bess, was on his Senate payroll, making $4,500 a year. Truman was certain—and correct—that this would come out if he were on the national ticket.

Truman was six years old when he first saw Elizabeth "Bess" Wallace at Sunday school back in Independence, Missouri. He was immediately smitten with her blond hair and blue eyes. It took him five years to work up the courage to talk to Bessie, when they attended fourth grade together.

She was the only girl he ever courted. In his twenties, he pursued Bess as persistently as he took on every other project, including a marriage proposal she rejected. Finally, after he returned from France and the war, they married in 1919. Truman was thirty-five years old.

For the rest of their lives, he talked most things over with his wife—personal and political. He took to calling her "the Boss." Their only child, Margaret, said whenever her father spoke in public, he always looked over to Bess for approval.

So when he put her on his Senate payroll, it was a real job. Bess was a trusted adviser and Truman's main speechwriter. She had no problem telling her husband exactly what she thought. One of the few areas where he didn't listen was his salty language.

Truman liked to tell a story about a speech in which he repeatedly used the word "manure." A friend leaned over to Bess and said, "I wish you could get Harry to use a more genteel word." Bess responded, "It's taken me years to get him to say 'manure.'" It was a good joke, but Truman worried about the politics when people found out—as they did—that his wife was "Payroll Bess."

His concerns didn't matter. On the opening day of the convention in Chicago, Robert Hannegan, chair of the Democratic National Committee, called Truman to his hotel suite. Party elders set it up so Truman could hear Hannegan on the phone with President Roosevelt, who was in San Diego.

"Bob," Roosevelt said, "have you got that fellow lined up yet?"

"No," Hannegan responded, "he is the contrariest goddamn mule from Missouri I ever dealt with."

The president declared, "Well, you tell the senator that if he wants to break up the Democratic Party in the middle of the war, that's his responsibility." Truman then took the phone, and after a little resistance, said, "I have always taken orders from the commander in chief. I'll do it."

Roosevelt promptly forgot about his running mate. And after their inauguration in January 1945, he kept his vice president out of high-level discussions, especially the planning and execution of America's war efforts in Europe and the Pacific.

But now it was noon on April 25. Truman was president. And Secretary of War Stimson walked into the Oval Office. He handed the president a short, typewritten memorandum and waited while Truman read it. The first sentence was a battering ram. "Within four months we shall in all probability have completed the most terrible weapon ever known in human history, one bomb of which could destroy a whole city."

The memo briefly laid out how the weapon had been developed in collaboration with the United Kingdom. But the United States controlled all the resources to construct and use the bomb, and "no other nation could reach this position for some years."

Still, it pointed out other nations would, no doubt, be able to develop the technology, starting "in the next few years" with Russia. And Stimson added: "The world in its present state of moral advancement compared with its technical development would be eventually at the mercy of such a weapon. In other words, modern civilization might be completely destroyed."

While Truman was reading, Army major general Leslie Groves was being ushered into the White House by a back way, through underground corridors. He walked into the Oval Office just after the president finished the memo. Pentagon officials had given this meeting a great deal of thought. They worried if reporters saw Stimson and Groves come in together, it would set off a wave of speculation.

Henry Stimson had been part of the eastern establishment from his birth in 1867. A graduate of Andover Academy, Yale, and Harvard Law School, he first served as secretary of war in 1911 under President William

Howard Taft. Herbert Hoover named him secretary of state in 1929. It was in that post that he ended the department's operation to break secret codes, famously stating, "Gentlemen don't read other people's mail."

In 1940, FDR appointed Stimson to run the War Department again. Stimson first learned of research into an atomic bomb in 1941. When the Manhattan Project was started to produce the weapon, Stimson was put in charge of what he called "S-1."

In fact, the man who was now briefing Truman had steered him away in June 1943, when the Truman Committee began asking questions about a defense project in Pasco, Washington. Stimson called then-senator Truman on the phone. "Now that's a matter which I know all about personally, and I am one of the group of two or three men in the whole world who know about it. . . . It's part of a very important secret development."

Truman got the point immediately. "I herewith see the situation, Mr. Secretary, and you won't have to say another word to me. Whenever you say that to me, that's all I want to hear."

Secretary of War Henry Stimson (left) with his aide, Colonel William Kyle.

Now at age seventy-seven, Stimson was somewhat frail. He was the only Republican in Roosevelt's Cabinet, and by appearances he seemed more comfortable in the nineteenth century than the twentieth. He sported a mustache and his hair was parted down the middle. He wore a gold watch chain across his vest. For all the important jobs he'd held, all his prestigious titles, he preferred to be called "Colonel Stimson," for his service as an artillery officer in France during World War I. But no one took him lightly. Stimson was still a highly respected figure of enormous influence in Washington.

Then there was General Groves, who took over the manufacturing phase of the Manhattan Project in 1942. He was the right man for the job. At six feet tall and 250 pounds, he was physically imposing. A thin mustache added to his intimidating presence. Groves played the part, using "my natural characteristics, which you can call domineering or dominant or brash or self-confidence, or anything else you want to, but there were certain characteristics there that led to very vigorous control."

The Groves family came to America eight generations before. Peter Groves, his great-great-grandfather, fought in the American Revolution. Leslie Groves spent his early years on military bases across the country, where his father served as an Army chaplain. He attended West Point and ranked fourth in his class.

Groves rose through the Army Corps of Engineers, and had already overseen one massive project—construction of the Pentagon in 1941 and 1942. At an estimated cost of $31 million, it was the largest office building in the world, with more than six million square feet of floor space on thirty-four acres, and two parking lots for eight thousand cars.

People who worked under Groves described him as ruthless. A fellow engineer said when you dealt with him, "a little alarm bell rang 'Caution' in your brain." He issued orders to officers even if they outranked him. While some called him a bully, he bulldozed the War Department's new headquarters to completion in less than a year and a half.

But big as it was, the Pentagon paled in comparison to the Manhattan

Major General Leslie R. Groves Jr.

Project. Creating an atomic bomb was a devilishly complex process. First, the country had to produce radioactive fuel. Then it had to figure out how to safely detonate the fission process—setting off an atomic chain reaction—at the right moment and in the right place. And it had to pull all of this off in complete secrecy.

By April 1945, more than 125,000 men and women were working on the project at installations all over the United States. Somehow, Groves had to ensure no hint of this massive undertaking leaked. They must keep the enterprise secret from the public, as well as most of the gossip-loving military.

In a sense, Groves owed his job to Adolf Hitler's hatred of Jews. In 1933, when Hitler came to power in Germany, Nazi persecution of the Jews prompted hundreds of the world's top scientists, professors, and researchers to flee the country.

University of Berlin physicist Leo Szilard found refuge in London, where he conceived an idea straight out of science fiction. He theorized that splitting an atom—the tiniest particle in an element—would trigger a chain reaction that would "liberate energy on an industrial scale." It could fuel an atomic bomb, something first envisioned in the 1914 H. G. Wells book *The World Set Free*.

Five years later, a pair of German scientists proved Szilard's theory by splitting uranium atoms by bombarding them with neutrons. The energy released—a process known as nuclear fission—was tremendous enough to power a bomb. But there were many, many steps between the controlled physics of a laboratory and the battlefield.

Szilard, who'd moved on to a teaching post at Columbia University in New York, worked with fellow physicist Enrico Fermi to confirm uranium was indeed the element most likely to precipitate a chain reaction. Szilard worried if German scientists developed an atomic bomb, Hitler would use the weapon to pursue his goal of Aryan world domination.

So Szilard called on an old teacher for advice on how to warn leaders of the free world about the threat—a fellow immigrant named Albert Einstein.

By the late 1930s, the German-born physicist was the most famous scientist in the world, his name synonymous with the word *genius*. Awarded the Nobel Prize in 1921, Einstein developed groundbreaking theories that led to new ways of looking at time, space, matter, energy, and gravity. In 1933, while Einstein was visiting the United States, Hitler came to power. Because of his Jewish background, Einstein settled in America, taking a position at the new Institute for Advanced Study at Princeton.

Now he took up Szilard's cause. In a letter dated August 2, 1939, Einstein told President Roosevelt: "A single bomb of this type, carried by boat and exploded in a port, might very well destroy the whole port together with some of the surrounding territory."

Einstein told FDR that scientists in America and Britain were already conducting nuclear research. And signs pointed to Germany doing the same. "I understand that Germany has actually stopped the sale of uranium from the Czechoslovakian mines which she has taken over." He noted that the son of a top German official was attached to the Kaiser-Wilhelm-Institut in Berlin, where some of the American work on uranium was now being repeated.

Roosevelt took Einstein's warning seriously, and set off a chain reaction of his own. The president established the Advisory Committee on Uranium, charged with stockpiling the material for ongoing research and development. The committee languished in relative obscurity until

Albert Einstein
Old Grove Rd.
Nassau Point
Peconic, Long Island

August 2nd, 1939

F.D. Roosevelt,
President of the United States,
White House
Washington, D.C.

Sir:

Some recent work by E.Fermi and L. Szilard, which has been communicated to me in manuscript, leads me to expect that the element uranium may be turned into a new and important source of energy in the immediate future. Certain aspects of the situation which has arisen seem to call for watchfulness and, if necessary, quick action on the part of the Administration. I believe therefore that it is my duty to bring to your attention the following facts and recommendations:

In the course of the last four months it has been made probable - through the work of Joliot in France as well as Fermi and Szilard in America - that it may become possible to set up a nuclear chain reaction in a large mass of uranium,by which vast amounts of power and large quantities of new radium-like elements would be generated. Now it appears almost certain that this could be achieved in the immediate future.

This new phenomenon would also lead to the construction of bombs, and it is conceivable - though much less certain - that extremely powerful bombs of a new type may thus be constructed. A single bomb of this type, carried by boat and exploded in a port, might very well destroy the whole port together with some of the surrounding territory. However, such bombs might very well prove to be too heavy for transportation by air.

Albert Einstein's 1939 letter to President Franklin D. Roosevelt.

-2-

The United States has only very poor ores of uranium in moderate quantities. There is some good ore in Canada and the former Czechoslovakia, while the most important source of uranium is Belgian Congo.

In view of this situation you may think it desirable to have some permanent contact maintained between the Administration and the group of physicists working on chain reactions in America. One possible way of achieving this might be for you to entrust with this task a person who has your confidence and who could perhaps serve in an inofficial capacity. His task might comprise the following:

a) to approach Government Departments, keep them informed of the further development, and put forward recommendations for Government action, giving particular attention to the problem of securing a supply of uranium ore for the United States;

b) to speed up the experimental work,which is at present being carried on within the limits of the budgets of University laboratories, by providing funds, if such funds be required, through his contacts with private persons who are willing to make contributions for this cause, and perhaps also by obtaining the co-operation of industrial laboratories which have the necessary equipment.

I understand that Germany has actually stopped the sale of uranium from the Czechoslovakian mines which she has taken over. That she should have taken such early action might perhaps be understood on the ground that the son of the German Under-Secretary of State, von Weizsäcker, is attached to the Kaiser-Wilhelm-Institut in Berlin where some of the American work on uranium is now being repeated.

Yours very truly,

A. Einstein

(Albert Einstein)

March 1941, when Churchill asked FDR to move the nuclear program to the "highest priority." The British had been aggressively studying atomic bomb physics under scientist Niels Bohr, but their facilities had been under constant attack by the Germans. And so was born the S-1 task force, with Groves in charge.

One of Groves's first hires was Oppenheimer, the scientific director. Top researchers were scattered across the country, and Groves realized he needed to bring them into facilities where they could work together to develop the weapon.

He decided the bulk of the work would take place in three sites, code-named X, Y, and W. Each would specialize in a particular aspect of the project. The massive, secure bases would be custom-built from the ground up. The first, Project X, went up in rural Tennessee, about twenty-five miles northwest of Knoxville. Engineers and contractors swarmed to the area, known as Oak Ridge, in February 1943, and built research laboratories, office buildings, and employee housing, all secured by protective fencing and sentry posts. Project X was an enrichment facility, the source of weapons-grade uranium for atomic bombs. Here workers separated tiny amounts of the chain-reaction isotope U-235 from tons of uranium, a time-consuming process. A "jug-sized" block of U-235 required thousands of tons of the raw material. The enriched uranium was stored in a hollowed-out bluff near an abandoned farmhouse. Groves wanted to stockpile as much fissionable nuclear weapons fuel as possible, so he built the world's first permanent nuclear reactor in Oak Ridge. It used uranium to generate a second source of nuclear fuel in the form of plutonium. Plutonium-239 possessed even greater explosive potential than its parent compound. Plutonium rarely occurs in nature, and fissionable plutonium-239 has no real use other than as a nuclear explosive. In a matter of months, Oak Ridge was generating stockpiles of U-235 and plutonium-239, but the Manhattan Project needed more than Oak Ridge could supply. Site W, another processing facility, went up in Hanford, Washington, in September 1944. Suddenly the United States needed uranium, and lots of it.

The only known deposits in the United States were in the Rocky Mountains, but Colorado didn't have nearly enough to meet the need. Groves turned to the Belgian Congo. Belgium had surrendered to the Nazis in 1940, but the Congo still remained on the Allied side. In 1943, the U.S. Army Corps of Engineers provided free construction services to a Belgian mining company that owned the Congolese uranium mines.

With a fuel supply in place, Groves still needed somewhere to assemble the bomb. Oppenheimer led Groves to Los Alamos, where the scientist spent part of his childhood. The remote site was perfect, and soon became the Weapons and Design Lab—code-named Y.

While Oppenheimer and Groves got along, the general insisted civilian employees in Los Alamos operate in utter secrecy and demonstrate military-like efficiency.

His brusque manner offended many of the independent-minded scientists, who dreaded his visits to Los Alamos. The disdain was mutual. Groves described the scientists as "children, crackpots and prima donnas."

"I am the impresario of a two-billion-dollar grand opera with thousands of temperamental stars," Groves said.

Now, on April 25, here in the Oval Office, the "opera" was getting close to its premiere. General Groves handed the president a twenty-four-page report that described S-1 in great detail. Truman read his copy, while Stimson and Groves shared another.

The memo started with the "Purpose of Development": "The successful development of the Atomic fission bomb will provide the United States with a weapon of tremendous power which should be a decisive factor in winning the present war more quickly with a saving in American lives and treasure."

Groves detailed the unimaginable power of this new superweapon: "Each bomb is estimated to have the equivalent effect of from 5,000 to 20,000 tons of TNT now, and ultimately, possibly as much as 100,000 tons."

The Groves report explained the explosive power of atomic fission in considerable technical detail. It described how the bomb was being manufactured. It reviewed the history of the Manhattan Project, from its genesis in 1939, to the transition to the manufacturing phase, to the "extraordinary security measures" that had been taken to keep the entire operation "top secret."

And the report discussed "foreign activities." It said since 1943, Russia "evinced a strong interest in our activities and through its diplomatic, information and espionage groups in the United States has made efforts to secure particularized information concerning the project."

As for Germany, the report noted the number of its scientists in the atomic field and said since 1941, there had been reports Germany "was about to use an atomic bomb of tremendous force." But with the Nazi regime in collapse, it stated, "There would no longer appear to be any possibility that Germany could use an atomic bomb in this war."

The report concluded: "Atomic energy if controlled by the major peace-loving nations, should insure the peace of the world for decades to come. If misused it can lead our civilization to annihilation."

Truman peppered Stimson and Groves with questions. He was shocked that a project of this size and expense, with plants across the nation, had remained a secret. When he asked how soon the bomb would be operational, Stimson repeated what he wrote in his memo: "Within four months."

Truman understood how the bomb could shorten the war dramatically. But he was also concerned with its short-term implications for international relations, especially with the Russians, and long-term consequences for the planet.

Truman bogged down several times while reading the highly technical report, and said it was tough to absorb in one sitting. "I don't like to read papers," he complained.

Groves answered that it was impossible to summarize more simply. "We can't tell you this in any more concise language. This is a big project."

The president left no doubt that he backed S-1.

All of this—the briefing and going over the memo—took only forty-five minutes. Truman decided not to keep his copy of the Groves report, feeling it was "not advisable." Stimson left the Oval Office to go home for his daily afternoon nap.

But the president was shaken by what he'd learned. He kept thinking about Stimson's grave warning, that the bomb might be "so powerful that it could end up destroying the whole world."

Truman felt the same fear.

COUNTDOWN:

90 DAYS

May 8, 1945

Washington, D.C.

The Oval Office was crowded with American and British military brass, Cabinet members, the president's wife and daughter, and a gaggle of newspaper and radio correspondents. At exactly 9:00 a.m., the radio microphones would go live, and Truman would make an important announcement to the nation.

Ten minutes remained, and the normally formal group was giddy with anticipation. Truman made jokes with the newsmen. Yes, it was his sixty-first birthday, but no, that wasn't the big news. He agreed to read his statement to them just before the broadcast, but they couldn't file anything until he was off the air.

"You needn't be uneasy. You'll have plenty of time," the president said.

The reporters laughed. The president cleared his throat and read aloud: The Germans had surrendered. The war in Europe was over.

No one in the room was surprised. It had been almost a year since Allied troops stormed the beaches of Normandy. Since then, the Allies had raced east to Berlin, while the Soviet Union charged west.

Germany had been on the brink of defeat for a while, especially after Allied forces crossed the Rhine River in March, giving them a clear path into eastern Germany and Berlin. Still, Hitler refused to surrender. General

Eisenhower warned, "No one knows what the German will do in his own country, and he is trying hard."

The Nazis made a tenacious last stand on their own soil. Hitler dug in for the final battle in a concrete bunker fifty-five feet beneath his Berlin headquarters.

By early April, the Allied forces captured the industrial centers on the Ruhr River. Entire cities were reduced to rubble by intense Allied bombing raids. On April 16, American troops reached Nuremberg, the stage for the Third Reich's massive Nazi Party rallies, and some of Hitler's most maniacal speeches. Hitler ordered the city protected at all costs, but it fell four days later, on April 20, Hitler's birthday.

As the Allies rolled onward to Berlin, they discovered the true evil of the Third Reich: dozens of concentration camps, factories of death where the Nazis exterminated millions of Jews, Gypsies, homosexuals, and "undesirables." The victims were killed in gas chambers, hung, starved, or beaten to death, their emaciated bodies stacked like firewood.

On April 30, as bombs rained down on his bunker, Hitler and Eva Braun, his bride of two days, committed suicide. (German soldiers later burned Hitler's body in the chancellery garden.) Germany surrendered a week later. Field Marshal Wilhelm Keitel signed the formal terms on May 7 and ordered German troops to lay down their arms.

Now it was time for Truman to share the news with his war-weary nation. The crowd of officials and reporters moved from the Oval Office to the Diplomatic Reception Room, where FDR made many of his radio broadcasts. There, on cue, Truman read his statement.

"This is a solemn but glorious hour. I only wish that Franklin D. Roosevelt had lived to see this day," the president said.

He reminded Americans of the terrible cost the Allies had paid to "rid the world of Hitler and his evil band."

"Let us not forget . . . the sorrow and the heartache which today abide in the homes for many of our neighbors. . . . We can repay the debt which we owe to our God, to our dead and to our children only by work, by cease-less devotion to the responsibility which lies ahead of us.

"If I could give you a single watchword for the coming months, that word is work. Work and more work. We must work to finish the war. Our victory is but half won."

Truman reminded Americans the war in Europe might be over, but the Far East was "still in bondage to the treacherous tyranny of the Japanese. When the last Japanese division has surrendered unconditionally, then only will our fighting job be done."

With that, Truman ended the broadcast. It lasted two and a half min-utes.

Tens of millions of Americans tuned in to Truman's announcement, then spontaneously took to the streets to celebrate. Taverns opened early and filled up fast. Strangers embraced and wept for joy. Newspapers across the country put out special editions with big, bold headlines: The *Pitts-burgh Press* led with "V-E Day Proclaimed. Japan Next." The *Hattiesburg (Mississippi) American* shouted, "Japs Being Measured for Burial Kimono." The New York *Daily News* headline was short and simple: "It's Over."

Oak Ridge, Tennessee

Ruth Sisson heard whoops and shouts in the entryway of the massive de-fense plant in Oak Ridge. She wondered what the commotion was about, and a coworker shouted down the corridor: "The Nazis have surrendered!"

"Isn't that wonderful?" said the woman on the nearest stool.

"Yes, it is," Sisson said with a big smile. "Thank the Lord."

Ruth felt her heart flutter for a moment. Her dear Lawrence was in Germany, last she'd heard. Maybe he would come home! Surely the mili-tary wouldn't need so many soldiers, now that Germany was defeated. But then again, the United States was still fighting in the Pacific. From what the papers and radio said, that part of the war wasn't getting any better.

Ruth wanted to clap and cheer with the others, but her mind kept running down the same old dark roads. What if the Japanese didn't surrender? What if the United States had to invade Japan? What if the men who escaped injury in Europe were shipped *there*? Her joy faded. What Ruth didn't know that day was that she was working on a secret weapon—one that could end the war and save her boyfriend's life. It was so secret, workers were warned not to ask any questions. Just show up for work, do your job, and go home.

While her coworkers took a break to celebrate, Sisson took the president at his word and went back to work, monitoring dials and meters on the giant machine in front of her. Work was soothing, if a little dull. It kept her mind off her worries.

Sisson's boyfriend, Lawrence Huddleston, used to write two or three times a week, but the letters had slowed down significantly since he'd gone into the battle zone. Lawrence was an Army medic. He had taken part in some of the bloodiest battles on the western front, including D-Day and the Battle of the Bulge.

That turned out to be the last German offensive of the war. It went on for six midwinter weeks, from December 16, 1944, to January 25, 1945. Thirty German divisions attacked battle-fatigued American troops across eighty-five miles of Belgium's densely wooded Ardennes Forest. Hitler's plan was to drive a wedge, splitting the advancing Allied forces in two. It almost worked. The U.S. Army defeated the Germans, but 100,000 American soldiers were either killed or wounded.

It was Lawrence's job to keep wounded soldiers alive. Ruth worried that witnessing so much horror and gore might erode her sweetheart's faith. He was such a quiet, spiritual man. His letters barely mentioned his work or the progress of the war. He always asked about home, about her: What was she doing this weekend? How were her mother and father? Ruth always wrote back straightaway, and tried to keep the news upbeat. She told him about the latest songs on the radio, about movies, family dinners, choir practice. She urged him to stay as safe as he could, so when he came home, they could start their life together.

Ruth hadn't had a letter for weeks now. She felt a tingling, like maybe this great day for America might be a lucky day for her, too. Maybe there was a letter waiting for her.

As soon as her shift ended, Ruth bounded for the bus stop outside the factory gates. The bus was nothing more than a cattle wagon towed behind a truck, with a few benches and a stove in the middle. When the wagon pulled up and the next shift of workers got off, Ruth jumped on board and settled on a bench. The passengers chattered about the morning's news.

Ruth stared at the spring flowers along the narrow dirt roads, the trees leafing out nicely. The bus stopped to let people off by farm gates or winding paths leading up into the hills. Her mind drifted back to Lawrence. She wondered where he was that day, what he was doing.

Ruth didn't have much of a life story. She was raised in Oliver Springs, a small town outside Knoxville. She'd graduated from high school in 1943, and moved to nearby Clinton to take a job in a hosiery mill. She lived in a boardinghouse on Main Street, a block away from the factory. She saved her wages so she could go to college to become a teacher.

Ruth was taller than most girls her age. She kept her shoulder-length brown hair tightly curled and pulled back from her face, which made her look more mature than her seventeen years. She liked to wear dresses and lipstick, but she had to wait until the occasional night out to indulge herself.

One evening, Ruth and her best friend, Chelsey Davis, dressed up and went to the Ritz Theater for a movie, then to the soda fountain at Hoskins Drug Store for a bite. The place was jammed; all the seats at the lunch counter were filled. The girls grabbed an empty booth near the back. Soon two friendly young men approached their table.

"Do you mind if we sit with you?" one of them asked, introducing himself as Lawrence. The girls agreed and the quartet soon was gabbing away over burgers and fries.

Ruth still remembered what was playing on the jukebox: Frank Sinatra's

"In the Blue of the Evening," and Benny Goodman's "Taking a Chance on Love." They talked a little about the movie, but mostly about where they worked and who they knew in common. Lawrence Huddleston was good-looking, about five feet eight inches tall with a barrel chest, a crew cut, strong hands, and a big smile.

Ruth agreed to meet Lawrence the next evening.

They watched the same movie they did the night before, then strolled down Main Street. It was a beautiful, cloudless summer night, with stars stretched across the sky. They walked up and down the street, talking about their lives. Ruth told him she was the oldest of seven children, the only girl. Her father operated a sawmill and kept a small farm with a big vegetable garden, with rows of tomatoes, potatoes, and fields of corn. During the Great Depression, he'd kept his workers going with food from that garden. Being the oldest, Ruth helped her parents plant, weed, and harvest, milk the cows, and bring in the hay. It was a tough life. She wanted something better for herself. College was her ticket out.

Lawrence said he'd been to college. He'd won a football scholarship to Tennessee Wesleyan College, and played offensive tackle. It was fun, he

Ruth Sisson with Lawrence Huddleston.

said, but then his father died, leaving his mother to raise his brother and four sisters alone. His brother joined the Navy. Lawrence dropped out of college and took a job at the Alcoa aluminum plant to help the family survive.

He paused for a moment. His daddy had died of a broken heart, he said. Like Ruth's dad, his father had a big farm that was all paid off. But the Tennessee Valley Authority—one of FDR's ambitious projects to pull the country out of the Depression—used eminent domain to seize the property to build the Norris Dam. The project brought electricity to that part of the Great Smoky Mountains, but hard feelings remained. His father bought another farm, but the government took that one, too—this time to build a defense plant in Oak Ridge that "went up overnight."

"They didn't give him what the land was really worth," Lawrence said.

As they walked, Lawrence reached out and took Ruth's hand. He had one more thing to tell her.

"I just got my draft notice," he said.

Ruth stopped.

"I haven't been inducted. I don't know when that will happen, but I'm dreading it," Lawrence said. "I'm not afraid to go and fight. I'm just worried about my mother. She hasn't been doing so well. She needs my wages from the plant, for the girls."

That was when Ruth started falling for him. A man who cared for his mama like that? That was a good man.

"You think there's a chance we could get together again?" he asked.

Ruth didn't hesitate. "I'd like that," she said.

They started dating. As summer turned to fall they walked the same street, singing, "Oh, What a Beautiful Morning," a cheerful new Bing Crosby song. Some nights, they drove to Knoxville in Lawrence's big black Chevrolet.

After Thanksgiving, Lawrence learned he would be inducted in January. It was time for Ruth to bring him home to meet her family. Her mother, Beulah Marie Sisson, never liked any of the boys she dated, but she adored

Lawrence. He was an easygoing, responsible man. Her parents gave him their blessing.

The night before Lawrence was inducted, he asked Ruth to marry him when he came home from the war. She'd already prepared an answer.

"I'd have to think about it," she said. As much as Ruth liked Lawrence, she was only a teenager. She wasn't ready for marriage. Not yet.

Lawrence promised that he wouldn't give up. He'd keep asking her until she said yes.

The Army soon discovered Lawrence had taken anatomy classes in college, so they trained him to become a medic. In March 1944, Lawrence wrote to say he was being deployed to Europe. Would Ruth come to the army base outside Gadsden, Alabama, to see him off?

Ruth asked her father for permission. He agreed to let her go, but only if she took her brother, W.D., as chaperone.

And so one early morning, Ruth and her brother boarded a Greyhound bus for the daylong trip. She was so excited that she couldn't stop talking. She told W.D. her worries about Lawrence's safety. The news said Allied forces were in North Africa, Sicily, Italy—places that didn't mean a lot to people in rural Tennessee. Would Lawrence be sent to one of those war zones? Sooner or later, they'd have to go into France, and then Germany. It was too scary to think about.

When they stepped off the bus, Lawrence was waiting, impressive in his brown uniform. The streets were busy with soldiers. Ruth and W.D. stayed two nights at a downtown hotel. Lawrence showed them around town, took them to restaurants and funny movies, trying to laugh away the worry he saw on Ruth's face. He assured her he was going to be okay, that he'd had no frightening premonitions, like some soldiers did. That wasn't enough. Sitting in a café booth, she stared into his eyes. "You have to take care of yourself," she said.

He nodded his head. "I will."

The trip went quickly. At the bus stop, when the time came to say good-bye, Ruth felt a knot in her stomach. She didn't know if she would ever see Lawrence again. She fought back her tears. She didn't want him to see her cry. They hugged and kissed each other. "I'll see you when I get home," he said softly.

"I love you," Ruth said. She turned around and stepped onto the bus, walking quickly past the driver. She collapsed into a seat and began sobbing. W.D. sat next to her, his arm draped around her shoulders.

Lawrence wrote often. He dared to use that four-letter word, too.

"I know we're a long way apart in miles, but honey, our hearts are close and maybe we can be back together before long," he wrote on July 9, 1944. "I love you, my darling, more and more every day. Keep your chin up for me, my love."

Time passed. Letters arrived, sometimes packages. Once, he sent a bottle of French perfume—D'Orsay Pino-Nice. Ruth didn't have many occasions to wear it, but every time she did, she thought of her faraway soldier.

It wasn't all romance. When Lawrence's mother died, Ruth was the one who told him the news. He'd made Ruth promise to tell him "if anything happened to mother." So, she kept her word. And as she was writing the sad news, something strange happened. Ruth felt like she couldn't live without this man. She was deeply in love. She told him—yes, she would marry him as soon as he got home.

In the meantime, Ruth heard rumors about a new job opportunity just down the road. A vast city of thirty thousand people had sprung up almost overnight, some kind of Army plant. No one knew much more than that— except that they needed lots and lots of workers, and right away. Ruth applied in August 1944. Her father applied, too.

When they went for their interviews, Ruth noticed the heavy security. The Sissons passed through one of seven gates in the miles-long perimeter fence. Her father was put to work in a machine shop in one part of the sprawling complex. Ruth was hired, too, but no one could tell her what her job entailed. She found out on her first day of work.

Ruth and her coworkers were going to help win the war, the supervisor said, but they couldn't say a word about anything inside the factory walls. Ruth already knew that. On her way in, she'd seen billboards with Uncle Sam's picture superimposed over three monkeys:

What you see here
What you do here
What you hear here
When you leave here
Let it stay here.

Ruth became a "cubicle operator." But the cubicles weren't like the ones crammed into offices across America. Hers was a tall chair stationed in front of one of 1,152 calutrons—machines that used an electromagnetic process to enrich uranium. Ruth monitored an essential step for building atomic bombs, but no one told her that. The cubicle operators never knew the science behind their machines. As the old military joke goes: "My job is so secret, even I don't know what I'm doing."

Most of the calutrons were more than eight feet tall, stretching from floor to ceiling. Each one had cockpit-like control panels with gauges and meters to monitor, and handles and knobs to adjust. Ruth was taught what to do if the needles on the meters went too far left or too far right. Ruth was supposed to "get it back to where it was supposed to be."

The women worked eight-hour shifts, sometimes the day shift, other times the overnight "graveyard" slot. The machines were monitored twenty-four hours a day, seven days a week. Ruth quickly noticed that the cubicle operators, as well as most of the workers in their part of the complex, were young women just out of high school. They all sat on stools in front of their big machines, eyes focused on the equipment.

Life slowly settled into a routine. Show up for a shift, go through security, check in with the supervisor, head to the cubicle. She sat there for

Ruth Sisson at work in her cubicle in front of the calutron machine. Ruth is the third person on the left.

eight hours, turning knobs to keep the meters balanced. If she couldn't balance the meters, she called her supervisor. If the supervisor couldn't do it, they closed down the calutron and called for maintenance.

They had to keep a close watch. Ruth had no idea what the machine was, or what the dials meant, or what happened when she turned those knobs. It wasn't her business. She didn't much care.

The calutron was developed only months before at the University of California, Berkeley, by Ernest O. Lawrence. The prototypes were operated by PhDs. There was some early concern about how women without scientific training would handle the equipment, but General Groves soon discovered the "girls" were more effective at the job than the scientists were. The physicists were too concerned with figuring out what atomic process was causing a needle to peg left or right, while the "Calutron Girls" simply alerted their supervisors when there was an issue. They also proved to have a better touch when adjusting the dials. The scientists constantly fiddled with them.

Keeping busy was the best way for Ruth to deal with her anxiety. When she was monitoring the calutron, she didn't have time to think dark thoughts.

The war was taking its toll on Tennessee. Ruth had recently attended a funeral for Army private Virgil Goodman, a childhood friend killed in action in Europe. They'd run together in the schoolyard, played red rover, sung in the church choir. When Ruth closed her eyes, she could see Virgil's grief-stricken family there by the grave in Butler Cemetery.

Ruth didn't want to be superstitious or think the worst, but how could she not? In quiet moments at work, or in bed at night, she whispered a prayer, "God, please keep Lawrence safe. Don't let him get killed."

The bus dropped Ruth right in front of her mailbox. She pulled out several letters. Nothing from Lawrence. She sighed and headed up the dirt path to the front door. It was dusk, the sky a riot of orange, red, and purple. A cool breeze was blowing, the scent of pine and jasmine in the air. As she did so often, there on the path, she wondered where Lawrence was just then.

She only hoped he wasn't on his way to the Pacific.

COUNTDOWN:
70 DAYS

May 28, 1945

Washington, D.C.

Colonel Tibbets fumed quietly in his chair as the generals took their seats for the high-level Pentagon meeting. Where the hell was Beser? It was almost guaranteed someone would ask questions about radar, including whether the enemy could prematurely trigger the bomb's fusing system. It was a question that no one but Beser, his top radar man, could answer.

Tibbets knew they had to work out every detail, answer every question. The bomb had to be tested before the end of the Potsdam Conference, an upcoming summit with President Truman, British prime minister Winston Churchill, and Soviet premier Joseph Stalin. The "gadget" wasn't just a weapon anymore. It was also a pawn—maybe a queen was more accurate—in a delicate international chess game.

Now that Germany had surrendered, the three leaders were to meet to set the borders of the new, postwar Europe, a subject first debated in February 1945 at Yalta. During that weeklong conference, Stalin promised FDR and Churchill that Russia would enter the war against Japan after Germany's defeat. Although the leaders remained committed to fighting a joint war in the Pacific, tensions between the three powers had been intensifying. Churchill had argued for free and fair elections in Eastern Europe. But Stalin was proving obstinate. He was reluctant to withdraw from parts of Eastern Europe, such as Poland, that his nation had taken from

Germany. The Allies feared that Stalin might never leave those countries, a move that could trigger another conflict.

An operational nuclear weapon would give the United States enormous leverage when negotiations resumed. No one could say for sure if the atomic bomb would even work. But Tibbets, Groves, and Oppenheimer had to assume the test explosion would be successful. They had to look beyond that and come up with a plan to use the bomb in combat.

That's why Tibbets was here, in this Pentagon conference room. He and the others at the table were waiting for the start of a meeting where they'd continue to engage in a grisly bureaucratic discussion. Which Japanese city should be immolated? Which would produce the most effective military destruction and psychological effects on the Japanese Empire?

The Target Committee had met twice in May at Oppenheimer's office at Los Alamos. Everyone agreed the first atomic explosion should be sufficiently spectacular for the importance of the weapon to be fully recognized internationally. They looked at places untouched by Allied bombing— still-thriving cities the Japanese felt were stable and safe.

They chose five potential targets:

KYOTO: *The former capital of Japan was an urban industrial area with a population of one million people, according to a Target Committee memo. "Many people and industries are now being moved there as other areas are being destroyed. From the psychological point of view there is the advantage that Kyoto is an intellectual center for Japan and the people there are more apt to appreciate the significance of such a weapon as the gadget."*

HIROSHIMA: *An important army depot and port of embarkation in the middle of an urban industrial area. "It is such a size that a large part of the city could be extensively damaged. There are adjacent hills which are likely to produce a focusing effect which would considerably increase the blast damage."*

YOKOHAMA: *"An important urban industrial area which has so far been untouched. Industrial activities include aircraft manufacture, machine tools, docks, electrical equipment and oil refineries."*

KOKURA: Home to one of the largest arsenals in Japan, it was surrounded by urban industry. *"The arsenal is important for light ordnance, anti-aircraft and beachhead defense materials."*

NIIGATA: *A strategic port city. "Its importance is increasing as other ports are damaged."*

As soon as he saw the list, Secretary of War Stimson saved Kyoto. He had a fondness for the city, which he'd visited long ago and remembered as "the shrine of Japanese art and culture."

Now, on this Monday morning, the Target Committee was meeting again. At 9:00 a.m., precisely, Tibbets glimpsed General Thomas Farrell, Groves's deputy, and his staff file into the room, right on time. An officer shut the big doors behind him and handed out "target-description files." Each thick folder contained large-scale maps of the targets, reconnaissance photographs and related data, as well as air-sea rescue procedures—just in case anything went wrong on the mission.

A few yards away, Lieutenant Jacob Beser thundered up the stairwell at the end of the hall and halted at the top to catch his breath. Tibbets had given him a weekend pass to visit his folks in Baltimore, and made him swear he'd be at this 9:00 a.m. meeting. He'd caught an early train, but it ran late. Once at Union Station, he struggled to find a cab. Still, he was only five minutes late. He stepped up to the conference room door, but a guard stopped him. "Restricted area," the guard said. The Women's Army Corps (WAC) officer at the reception desk chimed in. Beser must be mistaken, she said. A lieutenant wouldn't have any business in a meeting with "all *that* top brass."

Beser pleaded his case. But she had her orders, and she wasn't backing down. "Go get some coffee and forget you ever walked in here," she said.

Beser took a seat instead. He knew he wasn't getting in the room and that Tibbets was in there, seething about his absence. The colonel would chew him out once the meeting was over.

It was typical, Beser thought. Always in trouble, through no fault of his own.

Beser was short and skinny, with brown eyes and brown hair, slicked back and parted on the side. He had a big personality—a wise guy who had an opinion about everything, a "people person" who got along with everybody. That was no easy feat with so many alpha males in his squadron.

Beser twisted his hat in his hands and wondered what the men inside the room were saying. He hoped he wouldn't be officially reprimanded, not when he was so close to finally getting into the action. Back when Nazi Germany invaded Poland in 1939, Beser was too young to enlist without his parents' consent. He reminded his mother and father how they had met, a military romance in a hospital during World War I—a

Jacob Beser in 1945.

nurse named Rose fell in love with Nicholas, a handsome wounded soldier.

His parents said no. Beser returned to Johns Hopkins University's mechanical engineering program. He hit the books, and the bars, staying out late with his buddies in the joints along the Baltimore waterfront. He recalled spending Saturday night, December 6, 1941, swilling down oysters with "copious quantities of Arrow Beer" and Schenley's Black Label.

The following afternoon, Jacob was in bed with his hangover when his father barged into his room. "Pearl Harbor's been attacked," he said. "The nation's at war."

Beser joined his parents next to the living room radio. Commentator H. V. Kaltenborn said the Japanese had hit hard and without warning. "The United States has been attacked, and the United States will know how to answer that attack," he said.

Beser made up his mind. He'd go downtown the next morning and enlist as an aviation cadet in the U.S. Army Air Forces. He was still under age twenty-one. But now his parents said they'd sign the paperwork.

When he arrived at the recruiting office early the next day, Beser found a long line of men with the same idea. He finished basic training in October 1942 and was commissioned as a second lieutenant. He graduated near the top of his class of 250 cadets. But instead of heading into combat, he was deployed to Florida for special training on new, secret equipment called radar.

"Radio Detection and Ranging," an early warning system, had become an important new weapon in the war. Battles were often won by whoever was first to locate enemy airplanes, ships, or submarines. To give the Allies an edge, British and American scientists developed radar technology to "see" for hundreds of miles, even at night.

Radar worked by sending out a radio wave and analyzing the reflected wave after it bounced off any object in the air. Early in the war, England used radar to build an effective air defense network. It gave England an advantage during the Battle of Britain, when the German Luftwaffe did its best to bomb the country into submission. Not only could the radar system detect approaching enemy aircraft, but it could also estimate the distance, direction, strength, and altitude of the air force.

Radar had another important use, one that was relevant to the atomic bomb. For most of the war, artillery rounds had impact fuses. These smaller charges exploded when they struck a target, and set off the main explosives in the shell, which blew up into a cloud of shrapnel. But then scientists developed the proximity fuse, which operated like a miniature radar unit in the nose of a shell. If bombs and artillery shells were armed with proximity fuses, which used radio waves to detect their distance to an object, they could be detonated by radar in midair before they struck an enemy target, spreading lethal shrapnel over a wider area. In the case of enemy planes, which were hard to hit with antiaircraft shells, a proximity fuse could turn a miss into a kill.

Engineers at Los Alamos had been trying to create a proximity fuse for the atomic bomb. With a proximity fuse, the nuclear weapon could be detonated at a preset height. Scientists had already done the math. They had calculated that triggering a nuclear explosion in the sky above a Japanese city would have the maximum destructive impact. That's because the bomb's explosive force would shoot directly down to the earth below, then spread swiftly out to the surrounding areas. What was the ideal height to detonate the bomb? Probably two thousand feet above a city.

But Manhattan Project commanders and scientists knew that a radar-controlled proximity fuse came with a frightening vulnerability. A radar wave is basically the same as a radio wave, and if the frequency is known, it can be intercepted or jammed. If that happened, the atomic bomb might detonate too soon or too late, or not at all. The radar officer on the bombing mission had to be on top of everything. He'd need the latest equipment to detect and deflect Japanese radar.

There was no question Beser was among the best radar men in the military. He excelled in his classes, then went on to teach radar to new officers. Over time, Beser became a troubleshooter. During the war, defense companies developed new electronic equipment to improve the technology. When the equipment didn't operate correctly, Beser would work with companies to solve the problem. Sometimes that meant designing a new part—like special antennas—and then retrofitting units.

But Beser was miserable working behind the battle lines. Newspapers and radio newscasts made him crazy. In the spring of 1944, he told his family and friends, "There's a full-scale war in Europe and I'm not part of it."

His frantic effort for a transfer to the front lines landed him in a B-29 squadron in Wendover, Utah. He predicted it wouldn't be long before he was in the middle of the action. But when the Western Pacific Railroad train pulled into Wendover in September 1944, he wondered what the hell he had gotten himself into. He scanned the bleak surroundings—miles and miles of desert scrub. A sun-bleached town with a couple of shops along a ragtag main strip. He thought: "If the United States ever needed an enema, this is where they would insert the tube."

Beser didn't have time to settle in. As soon as he got to his post, the commander summoned everyone to a briefing outside headquarters. Tibbets didn't waste words. He introduced himself and warned the men that they were about to begin rigorous training. Those who stayed the course would soon be overseas, taking part in a mission to win the war. They'd learn more details later, Tibbets said, but not a word could be shared about it. Then, to the group's surprise and delight, Tibbets gave everyone a two-week pass—everyone except Beser, who was waved into Tibbets's office. Several people were already there, all in uniform. This doesn't look good, Beser thought.

"Lieutenant, you are about to be interviewed for a sensitive job," Tibbets said.

The men asked the usual questions: Where did you go to school? What military training have you received? What experience have you had since coming on active duty? Then one of the men looked Beser straight in the eye and asked, "How do you feel about flying combat?"

Beser found it hard not to shout. "Combat is precisely what I'm looking for," he said.

The officers smiled and asked him to wait outside. Fifteen minutes later, he was welcomed to the team.

They didn't tell Beser anything about what his job would be. But he couldn't help thinking his life insurance premium was probably going up.

It had been nonstop ever since. The day after the meeting, Beser flew with Tibbets to Kirtland Air Force Base in Albuquerque. When they got off the plane, they were picked up in a green sedan by Colonel Lansdale, the U.S. Army intelligence officer who'd been in Colorado Springs a few weeks before, when Tibbets had been chosen to lead the mission. Lansdale drove them sixty miles north, to the secret laboratory in Los Alamos. It was the first visit for Tibbets and Beser. As Lansdale drove, he reminded them about secrecy. "Don't volunteer anything you know."

The car stopped in Santa Fe to pick up another passenger, a man in a civilian suit. Norman Ramsey, a physicist, was the project's scientific and technical deputy. He was a tall, thin, clean-cut man with a boyish look. He can't be much older than me, Beser thought. Not all scientists were bearded, gray-haired professors. Over time, Beser would discover most of the scientists working in Los Alamos were in their twenties and thirties.

It was only another thirty-five miles to Los Alamos, but as they neared the destination, Beser noticed the landscape becoming more rugged and steep. They drove up narrow dirt roads, straddling the deepest ruts, to the top of a mesa with a breathtaking view of the Sangre de Cristo Mountains. When they reached the top, they were 7,300 feet above sea level, in a place that was isolated and virtually inaccessible.

Yes, the scenery was spectacular. Los Alamos? Not so much, Beser thought. A high fence topped with barbed wire surrounded what appeared to be some sort of prison. Once they passed through a security gate, Beser saw that many of the buildings were flimsy and hastily built. But the place was huge, bustling with thousands of military people and civilians.

The car pulled up in front of an anonymous-looking building. Lansdale escorted Tibbets to Robert Oppenheimer's office. Ramsey invited Beser to come and see his laboratory. Once inside, Ramsey filled in Beser on important details about the project. Beser would work with his division, called the "Delivery Group." They were responsible for bomb ballistics, and working out how to get the weapon to its target. They weren't nearly as far along as they should be, Ramsey admitted. Time was getting short. They were having some trouble designing the weapon's firing system. There were so many variables to consider when detonating a weapon above the ground: the geography, weather conditions . . . and radio waves.

Beser would soon know every detail of the bomb's firing mechanism, which contained a tiny radar system. He would learn to monitor enemy radar for attempts to jam or detonate the bomb's operating system. They needed to minimize its susceptibility to radio interference, Ramsey said. Beser would have to know how the bomb worked, step by step.

As he listened, Beser quickly realized that this was no ordinary mission. All missions were dangerous. But this one was as risky as it gets. It was clear to him that if he didn't do his job right, the bomb could go off on the way to the target.

Only a few scientists knew much about the program, Ramsey said. Beser would have to fly on each test run, then each bombing mission "until the medics say you've had enough." At this point, no one could guess how many bombs would be built, how many would be dropped—or whether they would even work.

Ramsey never said the words "atomic bomb." He talked about "fundamental forces of the universe being released," and "chain reactions taking place." He rattled off the names of other scientists involved in the project: Enrico Fermi, Niels Bohr, and Hans Bethe—all of them scientific royalty. Beser recognized their names from his physics classes. He had read some of their work.

After the briefing, Beser was introduced to several scientists who gave him a window into their work. They talked about creating "guns" using "atomic bullets" that, on impact, could trigger an explosion, whose light would be "brighter than a thousand suns." By the end of the day, Beser knew they were building an atomic bomb. *An atomic bomb.* Something straight out of a science fiction novel. The amazing part for Beser was that he, a Jewish kid from Baltimore, was going to be a part of history—if he wasn't killed first.

As days became weeks, and weeks became months, Beser learned more about the weapon as he shuttled between Wendover and Los Alamos. The weapons, to be more precise. There were two of them, two types: Little Boy and Fat Man.

Little Boy was a skinny, ten-foot-long, 9,600-pound bomb with a uranium core. Fat Man weighed 10,300 pounds and had a plutonium core. Both operated on the same theory: if sufficient force could be delivered to each weapon's radioactive core, it would set off a chain reaction, unleashing immense explosive power.

Inside Little Boy's bomb casing was a gunlike firing mechanism designed to detonate the weapon. The uranium was divided into two pieces: the "bullet" and the target. The bullet was a cylindrical stack of nine uranium rings inside a one-sixteenth-inch steel casing. The target was a hollow cylinder of more uranium. Once triggered by the radar-activated proximity fuse, the projectile would be fired into the target through a high-powered, six-foot-long aircraft-gun barrel. Traveling at 684 miles per hour, the projectile would fit like a plug into the target. The impact would create an explosive nuclear chain reaction. Little Boy was a terribly unstable weapon. Once the gun was loaded with the cordite propellant, anything that ignited it would cause a full-on atomic explosion.

Fat Man had the potential to be even more powerful than Little Boy, but it required a different trigger. (It would have needed a thirty-foot "gun barrel" to reach detonation velocity.) Instead, scientists designed an implosion mechanism to spark its atomic reaction. The plutonium core was packed inside 5,300 pounds of high explosives. After being triggered by the proximity fuse, thirty-two pairs of detonators would ignite simultaneously. The explosion would compress the softball-sized core into the size of a billiard ball, creating the necessary chain reaction.

Few people outside the Manhattan Project knew about these things. It was top secret. But Beser, a mere lieutenant now sitting in the waiting area outside the Pentagon conference room, knew more about the weapon than most of the men inside did.

He'd be on Tibbets's shit list for sure. Nothing I can do, he thought. Beser heard whispering. He looked up at the reception desk and saw an officer—a major—towering over the WAC. The officer looked in his direction. "Are you Beser?" he asked.

Beser said he was.

"What are you doing sitting there?" the man snapped. "You're needed inside." On his way into the conference room Beser smiled sweetly at the WAC.

He stepped inside and Tibbets motioned to the seat beside him. Beser tried to whisper an explanation about why he was late but was interrupted by a captain who had been addressing the committee. The captain wanted the Navy to place a submarine three miles off the Japanese coast and flash a LORAN beam—short for Long Range Navigation, a sophisticated new guidance system—to help them navigate their approach to the target. In the event of trouble, the beam could be used to guide the B-29 to the submarine for a possible sea rescue.

When the captain asked Beser for his opinion about the proposal, Beser didn't hesitate. "It's bullshit," he said.

Farrell asked Beser to elaborate. Beser said he didn't think it was possible to hold a submarine that steady because the tides would pull it off track. With the general's permission, Beser walked to a blackboard, picked up some chalk, and used a physics equation to prove his point. He scribbled a few numbers and Greek letters, then calculated the effects of wind and tidal currents. The submarine would need to be on the surface for the LORAN to work. "And in no way can a submarine remain surfaced three miles off the Japanese coast without coming under attack," Beser said. Farrell was impressed. Tibbets exhaled: Beser had delivered.

The committee went back to reviewing the targets. After several hours, the group agreed Hiroshima was the best choice for the first bomb drop. It was home to 285,000 people and 43,000 military personnel. The Second General Army, under the command of Field Marshal Shunroku Hata, was based there. His command force would defend the island of Honshu if and when Allied forces launched an invasion of the Japanese homeland. The surrounding area was dotted with military targets: shipyards, an airport, and an aircraft parts factory. While many of the buildings in the center of the city were built with reinforced concrete, the businesses and homes on the outskirts were mostly framed with wood. So many details still had to be worked out before they could even set a date for the mission. But, like the others, Tibbets knew Hiroshima would be the perfect target.

COUNTDOWN:

68 DAYS

May 30, 1945

Kimita, Japan

As another long day dawned, Hideko Tamura and her best friend, Miyoshi, bounded out of the school building and down dozens of steps to a small stream. There was no running water in the school, so the children of the Zensho Temple washed themselves in the creek. The girls shrieked as the cold water splashed on their faces and arms. Up the long steps they climbed, back into the school to get dressed.

A gong sounded, the signal for morning sutra. Hideko and Miyoshi grabbed their sutra texts, rushed into the chapel, and knelt on the tatami matting. Together the children belted out the *Namu Amida Butsu* chant: "Save us, merciful Buddha." Once that was done, the children tucked away their texts and lined up with their rice bowls for breakfast at a long row of narrow refectory tables. Hungry as they were, the girls were in no rush to finish. There was not a lot to look forward to at Zensho Temple, except another day of backbreaking chores.

Hideko hated the place, even though she knew why her parents sent her away from Hiroshima. Everyone feared U.S. warplanes. B-29s had fire-bombed many Japanese cities, but Hiroshima hadn't been hit yet. It was only a matter of time.

When the government evacuated children from Hiroshima to rural areas for their safety, their parents didn't protest. While they didn't want to be separated from their sons and daughters, they understood the risks of staying behind. They comforted themselves with government assurances that evacuees would be well-fed and schooled.

But once settled in the village of Kimita, Hideko quickly discovered that ten-year-olds went to class only on rainy days. The rest of the time they worked outdoors.

One group was made to dig out giant pine roots on the forest floor and construct hearths beneath to extract the pine oil for airplanes. Another group dug up heavy rocks. Hideko and her friend carried the stones in backpacks across the quarry, but the straps rubbed Hideko's shoulders raw. She was put on digging duty instead.

When food was scarce, they went out in small groups to the surrounding mountains to collect edible plants. Hideko was usually exhausted by the end of the day. "I'm hungry" was a familiar refrain among the students.

After almost two months in Kimita, Hideko was still deeply homesick. Her mother and father were kind, nurturing parents. Hideko's father, Jiro Tamura, was the second son of the founder of Tamura Industrial Group, a Hiroshima-based company that produced rubber goods throughout Japan and the Far East. Jiro had majored in law, but really wanted to be an artist. He had thick, dark brown curly hair that made him "look like the painter he always wanted to be," his daughter recalled. A good swimmer, he had broad, sturdy shoulders. Hideko smiled when she thought about the nights after supper, when he'd hoist her on his shoulders to walk the streets looking at the vendors' wares. She was proud to be seen with her papa.

Her parents met at a college baseball game in Tokyo. Jiro's school, Keio University, was playing Waseda, and there she was—a beautiful young woman sitting with her mother in the stands. After the game, Jiro followed them home and asked her mother for permission to court her. Her mother said no; it wasn't proper to accept such a bold request without a formal introduction. Courtship was done by interfamily arrangement, and in this case, the families were from different social classes. But Jiro was persistent.

Kimiko was beautiful, slender, and tall, with large expressive eyes and long, thick eyelashes. She held a job outside the house to help her widowed mother pay the bills. She loved Western culture and fashion. She preferred hats and heels over restrictive kimonos and obis. She went to movies and loved to read books and poems by Leo Tolstoy, Edgar Allan Poe, and Henry Wadsworth Longfellow.

Jiro's family objected to him courting a working-class girl, but he was in love. When he married Kimiko, his family disowned him. He took a sales job with Nissan Motors in Tokyo. A few years later Hideko was born, and Jiro's family reconciled. The young couple enjoyed entertaining. Their house in Tokyo was filled with friends and laughter.

Their bookcase featured Western classics. Hideko learned to read with Snow White, Sleeping Beauty, and later Robinson Crusoe and Huckleberry Finn. Her mother sang songs of spring to lull Hideko to sleep, and

Kimiko holding Hideko as a child.

through the window, the child could see her father in his smock, working inside his makeshift art studio. He spent hours in the little room making soft-colored landscapes. He admired the French Impressionists. His favorite painter was Paul Cézanne.

Then one dark day in 1938, the dreaded "red paper" arrived. Jiro was drafted into the Japanese Imperial Army, which had invaded China. Kimiko and little Hideko moved to Jiro's family estate in Hiroshima to wait out his three-year service.

The young officer was released from the army in 1941, but his veteran status couldn't save him from the war. Years later, Hideko remembered the voices on the radio, and the adults suddenly speaking in hushed voices. Hideko heard her aunt say Japan was at war with the United States and Great Britain. They were Japan's enemies now. Hideko didn't understand. *They're fighting us*? She asked if they could still see American movies. The little girl said she loved Charlie Chaplin. But her aunt warned Hideko to keep her voice down. "What if someone hears that and thinks we're unpatriotic?"

The adults assured her not to worry. But how could she not? She saw the looks on their faces.

A month after Pearl Harbor, the red paper came again. Jiro reported to the army base in Hiroshima.

Once again, Hideko and her mother moved in with her father's family. She was enrolled in the prestigious Seibi Academy, a wing of the Japanese military. It was a time of great patriotism, with lessons on Japan's mystical origins: how the land of the Rising Sun was created when a pair of gods stirred muddy waters, and droplets turned into the islands. Their celestial grandson was sent down to Kyushu Island to reign over all Japan. The students sang folk songs about Japanese people dedicating themselves to their country.

By 1944, the mood had changed. Families were losing loved ones in faraway places like Saipan and Guam. More and more ships were being destroyed. The government established a ration system for food and fuel.

Goods quickly disappeared from the market. Factories were being shut down. And Japanese cities were burning from relentless American B-29 raids. Still, Hideko was spared most of the hardship. Hiroshima hadn't been bombed. She played with her best friend, Miyoshi, and her cousins. Her father was stationed at a nearby army base and came home every night.

But by early 1945, Hiroshima was a different city. Bomb shelters were dug everywhere. Cisterns went up between houses throughout the neighborhood, for emergency water storage. Family life and school classes were interrupted for safety drills on how to extinguish fires started by incendiary bombs. Clothes had labels sewn in with the wearers' names and addresses. If the worst happened, their bodies could be identified.

Hideko's mother had survived the great Tokyo-Yokohama earthquake in 1923, which killed 140,000 people. She gave her daughter a detailed plan to follow if the "final assault" on Japan came to Hiroshima. The enemy would attack by air, Kimiko warned. If indoors, Hideko was to hang on to heavy furniture. That way, if the house was crushed, there might be space created at the bottom for protection, her mother instructed. Hideko would then have to find a way to leave the building as quickly as possible so the fire from incendiary bombs would not surround her. Once outside, the little girl had to run toward the river as fast as possible, making sure to protect her head with a hood or cushion during the escape. Airplanes often returned to kill off people fleeing an attack. Kimiko repeated these instructions over and over until they were etched in Hideko's mind. She listened with a sense of disbelief, never really believing tomorrow would not be just like today.

Until April 10, when the children of Hiroshima were evacuated from the city.

Hideko's mother worked feverishly at her sewing machine, preparing clothes and packing the belongings her little girl would carry to Kimita. She stayed up late the night before, fixing a box lunch for the long train trip. They went over the contents of her bundle in great detail. Kimiko saved a little pouch for last, which she placed in Hideko's hand.

"This is part of us," she said. "Papa's nail clippings and a lock of my hair."

Hideko was puzzled.

"This is a time of great emergency," her mother said. "We have to be prepared for anything. If something happens to me and Papa, you will still have something from us, to remember us."

Hideko was stunned. She didn't know how to process the information. She understood she was going away because cities were being bombed. They were too dangerous for children. But she hadn't connected that to *her* city, to *her* parents. It was unthinkable. Sensing her daughter's fear, Kimiko assured Hideko this was only in case of an extreme *if*. Chances were, they would be right here in Hiroshima waiting for her when the war ended.

"How long do you think that might be?" Hideko asked.

"I don't know," Kimiko said. She smiled then. "I survived the Tokyo earthquake. I can survive anything. I promise you I'll be around for a long time. And so will you."

In the predawn hours, a sea of children and their parents filled the Hiroshima Station Square. Many wept, or fought back tears. Officials gave reassuring speeches, praising those who endured hardships until victory was theirs. Children like Hideko were told to carry on.

Hideko was appointed leader of her girls' group, responsible for helping smaller children onto the train. When her turn came to board, she turned toward her mother to wave good-bye and saw Kimiko clutching a handkerchief to her eyes, trying to hide her tears. Hideko was independent and strong, just like her mother. But she was still a little girl. Overwhelmed, she burst into tears and sobbed all the way to her seat. She mustered enough strength to fulfill her duty. She called out the names of her classmates, made sure everyone was there. The whistle blew. As the train left the station. Hideko watched as the adults swarmed the train tracks, crying out and waving good-bye as if they might not see their children again.

The trip was a long one. Hideko tried to comfort the other girls, but hours after the train left, some were still crying. Outside the windows, mountain ranges and thatched-roof houses passed by. Day turned to night, and the train pulled into the station at Zensho Temple, Kimita. Time seemed to stop then. Hideko wondered when it would start again, when they would go home, if her parents missed her as keenly as she missed them.

The days were dull and difficult, and things were not improving. She decided to take action.

She knew school officials censored their letters home, that anything less than cheerful was never posted. Hideko determined to find a way around the censors and get letters out to their parents that told the truth about the forced labor, hunger, and squalor, and appealed for a rescue.

Life might be dangerous at home, but it couldn't be worse than this, Hideko thought. She needed her mother.

COUNTDOWN:

66 DAYS

June 1, 1945
Washington, D.C.

Henry Stimson's old bones ached. After two days of maps, black coffee, logistics, and wrangling, the Interim Committee was poised to make its final recommendation: Should they use this atomic weapon, or continue to grind out the war in Japan the old-fashioned way? Ultimately, it would be Truman's call, but this panel carried great weight.

It was heavy going. The venerable secretary of war listened carefully to all sides of the issue: the economic impact, the environmental damage, the morality of employing such a devastating weapon against fellow human beings. The more Stimson heard, the more he returned to the same question: How many civilians would die? Entire Japanese cities could be wiped out, millions of innocents destroyed, the landscape scorched and poisoned for decades after. The possibilities were disturbing.

But there seemed to be no other way to get Japan to surrender.

The country was tired of war. More than three years after the Pearl Harbor attack, every aspect of American life continued to revolve around the conflict. Factories churned out tanks and planes. Schools turned out young men who were still being drafted and deployed overseas. Women and children looked more and more like refugees because food, fabrics, clothes, and household items were still being rationed. There was a flutter of optimism when Germany surrendered. Maybe the war with Japan would be over soon, maybe most of the soldiers and sailors would be home by Christmas . . . but that hope flickered out a little more each day.

President Truman didn't mince words when he told Congress, "There is no easy way to win" in Japan. Victory would mean doubling the number of American forces in the Pacific to four million. Allies promised to pitch in, but Truman tamped down expectations. "We have not yet come up against the main strength of the Japanese military force of four million troops under arms and several million additional men of military age who have not yet been called to the colors."

Truman's message was a bucket of cold water on the hopes of America. Every time a war-weary citizen opened a newspaper, turned on the radio, or went to the movies, the news was an endless vision of battles, bombs, and casualty reports.

The newspaper on Stimson's desk reported the grizzled U.S. First Army, which had spearheaded the drive from Normandy to Berlin, was now being deployed to the Pacific. The American Baptist Foreign Mission found evidence of war crimes: apparently Japanese soldiers had beheaded eleven pastors and a pastor's nine-year-old son two years earlier in the Philippines. The inside pages enumerated the $280 billion America had already spent fighting the Nazis and the Japanese. Another story focused on Osaka, the latest city to burn in American firebombing raids. The reporter quoted General Curtis LeMay, the man in charge of the relentless air campaign: "No matter how you slice it, you're going to kill an awful lot of citizens."

Stimson abhorred this war of massive destruction. He was a soldier, yes, but also a humanist, a diplomat, a champion of international law and morality. He believed that war "must be restrained within the bounds of humanity." Airpower should be limited to "legitimate military targets."

But World War II had upended noble rules of engagement. Germany and Japan had ruthlessly targeted civilians in cities and towns and herded "undesirables" into death camps. America wasn't like that, he maintained. Deliberately targeting civilians for mass killing was immoral. But now his country was poised to unleash a weapon that would kill an incalculable number of people. And that was his conundrum: Stimson was both awed by the weapon's destructive power and appalled. Stimson had called the bomb both "a Frankenstein" and a "means for world peace."

Stimson had expressed his concerns to Truman. He told the president that the reputation of the United States for fair play and humanitarianism was "the world's biggest asset for peace in the coming decades. I believe the same rule of sparing the civilian population should be applied, as far as possible, to the uses of any new weapons."

With the date for the first test of the atomic bomb drawing closer, Stimson rushed to create a new policy, some guidelines for the proper use of nuclear weapons in war, as well as peacetime. With Truman's blessing, Stimson in early May established an Interim Committee, until a more formal nuclear control organization could be created.

Stimson was the director, and eight prominent industrial, scientific, and political figures filled out the panel, including Vannevar Bush, an electrical engineer who oversaw the government mobilization of scientific research during World War II, and James Conant, president of Harvard University. Four Manhattan Project leaders, including Oppenheimer and Enrico Fermi, represented the scientific community.

General Groves supported Stimson's idea. The committee would show the world that "the very important decision as to the use of the bomb was not made by the War Department alone but rather that they were decisions reached by a group of individuals well removed from the immediate influence of men in uniforms."

The committee, meeting for the first time on May 9, immediately began tackling the complicated issues. Stimson acknowledged the challenge facing the group. "Gentlemen, it is our responsibility to recommend action that may turn the course of civilization," he said.

It was important to regard the bomb as more than a new weapon. It was a "revolutionary change in the relations of man to the universe," he warned, that might mean "the doom of civilization."

The old soldier was not the only one concerned about history and morality. The committee was designed to sound out the doubts of a significant number of scientists at work on the project. The scientific critics were
led by Leo Szilard, the same physicist who urged Einstein to write Franklin
Roosevelt back in 1939, warning of the possibility Hitler was developing
nuclear weapons. Szilard was now having serious second thoughts.

He was the chief physicist at the Metallurgical Laboratory at the University of Chicago, a group charged with producing weapons-grade plutonium to fuel the bombs. Szilard felt uneasy about the military's dominant
role in managing the Manhattan Project. Two months earlier, Szilard organized his colleagues to demand limits on the use of atomic weapons. He
drafted an open letter to President Roosevelt, urging the president to practice restraint in using the bomb, and circulated it to the various Manhattan
Project locations. But the letter never reached the president's desk.

After Roosevelt died, Szilard arranged a White House meeting with
Truman, but was passed off at the last minute to James Byrnes, the president's representative on the Interim Committee. Szilard and two colleagues visited Byrnes at his home in Spartanburg, South Carolina. The
meeting didn't go as planned.

Szilard told Byrnes he'd spent many sleepless nights thinking about
"the wisdom of testing bombs and using bombs." Other nations were hard
at work on their own nuclear programs, and would likely have bombs of
their own in a few years. "Perhaps the greatest immediate danger which
faces us is the possibility our 'demonstration' of atomic bombs will precipitate a race in the production of these devices between the United States
and Russia," he warned.

But Byrnes, a former U.S. senator and Supreme Court justice, and
soon to be Truman's secretary of state, was a born politician. To him, the
atomic bomb represented U.S. power over other nations. It would defeat
Japan, he believed, and keep the Soviet Union from expanding its influence
in Asia and Europe.

Szilard left the meeting disappointed, saying Byrnes was more concerned about the Soviets' postwar behavior than the moral price of using a weapon of mass destruction. Szilard didn't give up. He collected the names of like-minded scientists and went to work persuading the American government not to use the bomb against civilian populations.

Manhattan Project scientists, led by James Franck, winner of the 1925 Nobel Prize in Physics, made the case in a top-secret report. It would be impossible to keep the United States' atomic discoveries a secret indefinitely, they said. They predicted a nuclear arms race, forcing America to develop armaments at such a pace that no other nation would think of attacking first, for fear of overwhelming retaliation.

The Interim Committee met four times in May—including the last day of the month—and reconvened on June 1. By then, they'd brushed aside the objections from Szilard and Franck. They had moved on to the bomb's potential destructive power, and the effect it would have on the Japanese will to fight.

At one point, a member tried to discredit the bomb's destructiveness, arguing that "it would not be much different from the effect caused by any Air Corps strike of present dimensions."

But Oppenheimer disagreed. Scientists were still unsure about the bomb's explosive force. It could equal anywhere from 2,000 to 20,000 tons of dynamite—but the visual effect "would be tremendous," Oppenheimer assured them. The blast would be "a brilliant luminescence which would rise to a height of 10,000 to 20,000 feet." The explosion would endanger all life for a radius of at least two-thirds of a mile. He said the weapon would be ideal for use against a concentration of troops or war plants, and predicted the bomb might kill 20,000 people.

Arthur Compton, a member of the committee's scientific advisory panel and a Nobel laureate, asked if they could arrange a nonmilitary demonstration, so the Japanese would see the futility of continuing the war.

Others rejected the idea. Byrnes said that telling the Japanese where a bomb would be dropped would prompt them to move American prisoners of war to the area.

Stimson was concerned about something else: What if the bomb didn't work? "Nothing would have been more damaging to our effort to obtain surrender than a warning or a demonstration followed by a dud. This was a real possibility," Stimson recalled later.

There was one more factor. They didn't have a bomb to waste. They hadn't produced enough U-235 or plutonium to make backup bombs. "It was vital that a sufficient effect be quickly obtained with the few we had," Stimson said.

Oppenheimer later summed up the debate: "The opinions of our scientific colleagues on the initial use of these weapons is not unanimous: They range from the proposal of a purely technical demonstration to that of the military application best designed to induce surrender. Those who advocate a purely technical demonstration would wish to outlaw the use of atomic weapons and feared that if we use the weapons now our position in future negotiation will be prejudiced. Others emphasize the opportunity of saving American lives by immediate military use and believe that such use will improve the international prospects, in that they are more concerned with the prevention of war than with the elimination of a specific weapon. We find ourselves closer to the latter views. We can propose no technical demonstration likely to bring an end to the war; we see no acceptable alternative to military use."

In the end, Stimson agreed with Oppenheimer. The only way to get Japanese emperor Hirohito and his military advisers to surrender was by administering "a tremendous shock which would carry convincing proof of our power to destroy the Empire." Stimson added, "Such an effective shock would save many times the number of lives, both American and Japanese, than it would cost."

Stimson knew that military planners were predicting massive casualties if U.S. troops invaded Japan. It was unclear how many Japanese would die defending their homeland. The fighting could go on for years. No one wanted that.

So after the June 1 meeting, Stimson was ready. His committee and scientific panel had discussed every possible scenario and reached consensus on three recommendations. Now Stimson would forward them to Truman:

- The atomic bomb should be used against Japan as soon as possible.
- It should be used on a military installation surrounded by houses or other buildings most susceptible to damage.
- It should be used without warning.

If Stimson and committee members thought that was the end of the issue, they were wrong. It was the start of a long, deeply felt debate that would last for decades.

COUNTDOWN:

53 DAYS

June 14, 1945

Omaha, Nebraska

They'd passed a long, hot week waiting for the souped-up B-29 to roll off the assembly line in Omaha, a week of whiskey and fisticuffs and what passed for fun in rented rooms. Captain Robert A. Lewis and his eight crew members were ready now to board the spanking-new Superfortress and return to Wendover for a few days. There they'd pack up their things, then join the rest of the 509th Composite Group on Tinian Island.

It wasn't supposed to play out this way. They'd shown up on June 7, ready to take delivery of the customized bomber and make a quick turn-around. The plane wasn't ready, so Lewis gave his men a chance to unwind.

And boy, did they ever. Booze, smashed glass, jealous husbands, policemen. Lewis managed to keep them all out of jail. It wasn't the first time, and despite his own reputation as a loose cannon, Lewis's men were deeply loyal to him.

Lewis was born in New York City, raised in New Jersey, and enlisted in the Army Air Corps after Pearl Harbor. A thrill seeker, he soon became a hotshot test pilot. His achievements included flying aviation legend Charles Lindbergh in a B-29. Lindbergh was impressed with the way Lewis handled the difficult plane, and told him he'd have been happy to have Lewis with him on his historic first flight across the Atlantic.

Then there was General Curtis LeMay, the colorful, cigar-chomping air commander. Lewis took LeMay on his first B-29 flight and showed him the challenges it presented. As soon as they landed, LeMay promoted Lewis to captain, right there on the field.

Lindbergh and LeMay weren't the only ones who praised Lewis. So did Tibbets, his commander in the B-29 test program. Tibbets had trained Lewis himself, and watched him become one of the best pilots of the new plane in the Air Forces. Lewis had flown the Superfortress hundreds of times, and survived two crashes due to mechanical failures. Lewis always kept a cool head in harrowing conditions.

When Tibbets was chosen to lead the atom bomb mission, he recruited Lewis right away. Tibbets respected Lewis's skills. But the two men did not always get along. Tibbets was a serious, by-the-book commander whose uniform never had a button out of place. Lewis was his antithesis, a twenty-six-year-old loudmouth, stocky and blond, who wore a tattered flying jacket. He was a street kid who settled disputes with his fists, but he wasn't a bully. Lewis looked out for the underdog and took good care of his crew. But he'd never flown in combat. That was a mark against him, which he found rankling.

Lewis got close to Tibbets while they tested out the Superfortress. But once Van Kirk and Ferebee—Tibbets's old buddies from Europe—arrived at Wendover for the secret program, the relationship shifted. The old team was like the Three Musketeers, sharing terrifying and funny memories of the skies over Germany, France, and England. Lewis had done plenty of white-knuckle flying, but he couldn't add anything heroic to their conversations.

He got along with Van Kirk and Ferebee. They played cards late into the night, but Ferebee was a card shark, practically a professional, and Lewis always seemed to lose a lot of money. Tibbets jokingly advised him not to gamble with Ferebee. "Stay in your own league," he said. That stung. Lewis thought Ferebee, with his suave mustache and Clark Gable looks, was arrogant.

Captain Robert A. Lewis in 1945.

It didn't help that Lewis was kept in the dark about their mission. All he knew was they were practicing for something big. In a November 24, 1944, letter to his parents, he expressed his boredom and frustration: "Today was typical for its routine. Morning briefing followed by bombing practice, back for lunch (good), then more practice. I don't ask why. Nobody does."

A couple of weeks later, Lewis cut loose. He wanted to visit his folks for Christmas, and he knew the 509th senior flight engineer needed a ride home to his wedding. On December 17, Lewis and the engineer "borrowed" a C-45 twin-engine transport plane and took off on the 2,500-mile journey to Newark, New Jersey. They ran into heavy weather. As they passed over Columbus, Ohio, the C-45's radio, altimeter, and compass failed. Lewis steered the plane toward the ground, trying to navigate by streetlights, but a blizzard reduced the visibility to near zero. Lewis just kept flying eastward, and eventually landed at Newark. There was almost no fuel left in the tank.

After Christmas, Lewis met the flight engineer and his bride back at the airport. Regulations prohibited civilians from flying in military aircraft, so Lewis put his flying jacket and cap on the woman and sneaked her on board. They hit another blizzard on the way back and were forced to land. Lewis and the happy couple finally returned to the base on December 29. Tibbets was furious and told Lewis he deserved a court-martial, prison, or expulsion. Lewis didn't think it was a big deal.

Tibbets thought about it for a week. He admitted it took steely nerves to fly a disabled plane in brutal weather. No question Lewis was an exceptional pilot, and the Air Forces was in critical need of his skills. In the end, Tibbets decided against pressing charges. The commander didn't want to ruin his life, he told Lewis, but from now on, Tibbets would watch him like a hawk. If he screwed up again, no more chances.

Lewis was on his best behavior in the six months since then. He hoped he wouldn't be held responsible for his crew's behavior in Omaha. If he was, maybe Tibbets would understand that this was their last chance to live it up a little before they headed to Tinian. Once they were there, who knew what would happen.

Lewis figured out he and his crew could well be on the plane for the secret mission, whatever that turned out to be. On most training days, Lewis was the chief pilot, but when Tibbets flew with them, Lewis was copilot.

Of course, Lewis's crew thought their captain deserved the place of honor. Tibbets was rarely around to fly; he was always busy with the top brass on administrative matters. Still, they knew Tibbets would probably be the one piloting the "first strike."

That's the way command worked. Tibbets was a proven combat pilot—trusted to shepherd General Eisenhower in the field. Plus, he had great organizational skills.

A month earlier, Tibbets had visited Omaha's Glenn L. Martin bomber plant to pick out the plane he would fly on the big mission. Tibbets advised aeronautic engineers to modify the design of the B-29s in the 509th to make them lighter and faster. They removed all but the rear gun turrets and most of the protective armor plating. Faster engines with reversible pitch propellers—enabling the plane to taxi in reverse—were added to improve the aircraft's speed and mobility. The bomb-bay doors were enlarged to accommodate Little Boy and Fat Man, and engineered to be pneumatically controlled, allowing faster opening and closing at the point of delivery.

Tibbets really didn't care if the flight crews liked him. He was focused on getting the 509th ready for its mission. They trained until they got it right. Part of his squadron spent the first three months of 1945 in Cuba, practicing high-altitude coastal and ocean flying and long-range navigation. High-altitude bombing was a new tactic, and Tibbets drove the crews relentlessly to increase the accuracy of their bomb drops. They practiced steep diving maneuvers—the only way, Tibbets believed, a B-29 would be able to escape an atomic bomb's blast. Back at Wendover, flight crews practiced dropping large "dummy" bombs modeled after the shape and size of the real bombs, to prepare for the big drop in Japan. And in late spring, almost everyone packed up and moved across the Pacific to Tinian, a tiny dot on the map.

Meantime, Tibbets was running from meeting to meeting between Wendover, Washington, and Los Alamos. He was responsible for 1,800 men, an elite group charged with dropping the first atomic bomb in history. He was too busy to bond with the men. Besides, Tibbets carried with him sobering intelligence he'd never shared with them: once they delivered the bombs, the shock waves from the explosion could kill the flight crew. No one could guarantee the bomb wouldn't explode on the way to the eventual target. He and his men were flying into deadly peril.

Lewis and his fellow crew members in Omaha didn't know any of that. So after their plane was ready, Lewis's crew inspected their shiny new B-29. They strapped into their positions. Lewis ordered the flight engineer to start the big engines, which sounded smooth as new silk. On this flight, and the long flight after it to Tinian, he'd be sitting in the pilot's chair.

COUNTDOWN:
49 DAYS

June 18, 1945
Washington, D.C.

Harry Truman was living by himself in the White House. Bess and Margaret and his mother-in-law had left two weeks earlier to return to Independence for the summer. The president was lonely, and he didn't like it.

He took to imagining that the noises he heard in the middle of the night in the big, empty house were the ghosts of Andrew Jackson and Teddy Roosevelt walking around and having an argument with FDR. He wandered into rooms and even closets he hadn't explored yet, feeling sorry for himself.

"Dear Bess," he wrote in one of his many letters to his wife. "Just two months ago, I was a reasonably happy and contented vice president. But things have changed so much it hardly seems real. . . . I sit here in this old house and work on foreign affairs, read reports, and work on speeches—all the while listening to the ghosts walk up and down the hallways and even right here in the study."

But as keenly as he missed his family, there was something much bigger troubling him—how would he end the war in the Pacific? He had learned about the Manhattan Project and its frightening potential. He had talked with top advisers and generals. He was getting a lot of different advice. He needed to decide on a path forward, even if it was just a placeholder.

Now, at 3:30 on the afternoon of June 18, President Truman convened a meeting of his War Cabinet, which included the Joint Chiefs of Staff and the top civilian officials from the War Department. In the room were some of the giants of mid-twentieth-century America. General of the Army George Marshall, who would later serve as secretary of state. Secretary of War Henry Stimson. Assistant Secretary John J. McCloy, who would go on to hold posts ranging from high commissioner for Germany to president of the World Bank to a member of the Warren Commission, investigating the Kennedy assassination.

Other participants were just as accomplished: Secretary of the Navy James Forrestal; Fleet Admiral William Leahy, who served Roosevelt and now Truman as chief of staff; Fleet Admiral Ernest King, who was chief of naval operations; and Lieutenant General I. C. Eaker of the Army Air Forces, representing General Hap Arnold, who was recovering from a heart attack.

The agenda for the meeting was as ambitious as the luminaries in the room: how to force Japan's unconditional surrender and end World War II. For weeks, Truman had listened to different opinions about the atomic bomb. The Interim Committee recommended using it as soon as possible against Japan—and without warning—"to make a profound psychological impression on as many inhabitants as possible."

Truman considered another option: staging a demonstration of the weapon prior to using it in combat. But there were two problems with that approach. If the weapon failed to work, it would only fuel Japan's resolve to fight on. And American prisoners of war might be relocated into the line of fire.

While most military leaders favored using America's new super-weapon, there were notable exceptions. General Douglas MacArthur, commander of U.S. Army Forces in the Pacific, believed Japan's "defeat was inevitable" and it was unwise to unleash such a destructive new weapon of war. General Dwight Eisenhower, supreme commander of Allied forces in Europe, made the same argument.

And then there was the president's chief of staff, Admiral Leahy, the nation's highest-ranking military officer, who was firmly on record against the atomic bomb for a different reason: the "damn thing" will never work, he said. He called it "all the biggest bunk in the world."

It was against this backdrop that Truman called his top military and civilian advisers to order on June 18. The president turned first to General Marshall, who said the situation in the Pacific now was "practically identical" to what they confronted in Europe before D-Day. And Marshall proposed a similar strategy—a major ground invasion of the Japanese homeland, beginning on the southern island of Kyushu on November 1, "cutting to a minimum Jap time for preparation of defenses."

Marshall turned to projected casualties. He noted the number of Americans killed, wounded, and missing in the first thirty days of Normandy was 42,000. American troops suffered similar casualties in the fierce fighting at Okinawa. But, Marshall said, "There is reason to believe that the first thirty days in Kyushu should not exceed the price we have paid for Luzon," a major battle in MacArthur's campaign to retake the Philippines that had cost fewer American casualties: 31,000.

He added, "It is a grim fact that there is not an easy, bloodless way to victory in war and it is the thankless task of the leaders to maintain their firm outward front which holds the resolution of their subordinates."

The proposed invasion of Kyushu already had a code name: "Olympic." And Marshall had a remarkably precise request for the number of troops that would be needed—766,700. Truman asked Chief of Staff Leahy for his estimate of casualties. The admiral noted American troops on Okinawa had lost 35 percent in casualties, which would translate to a quarter of a million to invade Japan.

Some estimates of potential losses were even higher. General Marshall's staff believed that the full ground campaign to defeat Japan—code name "Downfall"—would cost 500,000 to a million lives. The invasion of the main island of Honshu would not begin until March 1946. In other words, the war would drag on for months, perhaps years.

The president turned to Secretary Stimson. He asked if the secretary believed "the invasion of Japan by white men would not have the effect of more closely uniting the Japanese." Stimson said it probably would. Secretary Forrestal added that the full operation might take a year, or even a year and a half to complete.

Truman said he hoped to get a firm commitment from Russia to enter the war in August, and perhaps shorten Japan's resistance. Admiral Leahy raised the possibility of accepting less than the current American demand—unconditional surrender by the Japanese—fearing it would only make the enemy more determined to fight on and kill more Americans.

But the president knew softening the terms for surrender in any way would be politically explosive. He was not ready to try to change public opinion on the matter.

It was clear to Truman just how terrible the cost of invading Japan would be. The current campaign to capture Okinawa was vivid proof. U.S. military planners had predicted it would take two days to seize control of the island. The battle for the eight square miles was now in its seventy-eighth day. Even when the Japanese lost 100,000 of their 120,000 men on the island, and were obviously defeated, thousands of Japanese soldiers kept fighting, in many cases falling on their own grenades rather than surrender. If the enemy fought that fiercely for Okinawa, what would they do to defend their homeland?

Still, the president ended the discussion by ordering the Joint Chiefs to proceed with their plan to invade Kyushu, adding he would "decide as to final action later."

As the meeting was starting to break up and the War Cabinet was preparing to leave, Truman realized that John McCloy, his assistant secretary of war, had not said a word yet.

"McCloy," he said, "nobody leaves this room until he's been heard from. Do you think I have any reasonable alternative to the decision which has just been made?"

McCloy turned to his boss, Secretary Stimson, who said, "Go ahead."

McCloy was a more important figure than his title of assistant secretary indicated. He was a highly respected member of the New York legal community. Stimson brought him to Washington as his troubleshooter, and tried to ensure he got the chance to weigh in on every major decision about the war.

It turned out McCloy had plenty to say. For the last hour, there had been detailed discussions of invasions, troop levels, and casualties. But there had not been a single mention of the atomic bomb, which could potentially end the war more than a year sooner and save hundreds of thousands of American lives.

"Well, I do think you've got an alternative," McCloy told the president. "We ought to have our heads examined if we don't explore some other method by which we can terminate this war than just by another conventional attack and landing."

Then he did something no one else in the meeting had done—he brought up the bomb. Even though all of them were thoroughly briefed on the Manhattan Project, there was a deafening silence in the room. "As soon as I mentioned the word 'bomb'—the atomic bomb—even in that select circle, it was sort of a shock," he recalled later. "You didn't mention the bomb out loud; it was like mentioning Skull and Bones [the secret Yale student fraternity] in polite society at Yale. It just wasn't done."

Now McCloy pressed on. "I would tell them [the Japanese] we have the bomb and I would tell them what kind of weapon it is." If they still refused to surrender, "I think our moral position would be better if we gave them a specific warning of the bomb."

The pushback was immediate. What if the bomb didn't work? The United States would be embarrassed, and the Japanese would be more determined than ever. McCloy refused to back down. "All of our scientists have told us that the thing will go off," he said.

Having now heard from everyone in the room, Truman ended the meeting, saying the group should "discuss this." He approved plans for a ground invasion deploying 766,700 American troops.

It was clear that no decision would be made about using the atomic bomb until it was tested successfully. For now, it was an ambitious, terrifying science project.

Oceanside, California

Oceanside was beautiful, clean, and safe, a California beach oasis. After surviving a solid year of dangerous missions, Draper Kauffman was finding it hard to adjust to the quiet.

It wasn't like he was on vacation—this was the start of his next big assignment. There was plenty of planning to occupy his mind. But much as he tried, he couldn't get Okinawa out of his brain—the constant artillery fire, machine-gun rattle, bloodbath banzai charges, and screams of terror and death.

One night as Kauffman stood with the captain on the bridge of the *Gilmer*, he spotted a kamikaze airplane coming straight at them. The ship's guns fired and fired and hit the plane, but it streaked into the *Gilmer* like a "flaming torch." The plane struck the ship's forward turret, killing one sailor and injuring three. "The idea of someone literally throwing himself at you along with his bomb made for an exceedingly uncomfortable feeling," he wrote back home with considerable understatement.

After Okinawa, Kauffman was ordered to Subic Bay in the Philippines to "conduct a lecture course"—another term for training more frogmen. Subic Bay was fine with Kauffman. His father, a vice admiral, was based there. They could finally catch up.

James "Reggie" Kauffman worked closely with the staff of General Robert Eichelberger, whose Eighth Army was finishing up the long, brutal fight for the Philippines. Vice Admiral Kauffman's office was in a Quonset hut, and his son headed there as soon as he landed. They hadn't seen each other in years. Kauffman knew his father was proud of him. He quit his job and joined the American Volunteer Motor Ambulance Corps in 1940 without telling his father. America wasn't in the war then, and Kauffman recalled the long letter his father wrote him, questioning why he'd joined and urging him to come home.

"The whole thing is incomprehensible to me," he wrote. The military didn't need him. Was his son in trouble, running away from some secret? "Here again, you should come to me as I have never let you down in the pinches," he wrote. He knew his son was a grown man, that his appeal was probably futile. He ended, saying he would always be there for him. "I am very fond of you and I always have admired you and had the greatest confidence in you. Regardless of what you intend to do and what I may think of your decision, I want you to know I will do everything I can for you. Love, Dad."

He knew his father had followed his heroic exploits over the years: the British and American bomb squads, then the frogmen. It was a long five years, but it felt even longer. When Kauffman saw his father, it was a somber reunion. Both were exhausted. They missed home, holidays, and family. And they both knew what was next: the invasion of Japan.

Plans were still being drawn up, but both Kauffmans knew the Underwater Demolition Teams would play a major role. Draper would be on the front line of the fight. He'd survived this long. He was pushing his luck.

Five days later, Draper Kauffman was in Oceanside, where his commanders wanted him to get started with training several teams of new men. Now that Okinawa had fallen, the United States was creating a giant air and naval base there, a launchpad for the inevitable invasion of Japan's homeland. It couldn't happen overnight. First, they needed more equipment, more men. They'd have to train them all, work out a plan, and study every detail.

Japan was a series of big islands. Kauffman's teams were engineered for island warfare. They would clear the coast for troops landing on the beaches—mapping underwater obstacles, disarming hidden mines, sneaking ashore on reconnaissance missions. How many of them would be killed? Kauffman wondered. How much longer would this go on?

Kauffman knew the nation was looking to finish the fight. He could see the signs. California newspapers were full of stories about postwar projects, speculating on how America's economy would respond when all the soldiers were discharged. Would there be enough housing? Enough jobs? The American economy was humming, cranking out military goods. But at some point, the factories would go back to making cars and washing machines and ice cream.

Kauffman didn't know when the invasion would happen. He wasn't sure if his commanders knew, either. That decision would be made by the folks at the Pentagon. He had his own job to worry about. He started calling each of his twenty-four teams to Oceanside for a month of training, reeling them in from assignments all over the Pacific. The battlefield was so vast that commanders had created a new Underwater Demolition Flotilla. The corps would be split into two separate squadrons, each with its own flagship. It was a clear sign the Navy was preparing for a long fight.

Kauffman looked out over the California beach, saw a ship on the horizon, an airplane overhead, and he flashed to another horrific image of combat. He just couldn't shake his own fears. He knew how hard the Japanese had fought on those remote islands. He could only imagine how hard they'd fight on their own soil.

COUNTDOWN:
36 DAYS

July 1, 1945

Los Alamos, New Mexico

Only two weeks remained until the test date, and the pressure was building at Los Alamos. Truman would soon be on his way to meet with British and Russian leaders in Germany. The Trinity explosion was set for July 16. It was a gamble. And depending on the outcome, the president would know how strong a hand he had for ending the war with Japan and dealing with the Soviet Union.

Truman would not tolerate a failure. Groves wouldn't consider a delay. Oppenheimer couldn't imagine wasting all the years of work that had already been done, so he kept pushing himself and his staff even harder. He had no choice.

Two weeks weren't enough to solve all the mechanical problems that still plagued the bombs. The test site, a desert wilderness about 230 miles south of Los Alamos, was still being set up. They had to get this right the first time.

Scientists and engineers were on edge—and exhausted. Groves was calling for speed. No excuses. So, with the pressure of the approaching test, they worked endless shifts at Los Alamos and at the test site, where 100-degree temperatures burned late in the day. They were still tinkering with molds and castings for the bomb, and equipment to measure the nuclear effects of the blast. Some slept at their desks or in tents in the desert.

Oppenheimer was overwhelmed with details and forgot to eat. His weight dropped to 115 pounds. He looked so emaciated Groves worried he might collapse.

The tension wasn't only about short time and overwork. As the test date approached, the scientists grappled with existential questions about the atomic bomb, and the morality of creating and unleashing something so lethal and irrevocable. Physicist Philip Morrison spoke up at a Target Committee meeting to express scientists' concerns to Oppenheimer, Groves, and other military leaders. Morrison said the Japanese should be warned in advance the weapon was coming, to give them every chance to surrender beforehand. His idea was brushed off by the officers as well as by his own boss, Oppenheimer. Morrison was crestfallen. He left the meeting feeling that the warriors had control of the program, and scientists would have no influence on their decisions.

Leo Szilard's petition demanding limits on the use of atomic weapons made the rounds at Los Alamos, and many scientists agreed the military should demonstrate the bomb's destructive possibilities in a test explosion, rather than dropping it on a city filled with innocent civilians. Physicist Edward Teller brought the petition to Oppenheimer, but he refused to sign. Scientists "have no business to meddle in political pressure of that kind," Oppenheimer told him.

Dozens of Teller's colleagues signed the petition. Others were pondering the issue, including Lilli Hornig, one of the few female scientists at Los Alamos. She was a newcomer, a chemist. She moved to Los Alamos with her husband, Donald, a group leader in the Manhattan Project, only a year before. Signing the document might jeopardize her career. But Lilli Hornig had already overcome many obstacles in her male-dominated field. For her, this was a matter of principle.

Like so many of the Manhattan Project scientists, Lilli Schwenk was foreign born and Jewish, the daughter of a Czech chemist and a pediatrician. The family immigrated to the United States and settled in Montclair, New Jersey. From an early age, her parents encouraged her to pursue

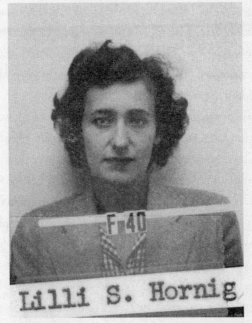

Lilli Hornig's security badge photo at Los Alamos.

Donald Hornig, left, and Lyndon B. Johnson, right, in December 1964.

a career in science. As a child, Lilli visited her father's laboratory, a huge room of sparkling glass beakers, test tubes, and flasks. Her father gave her micro-sized glassware for her dollhouse, and instilled in his daughter a deep love of chemistry. She majored in the subject at Bryn Mawr College, and continued on to graduate studies at Harvard in 1942.

At the time, few women went to graduate school and even fewer pursued degrees in hard sciences. At Harvard, she quickly discovered women were second-class students. Her professors made it clear to her that the handful of women they admitted were poor substitutes for the men who had gone to war. There was no ladies' restroom in the graduate school science building. The nearest was in another building, and the professor with the key had to be searched out.

Before taking her first class, she was summoned to meet with science department professors in the aptly named "Division Room." Inside was a long conference table overseen by portraits of past chairmen, all solemn white men. The professors sat at one end of the table and Lilli was told to take her place at the other end. They were blunt. They said girls always had trouble with physical chemistry. So, before she could move on, she'd have to take a Harvard undergraduate physical chemistry class.

Lilli was taken aback. She told them she was a grad student. She didn't come to Harvard to take undergraduate courses. The professors could see she wasn't going to be intimidated. So they made a deal. She'd have to take a qualifying exam in physical chemistry. If she passed the test, she could take the graduate course.

That's when Lilli turned to Donald Hornig, another student she met her first day at Harvard. Donald was a quiet, serious young man from Milwaukee who was working on his doctorate in physical chemistry.

Donald was immediately attracted to Lilli. She was small and slender, with pretty eyes. He was happy to lend her his notes and answer any questions she had. Lilli aced the exam, proving the professors wrong.

Lilli and Donald fell in love and married in 1943, the year they both graduated. His doctorate dissertation was titled "An Investigation of the

Shock Wave Produced by an Explosion," and he went to work at the Underwater Explosives Research Laboratory of the Woods Hole Oceanographic Institution in Massachusetts. Not long after, Donald Hornig's boss passed along a mysterious invitation, asking him to take an unspecified job at an unspecified location.

"That's interesting," Hornig said. "Who requested me?"

"I can't tell you that," the boss said.

"What kind of a job is it?" he asked.

"I can't tell you anything about it. It's a very secret matter."

"What part of the country is it in?" Hornig said.

Again, nothing.

"Can you at least tell me north, east, south, west, what have you?"

"I can't tell you that, either," his boss said.

So Hornig said no. Later that day, the lab intercom crackled: "Telephone call for Donald Hornig from Santa Fe, New Mexico," the voice said.

It was chemist George Kistiakowsky, who was leading efforts at Los Alamos to develop a specialized explosive charge for nuclear weapons. He reassured Hornig the request was legitimate, even though facts would be sketchy until they reached an agreement.

"Everyone's mad that you said no," Kistiakowsky said. "You're the first person who's said no."

Hornig told Kistiakowsky he had to talk to Lilli first, but another call came right away. It was Harvard University president James Conant, one of the few civilians who knew about the Manhattan Project. He was appointed by FDR as an early scientific liaison with the United Kingdom; he was also a member of the Interim Committee. Conant wanted to know "what the devil was going on," and if Hornig was "unpatriotic."

"Remember, Hornig, Uncle Sam is pointing his finger at you," Conant said.

Hornig didn't need Conant questioning his patriotism. He went straight home and told Lilli about the calls. She wasn't sure about the move, but when Kistiakowsky offered Lilli a position at Los Alamos, the decision was made. The couple bought a 1937 Ford with frayed tires and drove 2,200 miles to New Mexico.

Hornig went straight to work developing the firing unit that would detonate the plutonium bomb.

But when Lilli met with personnel officials at Los Alamos, they asked how fast she could type.

"I don't type," she snapped. A typing course had not been part of her master's degree in chemistry at Harvard.

Eventually she went to work on plutonium chemistry, testing the solubility and the radioactivity of various plutonium salts—a humdrum task, she felt. Concerns that radioactivity could cause reproductive damage to women led to her transfer to the explosives group, where she helped produce charges for atomic weapons.

Over time, the Hornigs adjusted to life at Los Alamos. Lilli was twenty-three, and her husband was twenty-four. They discovered that many of the scientists on the project were roughly the same age. When they weren't working, they led a busy social life, with dinner parties, hikes in the surrounding mountains, camping, and horseback riding outings. There was even a musical theater group. Lilli helped build the sets and Donald played violin in the orchestra.

But such activities were merely diversions. The Hornigs couldn't escape the fact that they were always under the shadow of the bomb, the project, the test. And as the day for the test drew closer, Lilli thought more and more about the possible outcome of all their labors. Scientists had a moral responsibility. This was the moment to speak up. The Hornigs signed the petition.

COUNTDOWN:
35 DAYS

July 2, 1945

Los Alamos, New Mexico

With the test approaching, General Groves worried more than ever about spies. He insisted on secrecy at every research and development site. Post Office Box 1663 was the sole address for Los Alamos employees. Their mail was routinely inspected. Billboards were posted with bold and sometimes cryptic warnings: "Loose talk—a chain reaction for espionage," or "Who me? Yes, you. Keep mum about this job!"

Security officers were a common sight at every laboratory, plant, and facility. When the program began, it seemed logical to focus security on potential espionage by Germany. Military intelligence assumed only the Nazis had the expertise and industrial capacity to make use of American technology or intelligence. Japan and Italy lacked the industrial infrastructure and raw materials to build an atomic bomb.

Then there was the Soviet Union. They had all the essentials. They were American allies, but they couldn't be trusted. Groves learned that early on. In his first week as military commander of the Manhattan Project, Soviet agents were discovered at the Lawrence Berkeley National Laboratory in California. The agents used American communist sympathizers to try to gain information from the scientists.

Groves immediately established American security aims: Keep Germans in the dark regarding American scientific achievements. Ensure that

One of the security gates at Los Alamos.

the first atomic bomb drop was a complete surprise. And finally, keep details of the U.S. nuclear weapons program out of Soviet hands.

Extensive background checks were a critical part of the counterintelligence operation. The military wanted to ensure the scientists and support personnel weren't vulnerable to blackmail—which meant examining everything in their personal histories. Any association with communists was suspect.

Groves abhorred communism, but he knew many of the scientists in the Manhattan Project had dabbled in the ideology. Europe between the wars was full of anarchists, socialists, and freethinkers of every stripe—and many of them were university professors and scientists. The Great Depression sparked sympathy for communist doctrine, and almost all the scientists on the program had been exposed to the propaganda or had friends on the far left. Many fled the fascist wave and went to work in the West, including Oppenheimer.

Oppie wasn't interested in politics until Hitler came to power in 1933 and Jewish professors were forced out of their jobs. He contributed to a fund to help displaced Jewish physicists. He read *Das Kapital*, in which philosopher Karl Marx expounded on his theory of how capitalist systems exploit workers. He associated with members of the Communist Party, but there was no evidence he ever joined the party himself. He supported desegregation and labor rights, and funneled money to antifascist forces in the Spanish Civil War, using communist associates as a conduit. Oppie's wife, Kitty, was a party member and the widow of a labor rights firebrand who volunteered for the Lincoln Brigades and died fighting fascists in the Spanish Civil War. When the Soviet Union signed a nonaggression pact with Germany in 1939, and joined forces with the Nazis to invade Poland, Oppenheimer disavowed the communist movement and became a dedicated foe of fascism.

With so many known or suspected communists in his circle, the FBI kept a fat dossier on Oppenheimer, labeling the physicist "a professor having Communist sympathies." When Groves presented Oppie's name to a military committee to oversee the Manhattan Project, several members said no. But Groves vouched for Oppenheimer's loyalty. Besides, where would the committee find a more qualified candidate to run Los Alamos? Groves's steadfast support eventually won out. But security agents still monitored the physicist, just to make sure.

Groves was a pragmatist. He understood that some of the Manhattan Project scientists might have been exposed to communism during the Great Depression. The Communist Party had devoted most of its energy to organizing the unemployed and championing the rights of working people. But Groves believed his men could ferret out anyone more loyal to the Soviet Union than the United States.

One of the biggest problems was screening and monitoring the large number of foreign-born scientists employed throughout the project. It was virtually impossible to examine much of their past activities. But Groves acknowledged that someone with disloyal intentions could slip through the screening process.

And Los Alamos was a security nightmare. Too many people worked together in one place, toward a common goal. To prevent espionage, General Groves insisted the project scientists keep their work compartmentalized, limiting the number of people who knew the overall scope and progress of the effort.

But Oppenheimer took the opposite tack. He encouraged scientists from different departments to meet, share their work, and cooperate. Oppie often moderated these group discussions himself. It fostered creativity, efficiency, and teamwork. But that approach made it easier for spies to gather information. If that happened, Groves knew it would haunt America long after the war was over.

COUNTDOWN:
34 DAYS

July 3, 1945

Los Alamos, New Mexico

A rumpled man walked slowly past the Quonset huts and makeshift labs of Los Alamos, staring into the notepad in his hands, smiling to himself. He didn't see the long twilight shadows, the sun glancing off the Sangre de Cristo Mountains. Both the beautiful and the banal went unnoticed.

William Laurence worked as he walked, organizing, editing, moving quotes around in his head. He had just finished a long interview with an important scientist. He had to make sure he got everything right, had to be sure he understood exactly what the man had explained.

His appearance seemed almost designed to escape notice. Laurence was an older man, in his late fifties, stocky, with a slight Eastern European accent and an oddly flattened nose. He wore his dark hair slicked straight back. His suit was too big, his tie so wide that even by Los Alamos's standards it was out of style. He could've been yet another scientist or engineer, except for that notebook and pen—and the entourage of Army security folks who always shadowed him.

At some point, Laurence would sit down and write out his day's work, try to fit it into the larger picture. But even after months of interviews at Los Alamos and every other Manhattan Project research site, it was still too early to start writing the big story. He was still gathering up the threads. He knew there were big events ahead that would shape his narrative.

William Laurence, the *New York Times* correspondent, on Tinian.

Laurence was a science writer for the *New York Times*, handpicked by General Groves to cover the historic project. Since April, he'd been given unique access to the inner workings of the Manhattan Project and Los Alamos—a secret world the reporter called "Atomland-on-Mars."

Laurence had an excellent reputation in his field. He was part of a team of reporters from several newspapers who'd shared the 1937 Pulitzer Prize for science reporting. Army intelligence had investigated Laurence carefully. He wasn't a risk, but his personal story was worthy of film noir.

He was born in Lithuania and named Leib Wolf Siew. As a rebellious teenager, he'd taken part in the Russian Revolution of 1905, when large numbers of angry workers across Russia went on strike to protest poor working conditions. The czar answered with violence, and hundreds of unarmed protesters were killed or wounded by his forces. Laurence owed his flattened nose to a policeman's rifle butt. To avoid arrest, his mother smuggled him out of Russia to Germany in a pickle barrel. Then he fled to the United States, where he started a new life with a new name: William Leonard Laurence. ("William" for Shakespeare, "Leonard" for Leonardo da Vinci, and "Laurence" for the street where he lived, in Roxbury, Massachusetts.) He went to Harvard, but dropped out of law school to enlist in the U.S. Army during World War I. Deployed to France, he worked as a translator in the Signal Corps, which was responsible for relaying messages between commanders and their fighting units.

Once he returned home, Laurence decided to become a newsman. He spent a couple of years at the *World* newspaper in New York City before joining the *Times* in 1930, where he became one of the first science reporters in the United States. An avid fan of science fiction novels, Laurence had a natural curiosity in physics and the universe. More important, he was able to explain complicated concepts to his readers.

In the prewar years, Laurence kept abreast of medicine and physics, chemistry and astronomy. As the science writer for the nation's preeminent newspaper, he had access to prominent scientists. During a visit to the Massachusetts Institute of Technology in 1940, Laurence attended an abstruse lecture on higher mathematics by J. Robert Oppenheimer. Afterward, Laurence approached the scientist and asked him to explain some aspect of his talk. Oppenheimer declared flatly that his subject was "not for the lay public."

Laurence didn't flinch. He said that he'd just have to go ahead and write it as he saw it, then.

"And how is that?" Oppenheimer asked.

Laurence explained portions of the lecture in simple, clear language a layman might understand. Oppenheimer was impressed. "I never thought of it that way," he said.

Laurence never had trouble with Oppenheimer again. The reporter saw the significance of atomic energy early on. At a Columbia University conference in February 1939, he learned about nuclear fission from physicists Enrico Fermi and Niels Bohr, and immediately recognized the military potential of an atomic "chain reaction." In a *Saturday Evening Post* article published in September 1940, "The Atom Gives Up," Laurence foretold the bright and dark potential of harnessing atomic energy. The story was so alarmingly prescient that in 1943, Groves asked the magazine to report to him "at once" if anyone requested a back issue with the story.

Laurence's biggest assignment began in April 1945, when Groves walked into the *New York Times* building in midtown Manhattan. The general knew at some point the government would have to disclose details of the atomic bomb to the public. He decided Laurence was the man for the job.

Groves told *Times* managing editor Edwin James that his reporter was needed for a secret project. He said Laurence would "disappear" for months, and couldn't publish anything until after the project was finished. It couldn't be an exclusive, either: Laurence's stories would have to be distributed to other news organizations.

James signed off on the agreement and called Laurence into his office. Groves made the same pitch, saying the position would require "absolute secrecy."

"You will, for all intents and purposes, disappear off the face of the earth," Groves said, adding that Laurence would be working not only with government approval but under government control. Not one article, one sentence, one word would go out until Groves gave the nod. Laurence also would be writing press releases and other official communications as needed.

Laurence didn't like the conditions, but he smelled a huge story, probably having to do with an atomic bomb. The newsman told the bosses he had one important condition: he wanted complete access. Groves said yes. Laurence was sold on the opportunity.

He told his wife, Florence, he was going away for a while and would get in touch with her as soon as he could. He'd been on the road ever since. He'd seen enormous uranium separation plants at Oak Ridge, Tennessee; plutonium-producing reactors of Hanford, Washington; the Metallurgical Laboratory at the University of Chicago, where in 1942 Fermi had achieved the first controlled chain reaction; and the nerve center of it all, the lab at Los Alamos.

Along the way, he interviewed scores of scientists. The more he learned, the more awestruck he was at the scale and scope of the project. He had to throttle back his enthusiasm at times, remember to keep his objectivity. He wasn't there to be a cheerleader.

Harvard president and member of the Interim Committee James Conant gushed about the project to Laurence. "They won't believe it when the time comes that this can be told. It's more fantastic than Jules Verne," he told the reporter.

"They'll believe it if it works," Laurence said.

Laurence loved the assignment. It was a journey to a scientific wonderland, tracking the story of a lifetime. All around him were "such stuff as dreams are made on." He said he felt like a "visitor on Mars."

It would be difficult to explain the principles behind the atomic bomb to nonscientists, but he didn't want to make it too simple, either. It was a balancing act. Laurence was forever scribbling on his pad, playing with words and images, stripping down complicated jargon to its simplest elements. Whatever words he finally chose would have to pass through military censors, so he had to be careful. It was the most pressure he'd ever felt as a reporter, but he loved it. To tell the story right, he'd have to start at the beginning.

"The key to atomic energy was found in 1939 when it was discovered that uranium of atomic weight 235 (U-235), a rare form of the element, could be split and made to yield a relatively enormous amount of energy from the nucleus, or core, of its atoms," he eventually wrote.

"The catch was that the atoms of U-235, as found in nature, were inextricably mixed with the atoms of ordinary uranium of atomic weight (U-238), the former only constituting seven-tenths of one percent of the mixture. Since both forms of uranium are twins (isotopes) possessing the same chemical properties, they cannot be separated by chemical means, while physical methods for its concentration were, from a practical point of view, non-existent as it would have taken 1,000 of the then best pieces of apparatus 1,000 years to produce one ounce."

Once through the heavy technical explanations, Laurence cut loose
with his prose. In the course of three years, he wrote, scientists and engineers had built a scientific "Never-Never Land," where the "impossibles
of yesterday were transmuted, by the magic of imagination, concentrated
brain power and a will-to-do, under the stimulus of a great national emergency, into actualities of staggering dimensions."

Laurence didn't know when his stories would be published. Everything depended on what would unfold in two weeks' time, when the
atomic bomb was to be detonated. He prepared his background stories and
explanatory sidebars as best he could, readied himself for a furious period
of deadline writing, and let himself feel the exhilaration of reporting one of
the biggest scoops in history.

He'd be at Los Alamos when they hit the trigger for the test. He would
witness the birth of the atomic age.

COUNTDOWN:
21 DAYS

July 16, 1945
Potsdam, Germany

Harry Truman woke up in Germany on his first foreign trip as president to an emotion he rarely felt. He was intimidated. He had been president for more than three months. But here he faced a daunting new challenge.

He had arrived in Germany the previous night for the start of the Potsdam Conference, where he would replace FDR in a Big Three Summit with British prime minister Churchill and Soviet premier Stalin. And for all his diligent preparations, he wasn't sure he was ready for the world's biggest stage.

Meanwhile, almost half a world away, in Alamogordo, New Mexico, after seven years of research, development, and construction, scientists were ready to detonate the world's first nuclear weapon.

Truman couldn't stop thinking about the test. In Europe, he was eight hours ahead of the team in New Mexico. All he could do was wait. But he was keenly aware that the test's results—still highly uncertain—could dramatically reshape the dynamics of great-power relations. If the bomb worked, he thought, "I'll certainly have a hammer on those boys."

Just the prospect of sitting down with Churchill and Stalin worried Truman for weeks. When he left the United States on July 7, he confided in his diary, "Talked to Bess last night and the night before. She wasn't happy about my going to see Mr Russia and Mr Great Britain—neither am I." He added, "How I hate this trip! But I have to make it—win, lose, or draw—and we must win."

In the days leading up to the conference, Truman ordered up a tutorial on the range of issues the leaders would discuss: the Soviet Union's alarming dominance in Eastern Europe; the future of a shattered Germany; Zionism; the strategy for winning the war against Japan. That last subject was Truman's big concern. Stalin had not kept the promise he made at the Yalta summit to join the effort against Japan. Now Truman wanted a firm commitment that the Russians would enter the fight.

Most of all, the new president worried about how he would get along with the two leaders. Roosevelt spent more than one hundred days with Churchill, often at the White House. The two men stayed up late into the night, talking about military plans, but also sharing stories about their long and eventful lives. FDR also thought he had developed a good working relationship with Stalin.

Truman was confident in his ability to deal with people. He felt that "complicated" problems really weren't so complicated. Once people sat down and discussed issues face-to-face, they could work through differences. Still, this was the world's biggest stage, a stage Truman had never seen before, let alone taken a lead role on.

The president, his top advisers, and a team of more than one hundred spent eight days at sea on the cruiser USS *Augusta*. He passed much of his time conferring and walking laps around the deck with his new secretary of state, James Byrnes. Each day, he received updates from the Advance Map Room, set up in the first lieutenant's office, with a direct communications link to the Map Room back in the White House. He worked his team hard, going over long memos prepared by the State Department on the big problems—and there were so many of them—the United States faced across the globe.

Every night at 6:00 p.m., a thirty-piece band played a musical program before dinner. At 8:00 p.m., a movie was shown in Byrnes's quarters.

The president didn't stick around, choosing instead to play poker in his room.

Truman and his team chatted over cards, but it wasn't your typical poker conversation. One subject was Churchill's prospects in the general election that Britain had just held. The votes were still being counted, but most thought Churchill would win.

Another topic was the atomic bomb. Truman's chief of staff, Admiral Leahy, continued to say it wouldn't work. "This is the biggest fool thing we have ever done," he maintained. "The bomb will never go off, and I speak as an expert in explosives."

Now, on the morning of July 16, Truman awoke in Babelsberg, a small wooded suburb just outside Berlin. He was staying at Number 2 Kaiserstrasse, a three-story stucco villa on Lake Gribnitz.

From the start, Truman was uncomfortable. "It is dirty yellow and red," he wrote in his diary. "A ruined French chateau-architectural style ruined by German endeavor to cover up the French. . . . The house as were all the others was stripped of everything by the Russians—not even a tiny spoon left. The American commander, however, being a man of energy, caught the Russian loot train and recovered enough furniture to make the place livable. Nothing matches." Despite its color, the villa was dubbed "the Little White House."

Officials told the president the home had belonged to a German filmmaker, the head of the Nazi movie industry, who was sent to Siberia. The truth was even darker. A prominent publisher had lived there with his family. Ten weeks before Truman arrived, the Soviets ransacked the house, raped the daughters, and ordered the family out within an hour.

The president had a suite on the second floor that included a bedroom, an office, and a bathroom he shared with his chief of staff. While he described the interior as a "nightmare," there was a bigger problem: there were no screens on the windows. In the summer heat, mosquitoes from the lake gave the presidential party a "working over" until the weather cooled.

President Harry S Truman at Potsdam villa, "The Little White House."

The conference was supposed to start later in the day. But that wasn't going to happen. Stalin had not arrived yet. And the Russians were not sharing any news of when he would show up. Churchill was ensconced in another villa in the compound. He paid a visit to Truman's quarters at 11:00 a.m. His daughter said he hadn't been up so early in ten years. Truman had been awake since 6:30.

Truman had never met Churchill, but like most of the world, he knew him well from newsreels and radio broadcasts—his stirring voice, his powerful words, his jaunty defiance of the Nazi war machine. But the Churchill who showed up at the Little White House was a diminished figure, seemingly older than his seventy years, tired and discouraged, the leader of a nation and empire in decline.

They talked for two hours, and it was largely a social call. Truman said he had prepared an agenda for the conference, and asked if Churchill had as well. The prime minister said he didn't need one. Churchill seemed to be impressed with the new president, noting afterward Truman's "obvious power of decision" and "a great deal of self-confidence and resolution." Before leaving, the two leaders "struck a blow for liberty" with a round of whiskey. A Churchill aide concluded that the prime minister was "delighted" with the president.

Truman was less certain. "He gave me a lot of hooey about how great my country is and how he loved Roosevelt and how he intended to love me etc. etc.," Truman wrote in his diary that day. "I am sure we can get along if he doesn't try to give me too much soft soap."

That afternoon, with Stalin mysteriously absent, the president decided to take an unscheduled tour of Berlin. It would make a great impression.

He rode in an open car with Secretary of State Byrnes and Admiral Leahy. About halfway to the city, they saw the entire U.S. 2nd Armored Division lined up along one side of the Autobahn. It was a remarkable show of force—eleven hundred tanks, trucks, and Jeeps. The president reviewed the troops from a half-track reconnaissance car. The line of men and equipment stretched so far that it took twenty-two minutes to drive the length of the formation.

"This is the most powerful land force I have ever seen," Leahy said. "I don't see how anybody could stop them if they really wanted to go somewhere."

The commanding general answered, "Nobody has stopped them yet."

From there, Truman rode into the center of Berlin. The destruction was astonishing. The world's fourth-largest city was gone, filled with piles of rubble after waves of pounding from British and American bombers, and then Russian artillery. The presidential caravan drove slowly through what little was left of Hitler's capital city—the Reich chancellery and the balcony where the Nazi leader addressed his followers, the Victory Column, the Brandenburg Gate, the Tiergarten.

"Hitler's folly," Truman observed in his diary. "He over reached [sic] himself by trying to take in too much territory. He had no morals and his people backed him up. Never did I see a more sorrowful sight, nor witness retribution to the nth degree."

President Harry S Truman, Secretary of State James Byrnes, and Fleet Admiral William Leahy inspecting Berlin rubble, July 16, 1945.

Truman had seen destruction as an artillery officer during World War I, but never anything like this. There were long, wandering lines of homeless German civilians—old men, women, and children—pushing or pulling all that was left of their belongings. The younger men were gone, sacrificed to Hitler's twisted dreams. And everywhere was the overwhelming stench of death in the July heat. But if Truman was shocked by the devastation, he was also clear-eyed. "I never saw such destruction. I don't know whether they learned anything from it or not."

The president was waiting for word of the first test of a nuclear bomb, a weapon so destructive that, if it worked, it would change forever the nature of war and man's ability to destroy his fellow man. It was on his mind as he reflected on what he saw in Berlin.

"I thought of Carthage, Baalbec [sic], Jerusalem, Rome, Atlanta, Peking, Babylon, Ninevah,—Scipio, Ramses II . . . Sherman, Jenghis Khan, Alexander. . . . I hope for some sort of peace—but I fear that machines are ahead of morals by some centuries and when morals catch up there'll be no reason for any of it."

Alamogordo, New Mexico

Perched like a watchman in a shed atop a hundred-foot-tall steel tower in the New Mexico desert, Donald Hornig huddled against the rain running off the eaves. On a platform beside him sat the "gadget"—the world's first atomic bomb. Thunder roared. The little shack rattled.

The tower stood alone like a giant lightning rod in the wide-open desert. What would happen if a lightning bolt struck it? Hornig didn't want to even consider that. The four-ton nuclear weapon was wired up and ready to go. If the thunderstorms would only stop, the test could get under way. Like Truman, on the other side of the planet, all Hornig could do was wait.

Six miles from the tower, Oppenheimer paced the control center. The gadget was supposed to be detonated at dawn, but the heavy storm threatened to delay the test. The Army meteorologist in the control center said the storm would pass soon, but that didn't ease the unbearable stress. People chewed their nails or chain-smoked—anything to relieve the tension. General Groves was growing angrier by the minute, holding the weatherman personally responsible for the storm.

No one wanted any more delays. They had worked so hard to get to this point. Oppenheimer had fought to conduct a test in the first place, while General Groves maintained they didn't have enough plutonium to waste on experiments. But Oppenheimer was adamant. Without a full-scale

The "gadget" at the bottom of the hundred-foot-tall steel tower at the Trinity test site.

The "gadget" just before the Trinity test on July 16, 1945.

test, he argued, doubt would remain about the weapon's effectiveness, especially in combat. The world had never seen a nuclear explosion before, and estimates varied widely on how much energy would be released. Some scientists at Los Alamos continued privately to have doubts it would work at all.

Testing the plutonium bomb was critical. They believed Little Boy—the atomic bomb with the uranium core—would work. But scientists weren't sure about Fat Man. They had to confirm the plutonium bomb's novel implosive design. Several plutonium bombs were now in the pipeline and would become available over the next few weeks and months.

The weapon next to Hornig on the tower was an atomic bomb with a plutonium core. In May 1944, Oppenheimer began searching for a test site. Manhattan Project leaders scanned New Mexico, Texas, and California for a flat, isolated stretch of wilderness where the bomb could be safely tested. Finally Kenneth Bainbridge, an experimental physicist charged with developing a place to explode the first atom bomb, found the perfect spot in the New Mexico desert. The site, some 230 miles south of Los Alamos, was in a remote corner of the Alamogordo Air Base, a section of desert called the Jornada del Muerto, or "Dead Man's Journey." Oppenheimer dubbed the test "Trinity," after a line in a John Donne poem.

It was Bainbridge's job to build a fully operational scientific laboratory in the middle of a desert. Not an easy task. Crews built the steel tower to hold the gadget, as well as three concrete observation bunkers where Manhattan Project researchers could watch in safety. Bainbridge leased a ranch house and turned it into a field laboratory and military police station. Rugged roads were flattened and paved to transport men and materials to the test site. Miles of wires and cables were laid to power the detonation and the research that would follow.

Scientists at ground zero were poised to measure key aspects of the reaction, the symmetry of the implosion, and the energy that would be released. The biggest concern was the radioactivity from the blast. They couldn't trust the weather to carry all the radiation into the upper atmosphere, so the Army stood ready to evacuate residents from the surrounding area. Technicians in the bunkers were given maps of possible escape routes, just in case.

With the Potsdam Conference looming, Oppenheimer scheduled the Trinity test for Monday, July 16, at 4:00 a.m. On the morning of July 11, he said good-bye to his wife, Kitty, and hadn't come home from work since. On July 14, he met in Albuquerque with military leaders who flew in from Washington to witness history. That night, scientists test-fired Hornig's triggering device, which had worked flawlessly—up until that moment. Hornig's boss, George Kistiakowsky, assured Oppenheimer and the brass it would work just fine on the gadget.

The morning of July 15, a truck backed up to the tower with its payload directly beneath the steel structure. The driver pulled away the canvas cover, unveiling the bomb in the bright sunshine. It was an awkward steel globe bristling with wires, switches, screws, and diagnostic devices. Inside its eight-thousand-pound shell were thirteen and a half pounds of plutonium bundled inside a mantle of explosives. Workers carefully moved the bomb into position and placed mattresses underneath.

A door opened in the floor of the corrugated steel shed atop the tower and let down steel cables. Workers hooked the bomb to the cables and an electric winch slowly hoisted it upward. As it rose to the top, one of the cables came loose and the gadget swayed sideways, drawing a gasp from the onlookers. But the weapon was righted and made its way through the door onto the floor above. Once the bomb was placed into position, technicians began the delicate work of inserting electrical detonators into openings on the steel casing.

Down below, Oppenheimer was a jangle of nerves. The weapon was so complicated, and so many people at the test site knew exactly how it worked that it would be easy to sabotage. He couldn't leave the bomb unattended through the night. Oppenheimer asked Hornig to "volunteer" to babysit the bomb until morning.

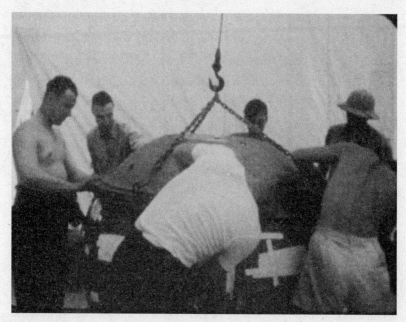

Oppenheimer inspecting the "gadget" before the July 16, 1945, Trinity test. He is standing in the back, second to the right.

Hornig had many hours to contemplate why Oppenheimer put him on the job. Maybe because he'd developed the trigger mechanism that had failed earlier that day. Maybe because Hornig was one of the Manhattan Project's youngest group leaders, making him the most expendable. Or maybe because Hornig was the only scientist able to climb up the hundred-foot tower. Whatever the reason, Lilli Hornig wasn't thrilled when he told her of his assignment.

He arrived at dusk, climbed the tower, and settled into the corrugated shed. The building was open on one side, with no windows on the other three. There was a telephone up there, a 60-watt lightbulb hanging from an overhead socket, and a folding chair. He pulled a paperback from his back pocket: *Desert Island Decameron*, a collection of humorous essays by H. Allen Smith. He sat down and opened the book.

Hornig had never been a security guard before. If a saboteur did show up, he didn't have anything but a telephone and a work of light literature to fight him off with. When darkness fell and lightning began flickering on the horizon, Hornig felt the first tremor of fear. Then the downpour started, and he decided the tower and ground were so wet, the power of a lightning strike would be conducted straight down to the desert floor. But another scenario niggled away: a sudden burst of electricity could trigger the bomb. If that happened, he would never know it.

Finally, the call he had been hoping for came through: come down from the tower and join Oppenheimer in the command bunker. Hornig took a final look around the shed and laid a hand on the ugly object inside it. No one would see it again.

Rain was bucketing down. In an area that had about three inches of rain annually, four had fallen already that year. The whole desert was underwater, and the roads were muck. When Hornig walked inside the control bunker, water was pooled on the floor. He had a cup of coffee at the canteen and joined the others waiting to see what would happen next. He was exhausted. He had been awake for seventy-two hours.

At 4:30 a.m., Hornig took his position for his next task: placing his finger on a console switch that would abort the blast, should anything go awry. He was the last person who could stop the detonation. The communication channel crackled to life. An operatic voice warbled a Spanish aria, radio signals skipping in from Mexico. What's next? Hornig thought to himself.

To relieve the tension, the technicians organized a betting pool to predict the size of the explosion. Edward Teller bet high—45,000 tons of TNT. Oppie bet a modest 3,000 tons. Groves became annoyed when Enrico Fermi started taking side bets on whether the bomb would ignite the atmosphere, and if so, whether it would destroy only New Mexico or the entire world.

Groves was afraid some of the more cautious scientists might convince

Oppenheimer to postpone the test. Fermi warned Oppenheimer that it wasn't a good time to detonate a nuclear bomb. The storm might drench them all with radioactive rain. The winds were gusting as high as thirty miles an hour. "There could be a catastrophe," he told Oppenheimer. Jack Hubbard, the Army meteorologist, assured everyone the storm would clear by sunrise, but Groves didn't believe him.

Oppenheimer and Groves had to make a decision. Neither wanted any more delays. What would Groves tell Truman? Oppenheimer was worried about his men. They had worked so hard to meet this deadline. They were stressed and tired. Would they be able to regroup quickly if the test was postponed? Groves and Oppenheimer decided to schedule the test for 5:30 a.m. and hope for the best.

As Hubbard predicted, the wind and rain stopped as morning arrived. Shortly after five, Groves traveled to another bunker to monitor the final countdown. Groves and Oppenheimer were positioned in different bunkers, just in case things went sideways. No one wanted to lose two key project leaders at the same time.

Meanwhile, on a hill twenty miles northwest of ground zero, *New York Times* reporter William Laurence took his position with VIP observers from Washington. They'd arrived from Albuquerque in a caravan of three buses, three automobiles, and a truck full of radio equipment. Laurence noted they were in the middle of the New Mexico desert, "miles away from nowhere, not a sign of life, not even a blinking light on the distant horizon." Compania Hill would be their encampment until "the zero hour."

They gathered in a circle for instructions on what they were to do at the time of the "shot." A soldier read out the directions by the light of a flashlight. At a short signal of a siren at zero minus five minutes, everyone was to find a suitable place to lie down. At a long siren signal at zero minus two minutes, everyone was required to "lie prone on the ground immediately, the face and the eyes directed toward the ground."

"Do not watch for the flash directly," the directions read, "but turn over after it has occurred and watch the cloud. Stay on the ground until the blast wave has passed (two minutes)."

Laurence watched several scientists smear sunscreen on their faces and hands in the pitch-blackness of the night, twenty miles away from the expected flash. They knew more than anybody about the "potentialities of atomic energy on the loose."

Back at the command center, the countdown sounded over the public address system. Observers at base camp picked it up on an FM radio signal. Thomas Jones, the Army intelligence officer, knew he'd be busy soon. His role was to make sure nobody noticed the massive explosion. He had men stationed around the test site as far south as El Paso and Amarillo, Texas. If ordinary citizens reported anything unusual, his team would mislead them. That was the only way to try to keep the test a secret. He hoped that was all he'd have to deal with. With this bomb, you just didn't know.

With only moments remaining, some scientists donned welder's glasses and assumed prone positions on the floor of the bunker, their feet pointed in the direction of the blast site. No one knew what would happen at zero, the moment of truth. This could be the end of everything.

At the two-minute mark, Oppenheimer muttered, "Lord, these affairs are hard on the heart." The last seconds ticked away.

Hornig's hand was poised at the "chicken switch." The ignition was controlled by an automatic timer. At 5:30 a.m., an electrical pulse would run from the bunker to the tower and into the firing unit of the bomb. Within a hundred-millionths of a second, a series of thirty-two charges would go off around the device's core, compressing the sphere of plutonium inside from the size of an orange to that of a lime. The gadget would explode. Now Hornig was the only person who could stop it. He felt a jolt of adrenaline. He was no longer tired. He heard the countdown. At thirty seconds before the explosion, four red lights flashed on the console in front of him, and a voltmeter needle flipped from left to right, showing his firing unit was fully charged. A good sign. Still, the final seconds dragged.

In another bunker, Groves clenched and unclenched his jaw. The silence was heavy. As he lay there, all he could think was what would happen if "the countdown got to zero and nothing happened."

Then a gong sounded in the control bunker. This was it. At 05:29:45, an electrical pulse traveled through the wires and hit the detonators. All thirty-two fired simultaneously, compressing the plutonium core at the center of the bomb, triggering a catastrophic nuclear reaction.

In thirty-millionths of a second, observers in the predawn darkness saw an intense flash of light, followed by a huge blast wave and a deafening roar. With the explosive power of 20,000 tons of TNT, a light "brighter than the noonday sun" was seen two hundred miles away, while the sound carried close to a hundred miles. A yellow and orange fireball stretched upward and spread across the sky. Then a spectacular

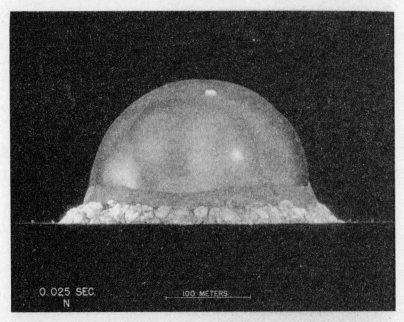

The huge fireball and mushroom cloud of the Trinity test on July 16, 1945.

mushroom cloud rose almost forty thousand feet in the air. Heat seared across the desert, vaporizing the steel tower and blasting a crater six feet deep and more than one thousand feet long in the desert floor. A herd of antelope that had been grazing near the tower vanished. There were no signs of life within a one-mile radius of the blast. Not a rattlesnake, not a blade of grass. No one could see the radiation generated by the explosion, but they all knew it was there.

The men huddled in the bunkers were filled with shock, joy, and relief. The gadget worked! Military observers were stunned by the display of sheer power. General Thomas F. Farrell, who was positioned in the control bunker, heard an "awesome roar, which warned of doomsday." For Groves, the blast was an awakening. At that moment, he knew the warfare business had changed forever. "I no longer consider the Pentagon a safe shelter from such a blast," he said.

On Compania Hill, the white light was so bright and lasted so long, James Conant thought the "whole world has gone up in flames." Edward Teller said the burst was like "opening the heavy curtains of a darkened room to a flood of sunlight." In the control bunker, Kistiakowsky said, "I am sure that at the end of the world—in the last milli-second of the earth's existence, the last man will see what we saw."

From above, the sight was just as impressive. Kneeling between the pilot and copilot in a B-29, Luis Alvarez, a physicist, was thirty thousand feet in the air and fifteen miles away from ground zero. Without warning, "intense light covered [his] whole field of vision." Then he saw a fireball and a mushroom cloud. He wanted to take pictures, but realized he had forgotten to bring a camera. So using his "mechanical drawing" skills, he sketched the nuclear cloud.

Concerned by the bright flash and the deafening roar, people living near the air base immediately began calling military authorities. Jones was ready with a bogus story. The military told residents and police an ammunition dump had exploded, but everything was under control. The

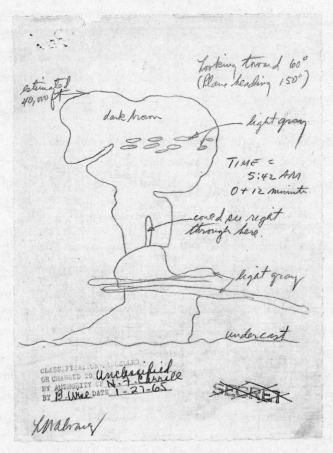

Luis Alvarez's sketch of mushroom cloud of Trinity test on July 16, 1945.

Associated Press reporter in Albuquerque was flooded with telephone calls from people wondering what had happened on the base. The reporter said if the Army didn't respond to comments he would put out his own story. Finally, the Army issued a statement:

Several inquiries have been received concerning a heavy explosion which occurred on the Alamogordo Air Base reservation this morning.

A remotely located ammunition magazine containing a considerable amount of high explosives and pyrotechnics exploded. There was no loss of life or injury to anyone. . . . Weather conditions affecting the content of gas shells exploded by the blast may make it desirable for the Army to evacuate temporarily a few civilians from their homes.

Meanwhile, reporter William Laurence was awestruck.

"The Atomic Age began at exactly 5:30 Mountain War Time on the morning of July 16, 1945, on a stretch of semi-desert land about fifty air-line miles from Alamogordo, N. M., just a few minutes before the dawn of a new day on this earth," he wrote.

"At that great moment in history, ranking with the moment in the long ago when man first put fire to work for him and started on his march to civilization, the vast energy locked within the hearts of the atoms of matter was released for the first time in a burst of flame such as had never before been seen on this planet, illuminating earth and sky for a brief span that seemed eternal with the light of many super-suns."

Meanwhile, the men who worked so long on the bomb had more prosaic reactions. When Groves greeted Oppenheimer, the general had a big smile on his face. "I'm proud of you," he said. All the usually loquacious Oppenheimer could say was "Thank you."

But Oppenheimer was proud, too. He believed the bomb would shorten the war. At the same time, he contemplated the future of civilization, remembering a passage of Hindu scripture from the *Bhagavad Gita*: "Now I become death, destroyer of worlds."

Some of the men celebrated and slapped one another on the back. Others were more subdued. Their euphoria gave way to sober reflections. Bainbridge, the test director, called the explosion a "foul and awesome display."

It was clear what would happen if the bomb were dropped on a Japanese city. Yes, it might shorten the war. But at what cost? When

Oppenheimer came to shake Bainbridge's hand, the soldier did not take hold. He looked Oppenheimer in the eye and said, "Now we're all sons of bitches."

J. Robert Oppenheimer and General Leslie Groves next to the charred remains of the steel tower at the Trinity test site.

COUNTDOWN:
20 DAYS

July 17, 1945

Potsdam, Germany

The next morning, President Truman was working at his desk on the second floor of the Little White House. It was where he had received the big news the night before.

Just after 8:00 p.m., Secretary of War Stimson and General of the Army George Marshall arrived with what aides said was important business. The fact that Stimson was even here in Germany was a bit surprising. Truman hadn't invited the secretary to Potsdam. Before the trip, he told Stimson, who was almost seventy-eight, that he wanted to save the secretary from "overexertion." Stimson wouldn't hear of it. He offered to get a letter from the surgeon general attesting to his good health. Truman gave in, recognizing how important the trip was to the elder statesman.

The president was meeting with Secretary of State Byrnes when Stimson and Marshall arrived. Stimson handed Truman a cable from Washington—the first report on the nuclear test he had been awaiting so anxiously.

"Operated on this morning. Diagnosis not yet complete but results seem satisfactory and already exceed expectations. Local press necessary as interest extends great distance. Dr. Groves pleased. He returns tomorrow. I will keep you posted."

Truman was thrilled. One of the central questions hanging over his brief presidency was now resolved: the atomic bomb worked. He was no longer the junior partner at this summit. He would begin the Potsdam Conference with a greatly strengthened hand. The successful Trinity test gave him a new confidence and optimism. The most powerful weapon ever created was part of his arsenal.

Now, just before noon on the seventeenth, Truman looked up from his desk. And there he was: Joseph Stalin, "the Man of Steel," dictator of the Soviet Union, the man Truman knew from newsreels towering over his generals, Communist Party leaders, and peasants. But here in person—all five feet five inches of him—Stalin looked to Truman like "a little bit of a squirt."

Stalin wore a plain khaki uniform. The chest of his military tunic was decorated with a single gold star—the Order of the Hero of the Soviet—and his pants had red stripes down the sides. His hair was brushed back from his prominent brow. His mustache was coarse and bristling. His eyes were yellow, as if stained by cigarette smoke. His skin was pockmarked and sallow—what in Moscow was known as "Kremlin complexion." His teeth were cracked and discolored. The former Missouri haberdasher greeted him in a light double-breasted suit, two-tone shoes, polka-dot tie, and matching handkerchief.

Stalin apologized for arriving a day late. Truman tried an "Uncle Joe" joke, as FDR used to do, but it didn't draw even a hint of a smile. The Russian was all business.

Truman told Stalin he didn't play diplomatic games. He usually said yes or no after hearing all the arguments about an issue. Stalin seemed to like that.

Then Stalin told Truman he would keep the promise he made at Yalta—to declare war on Japan by mid-August. The president was astonished—and greatly relieved. This was Truman's main objective in coming to Potsdam. And here he had just accomplished it before the conference even started. Truman put it bluntly in his diary, "He'll be in the Jap War on August 15th. Fini Japs when that comes about."

Cecilienhof Palace, site of the Potsdam Conference, July 1945.

It was time for lunch, and Truman decided to invite Stalin to join him. At first, Stalin refused. "You could if you wanted to," Truman pressed. Stalin finally agreed, and the mess staff added to the quantities of food already on the menu. A first course of creamed spinach soup and pumpernickel bread. The main course was liver and bacon. Stalin stroked his mustache in satisfaction. He praised the wine so much, the president later sent more than two dozen bottles to his villa.

When the president asked how Stalin thought Hitler had died, the generalissimo said he was probably still alive, hiding "either in Spain or Argentina." Stalin did not share that the Russians had an autopsy report that Hitler had committed suicide in his bunker. They talked about Spain and the Italian colonies in Africa. As Truman listened, he thought he could deal with Stalin. His read on the Russian: blunt, honest, and "smart as hell."

The Potsdam Conference began formally at 5:00 that afternoon. The meeting, code-named "Terminal" by Churchill, was held at the Cecilienhof Palace, the former summer home of the German crown prince. The flags of all three nations flew at the gatehouse—the Stars and Stripes, the Union Jack, and the Hammer and Sickle. But the Soviets were hosting the conference, and they left no doubt. Red Army soldiers with rifles and bayonets lined the long driveway. In the courtyard was a giant twenty-four-foot Russian red star of geraniums, pink roses, and hydrangeas.

The palace had 176 rooms and four wings, so each delegation had its own entrance and quarters. The conference itself was held in the oak-paneled reception room, big and dark, with high ceilings and a large window looking out on the lake. In the middle of the room was a round wooden table twelve feet in diameter, covered in cloth, with small flags of the three nations at the center. There were ashtrays for the participants.

Each delegation had five chairs at the table, with staff seated behind them. Truman sat in the center of the U.S. team. To his right were Secretary Byrnes and Admiral Leahy, and to his left were Joseph Davies, the former ambassador to Moscow, and Chip Bohlen, the State Department's Russia expert, who would serve as translator.

The British delegation was notable because Churchill had invited his Labor Party opponent in the general election, Clement Attlee, in case he should become the new prime minister once all the votes were counted.

Truman felt comfortable with the setup. It reminded him of a big poker table. But he was acutely aware that he was the new guy in this group—who'd been a county judge just a decade before—and Churchill and Stalin might think they could take advantage of him.

The first order of business was to name a chairman. And as someone comfortable in high-stakes games, Stalin made the first move. He nominated Truman, pointing out that he was the only head of state present. Churchill readily agreed.

The president did not relish the job, but as usual, he was prepared. He said he wanted the agenda for the next day's meeting to be set before they adjourned each day. "I don't want just to discuss," he made clear. "I want to decide." And despite the fact that both Churchill and Stalin were notoriously late-risers, he wanted talks to start at 4:00 p.m., not 5:00. The others agreed.

But sharp differences quickly began to surface. Truman brought up promises Stalin had made to FDR and Churchill at the Yalta Conference in February—especially his pledge to establish freely elected governments in countries in Eastern Europe liberated from the Nazis. In fact, as the Soviets had advanced toward Germany, they had set up puppet regimes in Poland, Hungary, Czechoslovakia, and other countries. Stalin also wanted his share of the German navy, which was now in British hands. Truman ended the session after one hour and forty-five minutes.

With the meeting over, the Russians ushered the delegations to an elaborate buffet dinner, including goose liver, caviar, endless varieties of meat and cheese, and impressive choices of wine and vodka. Truman would come to understand this was a typical spread for the Soviets.

Shortly after 7:00 p.m., he was on his way back to the Little White House. But during the ten-minute drive, the president's car was stopped by Russian soldiers at a checkpoint. Soon a Soviet lieutenant showed up and yelled at the troops for interfering with the American leader. Admiral Leahy whispered to Truman, "I'll bet that lieutenant is shot in the morning."

The president was pleased with how the day had gone, and wrote to Bess, whom he already missed, that night. "I was so scared I didn't know whether things were going according to Hoyle or not. Anyway a start has been made and I've gotten what I came for—Stalin goes to war August 15 with no strings on it. . . . I'll say that we'll end the war a year sooner now, and think of the kids who won't be killed. That is the important thing."

The atomic bomb had been tested. And early indications were it was a success. But Truman was still thinking of a ground invasion of Japan, and a long and bloody conflict.

COUNTDOWN:
19 DAYS

July 18, 1945
Potsdam, Germany

The next morning, Secretary Stimson rushed to Truman's villa and handed him a cable that came through overnight from George Harrison, his special assistant on the Manhattan Project back in Washington.

"Doctor had just returned most enthusiastic and confident that the little boy is as husky as his big brother. The light in his eyes discernible from here to Highhold and I could have heard his screams from here to my farm."

The decoding clerks at the Army message center were mystified, speculating about whether Stimson was a new father at seventy-seven. But the secretary translated the cable for Truman.

The "doctor" (General Groves) believed the plutonium bomb that was tested two days earlier was as powerful as the still-untested uranium bomb. The flash from the explosion had been visible for 250 miles, the distance from Washington to Highhold, Stimson's estate on Long Island. The explosion could be heard fifty miles away, the distance from D.C. to Harrison's farm in Virginia.

Truman, who was scheduled to have lunch with Churchill, was buoyed by the new details. He walked the six minutes to the prime minister's villa with the telegram folded in his pocket. The two leaders ate alone. Churchill and FDR had partnered on the Manhattan Project from the start. The night before, Stimson had shared the first sketchy report about the successful test with the prime minister. Now Truman filled him in on the latest news.

Churchill seemed just as delighted as the president. Truman knew that his counterpart hated the idea of invading Japan, fearing it could cost a million American lives and perhaps half as many British. Now there might be a way out, and the nightmare of another year or more of bloody conflict could be avoided. Churchill thought that this "supernatural weapon" might be able to end the war in "one or two violent shocks."

The two leaders discussed if or when they should tell Stalin. Truman said they should wait till the end of the conference. Churchill suggested they inform the generalissimo sooner, to make it clear they weren't keeping it from him. Truman agreed to share the news after one of the sessions. But Churchill cautioned that Stalin should be told "the Great New Fact," but none of "the particulars."

The prime minister added that the bomb made Russia's promised entry into the war irrelevant. It would be over before the Soviets crossed into Japanese-held Manchuria. Truman agreed, at least for the moment. He wrote in his diary that night, "Believe Japs will fold up before Russia comes in. I am sure they will when Manhattan appears over their homeland."

After lunch, Truman paid a courtesy visit to Stalin's villa. Despite having just eaten, he was confronted with another elaborate Russian buffet and numerous toasts. Finally, the two leaders went off by themselves.

Stalin handed Truman a note he had received from the Japanese. Tokyo's ambassador to Moscow said Emperor Hirohito wanted to negotiate an end to the war. The Americans and British had expected the Japanese to try to divide the Allies, angling to get the best deal they could. Stalin suggested asking for more details, to "lull the Japanese to sleep." The president replied he had no confidence in the good faith of the Japanese.

Truman was impressed that Stalin was so open about revealing the message from the Japanese, and in discussing how to respond to it. Perhaps the Soviets were ready to deal honestly with their allies. But throughout the Potsdam Conference, all sides were anything but transparent with each other. American cryptographers had already broken the Japanese code, and Truman had read the message from Tokyo. But with Stalin, he pretended to be surprised.

By 4:00 p.m., the earlier start time the president insisted on, the Big Three were back at the conference table. Truman was just as businesslike as he was with his own Cabinet. His demeanor was described by one observer as "crisp and to the point. . . . Where Roosevelt was warm and friendly with Churchill and Stalin, Truman was pleasantly distant."

But if Truman was crisp, Churchill was not. He made long, rambling speeches and seemed unprepared. One of the main topics was how the Allies would deal with postwar Germany. "What do we mean by Germany?" Churchill asked. Stalin had already seized a large swath in the eastern part of the country.

The Russian answered sharply. Germany, he said, "is what has become of her after the war. No other Germany exists." Truman was impressed and paid his Russian counterpart the highest compliment, telling an aide, "Stalin is as near like Tom Pendergast as any man I know," comparing him favorably to the Kansas City political boss.

At one point during the session, Truman wrote a note and passed it down to former ambassador Davies. "Joe, how am I doing?" he asked. Davies wrote back, "You are batting 1000 percent. You are holding your own with the best at this table."

But just two days into the conference, the hard-charging and decisive president was already frustrated with the slow pace of great-power diplomacy. He thought Churchill talked all the time, while "Stalin just grunts but you know what he means."

He complained to his diary, "I'm not going to stay around this terrible place all [summer] just to listen to speeches. I'll go home to the Senate for that."

Winston Churchill, Harry S Truman, and Joseph Stalin at Potsdam, July 1945.

COUNTDOWN:
18 DAYS

July 19, 1945
Oak Ridge, Tennessee

Voices boomed across the living room from the Crosley radio. Ruth Sisson listened to the evening news as she ironed the family's blouses and shirts. U.S. planes were turning Japanese cities into raging infernos. American bombers hit targets three hundred miles inside Japan. Tokyo reduced to rubble. It seemed like it might be over soon, but Japan refused to surrender.

Why wouldn't the emperor call it quits? asked one educated Yankee voice. Would they fight to the last man? Ruth wanted to turn off the radio, but her father was following every word, hunched in his usual spot on the sofa.

Ruth examined the collar of the pink floral dress spread out on the ironing board. She was wearing that dress when Lawrence said good-bye. It was frayed all along the seam now, almost worn through. Maybe her mom could mend it. There wasn't any money for a new one.

Her mother, Beulah, listened from the kitchen as she prepared supper. The kids ran in and out of the house, slamming the screen door. Just another couple of years, and my brothers will be drafted, Ruth thought.

"I think he'll be coming home soon," William Sisson said to Ruth.

She gave him a smile, hung up the dress, and shut off the iron. On the front porch, she stared at the line of trees at the edge of the farm. He was out there somewhere, her fiancé, Lawrence Huddleston. His last few letters came from England, but he didn't know how long he would be stationed there. "I may see you in a few months," he wrote. He couldn't wait to get home. He couldn't wait to hold her. He couldn't wait until they got married. She tried to read between the lines. He had seen a lot of terrible things, and the future might bring more. He didn't elaborate. That's what worried Ruth.

Almost three months after the Nazis surrendered, most American soldiers and sailors who'd fought in Europe were still there. At the defense plants and throughout the mountain communities in eastern Tennessee, women were saying their husbands, boyfriends, brothers, and sons were being sent straight from Europe to the Pacific without coming home at all. Could that be why Ruth hadn't heard from Lawrence? Maybe he didn't want to break the bad news to her.

Parents, cousins, friends, the radio, people on the bus—everyone talking about the war. Ruth was sick of it. When the fight ended in Europe, she thought they wouldn't need so many people at the plant, but she was wrong. They were still hiring, and so were many of the factories making weapons for the military. Alcoa, Lawrence's old employer, was advertising in the *Knoxville Journal*, looking for people to work forty-eight-hour weeks. Teenagers had their pick of part-time jobs.

It was clear the soldiers weren't returning anytime soon. The government was gearing up for a final deadly push into Japan. Lawrence would be there, once again on the front lines. That thought paralyzed Ruth with fear. As a medic, how many more young men would he have to save? How soon before he was wounded? Or killed? Everything was so secret. Everyone tried to figure out what would happen next the best they could, so rumors circulated constantly.

Ruth's father came outside, stretched, and yawned. "You okay?" he asked.

She nodded her head yes.

He stood near, silent. He didn't have to say a word. She knew he cared. Nothing he could say would lift her spirits.

Ruth's cousins Mary Lou and Thelma were coming over. Maybe they could take her mind off things.

Ruth walked back inside, picked up the newspaper to check the movie-house ads. As she turned the pages it was just more war: Potsdam Conference, Soviet Union. She avoided politics. After the war, she wanted to go to college, get a degree in education, become a teacher. She wanted to see movies, get married, buy a house, raise a family. Someday, when this war was over. If that day ever came.

Ruth Sisson (right) with cousins.

COUNTDOWN:

17 DAYS

July 20, 1945

Potsdam, Germany

Truman's mood had gotten even worse. As the conference spent days accomplishing almost nothing, the long-winded Churchill continued to ramble on, while Stalin was terse and blunt in refusing to give his allies any concessions. Truman was "sick of the whole business."

He wrote to Bess, "I have to make it perfectly plain to them at least once a day that so far as this President is concerned Santa Claus is dead and my first interest is U.S.A. Then I want the Jap War won and I want 'em both in it."

As discussions about Europe bogged down, Truman spent more and more time on the question of how to deliver a final ultimatum to Japan. And the central issue was what the status of Emperor Hirohito would be if the enemy surrendered.

Using what was called "Magic" equipment to break codes, Truman was reading "ultra top secret" communications from Foreign Minister Togo to Japan's Ambassador Sato in Moscow. The Japanese hoped to get Stalin to sign on to a peace deal, weakening the leverage of the United States and Britain. Togo laid out the terms: "If today, when we are still maintaining our strength, the Anglo-Americans were to have regard for Japan's honor and existence, they could save humanity by bringing the war to an end. If, however, they insist unrelentingly upon unconditional surrender, the Japanese are unanimous in their resolve to wage a thorough-going war."

"Honor and existence" meant allowing the emperor to remain in some position of power. That would bring "the war to an end." But if the United States continued to insist on "unconditional surrender" and the emperor's removal from the Chrysanthemum Throne, the Japanese would continue "to wage a thorough-going war."

Truman's team was split sharply over what to do. The U.S.-British position on Japan had always been "unconditional surrender"—just like with the Nazis in Europe. No terms, no provisions. Just capitulate. But now Secretary Stimson and Admiral Leahy both advised the president that the United States should drop its demand for "unconditional" surrender. They knew any decision by the Japanese to end the war would ultimately have to be approved by the emperor. And he would be far less likely to go along if his own standing was in jeopardy.

Secretary of State Byrnes disagreed. Since the "infamy" of the Japanese attack on Pearl Harbor, the U.S. position had always been total surrender, without any conditions. FDR stuck to that throughout the long and bloody conflict in the Pacific. Byrnes felt if Truman now softened the terms in his first months in office, the American public would "crucify" him.

The other issue was Russia entering the war. The concern was if the Soviets moved into China and Korea, and then Japan, they would look to establish the same kind of domination in Asia that they were now consolidating across Eastern Europe. Secretary Byrnes was especially insistent that the United States do all it could to end the war before the Soviets got in.

But that meant using the atomic bomb. And Truman still had doubts, both about whether it would work in a war setting, and, even if it did, whether it would force the Japanese to surrender. Truman still wanted Stalin and the Soviets to join the fight to ensure victory, regardless of possible long-term consequences.

With the lack of progress at the conference table, and major issues still to decide about Japan, plus the relentless heat in the villa all combining to make the president even grumpier, Truman invited Generals Dwight Eisenhower and Omar Bradley to lunch.

Ike was the face of the Allied victory in Europe. He led the successful campaigns in North Africa and Italy before being appointed supreme commander of the Allied Expeditionary Force in 1943. In that role, he was responsible for the invasion of Nazi-occupied Europe, which commenced on D-Day, June 6, 1944. More than 150,000 Allied troops stormed the beaches of Normandy. The invasion turned the tide of the war in Europe decisively toward the Allies. Eisenhower was now one of the true American heroes of the war.

Bradley was not as well known, but he was also a formidable military leader. He was the field commander of American soldiers on D-Day. His forces were the first to invade Germany, and controlled much of that country when the war ended. Bradley had something else going for him. Like Truman, he was from Missouri, and he liked his new commander in chief, judging the president as "direct, unpretentious, clear-thinking and forceful."

During lunch, the three men discussed strategy in the Pacific and whether to drop the bomb. Truman gave Bradley the impression that he'd already made up his mind to use the new superweapon. The president didn't ask either man for advice, but Eisenhower decided to give his anyway.

When Stimson first informed him about the bomb three days before, Eisenhower was engulfed by a "feeling of depression." Now he told the president about his "grave misgivings." First, Japan was already defeated. Using such a fearsome explosive was unnecessary. Second, he thought the United States "should avoid shocking world opinion" by being the first nation to so dramatically escalate the nature of warfare by deploying a true weapon of mass destruction.

Eisenhower also advised Truman to be in no hurry to get Stalin to enter the war. Like other presidential advisers, Ike was worried about what the Soviets would do in the Far East. But Truman still wanted the Russians in the fight.

The conversation with two of his top generals gave Truman even more to think about. In addition to his doubts about the bomb working outside of the carefully controlled conditions at Alamogordo, and whether a successful attack would be enough of a "shock" to force Japan's surrender, he still had to come to terms with the consideration that Eisenhower raised. Did he want to be the man to usher in a new age of human conflict with a terrifying new technology?

For now, he would keep the plans for invading Japan on track. But Truman knew he would have to decide—and soon—whether to use his new weapon.

COUNTDOWN:
16 DAYS

July 21, 1945

Tinian

Colonel Tibbets had just finished up his notes for another big meeting. He rubbed his eyes, yawned, and stretched out on his bunk for a quick nap. Every day, another damn thing; some new complication, confrontation, or snafu. The pace only picked up after Tibbets got General Groves's coded message.

The test in New Mexico was a success. Until now, the whole project had been theoretical. Two billion dollars had been invested in equations and formulas. Now the atomic bomb was a reality. Whatever doubts Tibbets might have had were gone. So he started drilling his men even harder. He knew the next atomic bang would be the real thing.

Tibbets's crews were flying sorties over Japan, dropping "pumpkin bombs"—orange globes that contained 5,500 pounds of high explosives and a proximity fuse that detonated in the air above the target, just like the atomic bomb. It was great practice.

Only one man was grounded: Lieutenant Jacob Beser.

Every time Beser asked to fly a sortie, Tibbets said no. Beser was the best radar man in the military, and Tibbets couldn't risk losing him before the big mission. Beser was insurance against Japanese radio signals triggering the nuclear weapon before it reached its target.

Beser couldn't stand watching everyone heading for the flight line,

leaving him behind again. He decided to try one more time. He barged
into Tibbets's quarters, ready to make his case. "Colonel, it's just one raid,"
he said, coming around the corner, seeing the boss flat out on his cot.

Tibbets looked up and sighed. He liked Beser. They had spent a lot of
time together over the last year in Wendover, Los Alamos, and the Pentagon. But lately, Tibbets was under more pressure than usual. It had been
like that since May, when the 509th Composite Group arrived on Tinian,
an island whose terrain was parklike, with groves of trees and sprawling
sugarcane fields. Its wide-open landscape was perfect for airfields. The
Navy construction battalions, known as the Seabees, rolled in with bull-
dozers mere days after the island was secured in July 1944.

A Seabee from New York realized the island from the air bore a geo-
graphical resemblance to Manhattan, so he laid out the streets on the grid
of the Big Apple. Broadway and Forty-Second Street was the busiest in-
tersection, and many homesick GIs were delighted to find themselves
living on Park Avenue, Madison Avenue, or Riverside Drive. The 509th
Composite Group was on the corner of 125th Street and Eighth Avenue.
They called their neighborhood "Columbia University," even though that
address in the real New York was in the heart of Harlem.

The island soon became almost as stressful, noisy, and congested as
a big city. It was a major U.S. military air base, perfectly positioned for
launching air attacks against the Japanese mainland.

The U.S. military referred to Tinian by the code name "Destination."
And so it was for Tibbets's 1,200 men and their eighteen specially modi-
fied B-29s. The 509th was a self-contained unit consisting of the 393rd
Bomb Squadron, the 320th Troop Carrier Squadron, the 390th Air Service
Group, 603rd Air Engineering, and the 1027th Air Materiel squadron. A
special unit arrived afterward, dubbed the 1st Ordnance Squadron: specialists who would handle the atomic bombs.

From the day he landed, Tibbets was busy meeting with the top brass,
including General LeMay, then commander of the Twentieth Air Force,

An aerial view of Tinian.

and Admiral Nimitz, the commander in chief of the Pacific Fleet. His men had been living in relative isolation near North Field, one of two air bases on the island. The 8,500-foot-long runway was the longest in the world—just enough for planes carrying heavy loads of bombs to depart nightly on the twelve-hour round trips to hit the enemy.

The last few months had been the most frenzied of Tibbets's career. Problems large and small popped up every day, and each one seemed to require his attention. He was frustrated and exhausted in turn, and it was a rare night that he got more than a few hours of sleep.

Much of the trouble came from the veil of secrecy the 509th lived under. Even high-ranking officers had to be briefed in a general way.

Tibbets's mission was very different from the routine bombing strikes the other squadrons were carrying out now. The other commanders didn't understand what was going on. No one did. To the other outfits on Tinian, the men of the 509th were a "bunch of pampered dandies." They were taunted. Someone even wrote a sarcastic poem about the 509th that was mimeographed and circulated on the island. It included the lines:

> *Into the air the secret rose,*
> *Where they're going, nobody knows,*
> *Tomorrow they'll return again,*
> *But we'll never know where they've been*
> *We should have been home a month or more*
> *For the 509th is winning the war*

Brigadier General John Davies, commander of the 313th Bombardment Wing, was intrigued by Tibbets's group and kept asking questions about their mission. When Tibbets said he couldn't talk about it, Davies got angry. He resented Tibbets's presence. Davies's crews had lots of combat experience over Japan, and the brigadier said Tibbets's men would benefit from briefings offered by his most proficient officers. Tibbets shrugged his shoulders and sent three of his crews to one of the sessions. That afternoon, Davies asked to talk to Tibbets.

"Are all of your crews like the ones you sent here this morning?" he asked.

Tibbets said they were.

"Goddamn it," he snapped. "They're demoralizing my whole school. They know more about airplanes and navigation than my instructors know."

That ended the briefings. But there were plenty of other rivalries to handle. There was Bill Irvine, General LeMay's director of materials. He centralized maintenance for the hundreds of B-29s on the island, and he didn't see why Tibbets's hotshot outfit should have its own separate facilities. As far as he was concerned, a B-29 was a B-29. He insisted Tibbets pool his maintenance people with the others, and send the 509th's airplanes to central maintenance for tune-ups and repairs. But Tibbets didn't want anyone but his mechanics fooling around with his specialized aircraft. Again, the colonel stood his ground.

In just a month, Tibbets traveled back to the United States three times for meetings with military leaders. He was set to witness the Trinity test in New Mexico, but Tom Ferebee, his trusted bombardier, called him back urgently to Tinian.

The message arrived just as Tibbets landed at Lunken Airport in Cincinnati. He'd planned a visit with his old mentor Dr. Alfred Harry Crum, the man who'd told him to forget about medicine and pursue a career in aviation.

Ferebee gave no details, but Tibbets dropped everything and hurried back to Tinian. When he walked off the plane, Ferebee was waiting. "It's bad news, Paul, really bad news," Ferebee said. There was a move under way to give the atomic bomb mission to another unit. Tibbets said he would get to the bottom of it.

General LeMay was behind the plot. Tibbets knew LeMay really didn't understand how much training, time, and effort had gone into this mission. LeMay had not been privy to the atomic secret until recently, and he was only given the basics: the weapon existed and was to be used soon. LeMay was authorized to tell his operations officer, Colonel William Blanchard, about the atomic bomb, and in Tibbets's mind, Blanchard spelled trouble. He was a smart, ambitious man, political enough to understand that the atomic bomb, if successful, would bring credit for ending the war to an obscure outfit that had just arrived in the Pacific. Blanchard clearly wanted a piece of the glory for himself and his men.

What Blanchard didn't know was the technique, developed over months of practice, for delivering the weapon. Tibbets had eighteen pilots infinitely more skilled at this specific job than anyone under LeMay's command. Tibbets could go over LeMay's head, and maybe that would have ended it then and there. But Tibbets decided to confront the general himself. He wasn't going to let LeMay take over. Tibbets walked into Le-May's office and asked him if the rumor was true. LeMay confirmed it.

When he was a brash young officer, Tibbets might have raised his voice and showed his anger. But over the years, he'd learned better. He took a deep breath, then "politely but firmly" said he intended to fly the mission himself. The 509th must be allowed to operate as intended from its formation, without outside interference. If anyone on General LeMay's staff wished to check out their proficiency, they were welcome to join one of their practice flights.

The following day, Blanchard was assigned to join Tibbets on a training flight to the nearby island of Rota, which was still in Japanese hands. They would drop pumpkin bombs on an airfield there. Blanchard strapped himself in. Tibbets fired up the engines and signaled "all go" to his A-team: Tibbets in the pilot seat, Robert Lewis as the copilot. They gave Blanchard a ride he'd never forget.

The B-29 arrived over their aiming point at the exact time navigator Dutch Van Kirk estimated. Ferebee dropped the bomb, and it landed squarely on the target. At that moment, Tibbets pulled the plane into a hair-raising 155-degree turn—one that Tibbets knew he'd have to use on the secret mission to get away from the blast. Blanchard was almost paralyzed as the g-forces pinned him to his seat. His face turned white. "That's enough," he gasped. "I'm satisfied."

"We're not through yet," Tibbets said.

For extra measure, Tibbets gave the colonel an idea of the souped-up plane's performance, like a stunt driver on a movie set. Despite the tricks, the B-29 returned to Tinian within fifteen seconds of the time that Van Kirk had said it would. Blanchard scrambled from the plane as soon as the door opened.

Tibbets didn't hear anything more from him or LeMay about the 509th's qualifications.

But Beser? He was relentless. Tibbets knew Beser had enlisted so he could fly combat missions over Germany. He told his story countless times to countless people. But he had not yet flown on a single combat mission.

"Paul, all I want to do is just this one mission, to see what it's like!" Beser cried.

Tibbets snapped. He leaped from his bed. "Goddamit, Lieutenant Beser, I've said no and I mean, *no*. Now, get the hell out of my room and go about your business. And the next time you come with a request, it's Colonel Tibbets, understand?"

Beser wheeled around and bounded out of the hut.

Word soon spread across the base: "The Old Man is on a rampage."

COUNTDOWN:
13 DAYS

July 24, 1945

Potsdam, Germany

Harry Truman was running out of time. It was the morning of his tenth day in Potsdam, and he knew that if he was going to use the atomic bomb, he had to decide soon. The military could not move forward without an order from the president. But he was still wrestling with the monumental decision he faced.

A little after 9:00, Secretary of War Stimson arrived at the Little White House and was ushered into the president's second-floor office. He brought a coded message from Washington:

> TOP SECRET
> OPERATIONAL PRIORITY
>
> WAR 36792 SECRETARY OF WAR EYES
> ONLY TOP SECRET FROM HARRISON.
>
> Operation may be possible any time from August
> 1 depending on state of preparation of patient
> and condition of atmosphere. From point of view
> of patient only, some chance August 1 to 3, good
> chance August 4 to 5 and barring unexpected re-
> lapse almost certain before August 10.

Truman understood what the message signified: the bomb was ready to be used against the Japanese in eight days. It was the news they had been waiting for. But Truman told Stimson that he was still thinking about giving the Japanese a warning. Even at this late date, with everything ready—the flight crews, the science, all the millions of man-hours and billions of dollars spent since FDR authorized the Manhattan Project in 1942—Truman still wanted to give the Japanese one last chance to surrender.

Three days earlier, Truman had received another briefing from Stimson at the Little White House, this time a report from General Groves. It was the first full description of the bomb test a week before. It took so long to get to the president because Groves refused to send it by cable, instead giving the dispatch to a courier to hand-carry across the Atlantic by airplane.

Truman listened as Stimson read the report out loud to him and Secretary of State Byrnes. It was fourteen pages double spaced. Stimson was so excited that he kept stumbling over the words. It took him almost an hour to get through it.

The Groves memo said the test exceeded all expectations. "For the first time in history there was a nuclear explosion. And what an explosion! . . . I estimate the energy generated to be in excess of the equivalent of 15,000 to 20,000 tons of TNT."

But it was the physical description of the explosion that was most riveting. "For a brief period there was a lighting effect within a radius of 20 miles equal to several suns at midday; a huge ball of fire was formed that lasted for several seconds. . . . The light from the explosion was seen clearly at Albuquerque, Santa Fe, Silver City, El Paso and other points generally to about 180 miles away. . . . A massive cloud was formed which surged and billowed upward with tremendous power, reaching the substratosphere at an elevation of 41,000 feet."

Groves quoted his deputy, General Thomas Farrell, head of field operations at Los Alamos, on what this meant for war with Japan. "We now had the means to insure its speedy conclusion and save thousands of American lives."

As the president listened to Stimson finish the report, he felt "an entirely new confidence." Stimson had taken the Groves dispatch to Churchill the next day. The prime minister responded with his inimitable sense of history and theater: "Stimson, what was gunpowder? Trivial. What was electricity? Meaningless. The atomic bomb is the second coming of wrath."

But if the bomb gave Truman greater assurance he could end the war on his terms, he continued to hope he would never have to use it. He was still looking for a way out. And that would take the form of a carefully worded ultimatum to Tokyo, to be issued by the three nations at war with Japan—the United States, Britain, and China—as the Potsdam Declaration.

The document still called for Japan's unconditional surrender. And while Truman didn't mention the bomb specifically, the declaration did issue this threat: "The full application of our military power, backed by our resolve, will mean the inevitable and complete destruction of the Japanese armed forces and just as inevitably the utter devastation of the Japanese homeland."

Once again, Stimson tried to convince Truman to drop the demand for "unconditional surrender." He said the Japanese would read the declaration as a statement that they must give up their emperor. He wanted to change the language to something more ambiguous: the Allies would "prosecute the war against Japan until she ceases to resist." Leave the emperor out of it.

But Secretary Byrnes wouldn't have it. He reminded Truman that he had reaffirmed "unconditional surrender" as U.S. policy in his first speech to Congress just four days after becoming president. These were the terms under which the Nazis capitulated. And American public opinion against the Japanese and their emperor was still running hot.

Newspapers were filled with stories of the enemy's atrocities. In May, a photograph was widely circulated of a blindfolded American prisoner of war on his knees, hands tied behind his back, about to be beheaded by a Japanese soldier.

A Gallup poll in June found only 7 percent of Americans believed the emperor should stay on his throne, even as a puppet. One-third of respondents wanted him executed as a war criminal. Unconditional surrender had been the demand ever since Pearl Harbor. Anything else would be seen as appeasement.

Before the president sent the ultimatum to Tokyo, he needed to show it to the Chinese for approval. Japan would get one last chance to avoid the kind of destruction unprecedented in human history.

Despite all his misgivings, Truman knew he had to drop the bomb. The Manhattan Project had given him a weapon to potentially end the war. And no matter how devastating their losses, the Japanese refused to surrender. They left him no choice.

But that didn't make his decision any less wrenching. The next day, what he wrote in his diary shows he fully understood how momentous his choice was. "We have discovered the most terrible bomb in the history of the world. It may be the fire destruction prophesied in the Euphrates Valley Era, after Noah and his fabulous Ark." But those were thoughts for his long, sleepless nights.

Now, on the morning of July 24, sitting in his office in the Little White House, the commander in chief turned to operational considerations. As Truman would later recall, "This weapon is to be used against Japan between now and August 10th. I have told the Sec. of War, Mr. Stimson, to use it so that military objectives and soldiers and sailors are the target and not women and children. Even if the Japs are savages, ruthless, merciless and fanatic, we as the leader of the world for the common welfare cannot drop this bomb on the old capital or the new (Kyoto or Tokyo)."

At 11:30, Churchill and his military team came to the villa's dining room for a conference of the chiefs of staff of both the United States and Britain. Perhaps Truman still had nagging doubts about dropping the bomb. What he heard only reinforced his decision to go ahead.

Truman turned once again to General of the Army George Marshall. The president asked for the latest estimate of what it would take to defeat the Japanese on their home islands. Marshall recounted the bloody campaign they had just waged at Okinawa, where U.S. forces killed more than

100,000 Japanese without a single surrender. Marshall said even their civilians would commit suicide rather than be taken prisoner.

It was the same story with the U.S. firebombing of Japanese cities. After the United States killed more than 100,000 people in Tokyo in one night, Marshall said, "it had had seemingly no effect whatsoever. It destroyed the Japanese cities, yes, but their morale was not affected as far as we could tell at all."

Marshall told Truman that he needed "to shock [the Japanese] into action." One way to shock the enemy would be to invade the Japanese homeland. Marshall said it would "cost" between 250,000 and 1 million U.S. casualties, with a similar loss on the Japanese side. The other military leaders there agreed with Marshall's estimate. The goal, they said, would be to end the war by November 1946.

Truman then turned to the other option. He asked Stimson which Japanese cities were devoted exclusively to war production. The secretary went down the list, mentioning both Hiroshima and Nagasaki. Truman told the men in the room that he had reached a decision: he would use the atomic bomb. He had given it "long and careful thought" and "did not like the weapon." But he felt it was inescapable that if the weapon worked, he must be willing to use it.

And there was the chilling cost of failing to use it. The closer U.S. forces got to the Japanese homeland, the more fiercely the enemy fought. In the three months since Truman took office, American casualties in the Pacific were almost half as great as during the previous three years of war. Not a single Japanese unit surrendered. And the enemy homeland was mobilizing for an invasion and the bloodiest battle of all. Japan had more than 2 million troops stationed there. And every civilian had been armed and trained to fight.

Truman said later, "It occurred to me that a quarter of a million of the flower of our young manhood were worth a couple of Japanese cities."

Now that the decision was made, the president couldn't put it off any longer: he needed to tell Stalin about the Manhattan Project and the existence of the new superweapon. At 7:30 p.m., after that day's session at the palace, Truman walked over to the Soviet delegation and talked to the premier through the Russian translator. He didn't ask for a private meeting. He "casually" mentioned to Stalin that the United States had a new weapon of unusual destructive force.

Truman braced himself. He didn't know how Stalin would react. Would he be angry the United States had undertaken a major research and development project, created a devastating new bomb, and kept it secret from an ally for years?

Stalin said he was glad to hear it and hoped the United States would make "good use of it against the Japanese."

That was it. No questions about the nature of the weapon. Nothing about sharing it with the Russians. American and British officials were shocked. The U.S. translator wasn't entirely sure that Truman's message had gotten through.

Afterward, Churchill came up to Truman and asked, "How did it go?"

"He never asked a question," the president replied.

But Stalin was interested. He just wasn't surprised. The Soviets had been conducting their own research for three years. And they had a spy inside the Manhattan Project. A German-born physicist at Los Alamos named Klaus Fuchs had supplied Moscow with valuable information.

Fuchs had been a communist for years, ever since his family was persecuted for speaking against the Third Reich. (His father was sent to a concentration camp and his mother was driven to suicide.) Fuchs joined the German Communist Party because he felt they were the only ones who could effectively oppose the Nazis. Fuchs eventually fled Germany and finished his physics doctorate in England. In 1942, he went with several other British scientists to New York to work with a Manhattan Project team at Columbia University. There he met a Communist Party member named Raymond, a courier for Soviet spies.

Fuchs began working at Los Alamos in 1944. On June 2, 1945—six weeks before Truman told Stalin about the weapon—Fuchs met Raymond in Santa Fe. Sitting in his car, Fuchs opened his briefcase and handed Raymond an envelope filled with classified details about "Fat Man," including the plutonium core, initiator, and high explosive leads system. He included a sketch of the atomic bomb itself. Even though Fuchs was welcomed by the American scientists at Los Alamos, he was a true believer in the communist cause. His loyalty was to the Soviet Union, not the United States.

For all of Stalin's seeming indifference about Truman's disclosure, a member of the Russian delegation heard Stalin and Foreign Minister Vyacheslav Molotov discuss it that night. Molotov said it was time to "speed things up" in developing a Russian bomb. A historian would later note, "The Twentieth Century's nuclear arms race began at the Cecilienhof Palace at 7:30 p.m., on July 24, 1945."

COUNTDOWN:
12 DAYS

July 25, 1945

Los Alamos, New Mexico

They partied in the streets of Los Alamos when they got the news of the Trinity test at Alamogordo. Whiskey flowed, bongo drums sounded, and scientists and technicians danced through that first great day.

As time passed, eyewitnesses excitedly recounted what they'd seen and felt that morning in the desert. A sudden flash, a searing bright light, followed by an enormous ball of fire that changed from yellow to orange to red as it grew. A mushroom-shaped cloud that climbed thousands of feet in the sky. A massive bang followed by the rumble of man-made thunder that could be heard for miles.

The scientists, engineers, and soldiers had been working so long and so hard, they had to talk about it. These were momentous times, and they'd seen something utterly marvelous. Led by Oppenheimer, the man they considered the genius of the age, they'd combined their efforts to unlock a secret of the universe.

And then the euphoria died down.

Some of the scientists began to face the stark truth: they'd created a means for mass destruction. In all likelihood, the device they'd so enthusiastically created would soon incinerate a Japanese city full of men, women, and children.

Work slowed at Los Alamos. Scientists began openly debating the morality of using atomic weapons. Kistiakowsky, the chemist who helped develop a specialized explosive charge for the nuclear weapon, said the new bomb was no worse than the ongoing firebombing of Japanese cities. Others argued that it was a trade-off: a Japanese population would die so another population of Allied soldiers wouldn't have to.

Physicist Robert Wilson was having a particularly difficult time. "It's a terrible thing we made," he told a colleague. Others felt guilty for waiting so long to take a moral position—they should have spoken up with Szilard and Franck. Some believed there was still time to convince military leaders not to use the atomic bomb without first warning the Japanese.

Oppenheimer had battled depression for most of his life, and he felt the familiar darkness closing in. In boardrooms with military leaders hashing out details of Japanese target cities, Oppenheimer imagined what would happen on the ground beneath the explosion, how the holocaust would unfold over city blocks and neighborhoods. His secretary, Anne Wilson, saw the change. He walked from his house to the Technical Area, mumbling, "Those poor little people. Those poor little people." She knew what he meant.

But somehow Oppenheimer was able to compartmentalize his second thoughts. He continued working with Groves to ensure the explosion delivered maximum psychological impact on the Japanese. General Thomas Farrell and Colonel John Moynahan, two officers in charge of the bombing of Hiroshima, were given a list of instructions.

"Don't let them bomb through the clouds or through an overcast," Oppenheimer wrote. "Got to see the target . . . Of course, they must not drop it in rain or fog. . . . Don't let them detonate it too high . . . or the target won't get as much damage."

Oppenheimer's monster was almost loose. Unlike Dr. Frankenstein, there was no way to destroy it now. He could only try to contain the damage.

Potsdam, Germany

Harry Truman prided himself on his ability to make a decision. But no one had ever had to make a decision like this. And even Truman struggled now. He was having trouble sleeping at the Little White House in Babelsberg. Maybe it was the unrelenting heat, or the strange surroundings. Maybe not.

He missed his family. After one phone call with Bess, he wrote he was "trying to think up reasons why I should bust up the Conference and go home." He complained he wasn't getting many letters from her or his daughter, Margaret. He wrote his wife to "tell the young lady her dad can still read." Other times, he instructed Bess to "Kiss the Baby." Margaret was then a grown woman of twenty-one.

When he did hear from his wife, he took great pleasure in it. "No your taste in hats is not screwy," he responded to one of her letters. But the relief didn't last long. Truman complained of fierce headaches during this period—a condition he suffered from throughout his life whenever he was under serious stress.

The choice might have been clear. General Marshall had laid out the terrible casualties if the United States invaded the Japanese homeland: more than another year of war, and hundreds of thousands of Americans dead or injured. But dropping the first atomic bomb meant the destruction of an entire Japanese city and tens of thousands of civilians. More than even that, it meant the introduction of a destructive new force to mankind. Truman understood the consequences. As he wrote in his diary that day, "We have discovered the most terrible bomb in the history of the world."

Despite the turmoil he felt so deeply, the president told Secretary Stimson to proceed—a monumental decision reduced to bureaucratic language.

Top-secret instructions went out to key military leaders: General Carl Spaatz, commander of the U.S. Army Strategic Air Forces; General Douglas MacArthur, commander of the U.S. Army Forces Pacific; and Admiral Chester Nimitz, commander of the U.S. Pacific Fleet.

"The 509 Composite Group, 20th Air Force will deliver its first special bomb as soon as weather will permit visual bombing after about August 3 1945 on one of the targets: Hiroshima, Kokura, Niigata and Nagasaki. To carry military and civilian scientific personnel from the War Department to observe and record the effects of the explosion, additional aircraft will accompany the airplane carrying the bomb. The observing planes will stay several miles distant from the point of impact of the bomb."

Truman knew that if the first atomic bomb did not end the war, the United States had one more in its arsenal. And the second one was fueled by plutonium, instead of uranium. That meant it was even more destructive.

But even now, just maybe, Truman thought there might be a chance he would not have to go ahead and use the bomb. Perhaps the Japanese would still surrender. That may explain why the president was so furious when he learned American diplomats in China had still not received the draft of the Potsdam Declaration that had been cabled there the day before. And when they finally did get it, they couldn't find Chinese leader Chiang Kai-shek, who needed to approve the ultimatum before it could be sent to the Japanese.

All of this was on the president's mind. He wrote in his diary, "We will issue a warning statement asking the Japs to surrender and save lives. I'm sure they will not do that, but we will have given them the chance. It is certainly a good thing for the world that Hitler's crowd or Stalin's did not discover this atomic bomb. It seems to be the most terrible thing ever discovered, but it can be made the most useful." Once again, Truman used that word: "terrible."

There was more drama at the conference that morning. Churchill needed to return to London to hear the results of the general election that had been held three weeks earlier. And the formidable prime minister was worried. He had a dream the night before that he shared with his doctor. "I dreamed that life was over. I saw it—it was very vivid—my dead body under a white sheet on a table in an empty room. I recognized my bare feet projecting from under the sheet. It was very life-like." Churchill provided his own analysis: "Perhaps this is the end."

But if Churchill was worried, so was his possible successor, Clement Attlee, leader of the Labour Party, who was part of the British delegation from the start. Attlee was a mousy figure, with a bald head, a trim mustache, and round glasses. He wore a three-piece suit even in the German summer. Churchill liked to call his opponent "a sheep in sheep's clothing." After sizing him up at the conference, Stalin said, "Mr. Attlee does not look to me like a man who is hungry for power."

At the end of the session, the Big Three stood outside the palace for what would turn out to be a final photograph. Truman took his place in the center, his arms crossed so he could shake hands with both of his counterparts. All three smiled for the still and newsreel cameramen, masking their emotions.

Truman was driven back to his villa, along with former ambassador Davies. The conference was not going well. Stalin refused to agree to any compromises on how to set the course for postwar Europe.

But that was one of many things on Truman's mind. He was stressed and exhausted. And now he worried about how Congress would react to the lack of progress at Potsdam. If the House and Senate failed to back how he had conducted diplomacy in his first time on the world stage, he told Davies, he was thinking of resigning the presidency.

Was it just the conference? Or was it turmoil over the decision he had made about how to end the war in the Pacific? Trying gently to lighten the mood, Davies told the president this would "bear thinking over."

COUNTDOWN:
11 DAYS

July 26, 1945

Tinian

Captain James Nolan and Major Robert Furman never fit in on the USS *Indianapolis*. They'd been ten long days and nine thousand miles in transit from San Francisco, sailing through waters infested with Japanese submarines, pretending they weren't really a doctor and an engineer. They took turns hanging around a cabin with an odd, bucket-shaped canister welded to the inside bulkhead.

Only Nolan and Furman knew what was inside the lead-lined container. Their orders were simple: one of them had to guard it at all times. Inside was $300 million worth of weapons-grade uranium-235 destined to fuel America's first combat-ready atomic bomb.

The ship's crew didn't know the specifics of the mysterious payload, but its importance was unmistakable. They had strict instructions: if the *Indianapolis* started to sink—before they could even save themselves—they had to place the canister aboard a raft and set it adrift. To maintain absolute secrecy, the old cruiser traveled alone, isolated from any other ships or aircraft.

Cruisers were not designed to search for submarines—a task that fell to destroyers—and the *Indianapolis* was not equipped with sonar, making it even more vulnerable to a sneak attack.

Nolan and Furman were unlikely security guards. Nolan was a medical doctor, a specialist in radiology, obstetrics, and gynecology. He enlisted in the Army in 1942 and was recruited for the Manhattan Project. At Los Alamos, Nolan set up a post hospital, where he delivered dozens of babies, including Oppenheimer's daughter. With time he took on another role: measuring and understanding the effects of atomic radiation on human health.

Furman, a Princeton graduate, was an engineer who worked closely with General Groves at the Pentagon. Groves later appointed him chief of foreign intelligence for the Manhattan Project. He was a spymaster, responsible for snooping out the extent of Nazi efforts to build the atomic bomb. He coordinated harrowing espionage missions to kidnap German scientists and seize caches of uranium ore. He once led a team of commandos to Belgium, where, under German sniper fire, they seized thirty-one tons of uranium. Somehow Furman managed to get the ore safely to port and shipped to the United States.

The odd couple met at Los Alamos on July 14 and encountered a series of near-disasters on the way to San Francisco. While driving near Albuquerque, a tire blew, sending their car careening toward the edge of a mountain road. They boarded the *Indianapolis* with the bomb-making materials after learning of the Trinity test success. They traveled disguised as Army artillery officers, and had a hard time keeping their cover. The ship's crew quickly grew suspicious.

When a sailor quizzed Nolan on what size shells he worked with in the Army, he didn't have an answer. He just gestured with his hands. Nolan was a poor sailor, and he kept to the cabin claiming seasickness for much of the voyage. Meanwhile, a fifteen-foot crate carrying the bomb's firing mechanism was lashed to the deck and protected by armed Marines. Rumors spread about the cargo. Was it some secret weapon? Nolan and Furman weren't going to tell anyone. Captain Charles McVay II knew little more than the enlisted men.

The voyage over, the *Indianapolis* dropped anchor half a mile off Tinian and winched the crate from the deck onto a landing craft. Nolan and

An overhead shot of the USS *Indianapolis* in 1944.

Furman left the ship by ladder, struggling with the heavy canister as they stepped into the waiting boat. When the boat reached the shore, workers were already there, ready to handle the special delivery. The uranium and the firing mechanism were unloaded, placed on a truck, and taken to an assembly hut where they'd be fitted into the bomb casing.

A second portion of uranium had yet to arrive, the so-called bullet that would be shot into the larger cylinder and trigger the explosion. That was flying to Tinian on a B-29 from Hamilton Air Force Base in California. Two other B-29s would leave at the same time, carrying plutonium for the second bomb.

Having finished its part of the secret mission, the venerable *Indianapolis* turned toward the Philippines, where warships were gathering for the invasion of Japan. The cruiser never arrived. Four days after delivering the uranium, the *Indianapolis* was torpedoed by a Japanese submarine and sank to the bottom of the Pacific. Only 317 of the 1,200 sailors on board survived.

In the meantime, Truman and other leaders were faced with stunning political news: Churchill had lost the general election. The man who led Great Britain through its darkest hour was no longer the prime minister. Clement Attlee would head the British government. Stalin postponed the conference for a few days.

Despite the upheaval, the Potsdam Declaration was released, warning Japanese leaders that failure to offer an unconditional surrender would result in their "inevitable and complete destruction."

To the Japanese, it may have sounded like saber-rattling. But Truman was ready with a weapon that could turn his threat into a fearsome reality.

COUNTDOWN:
8 DAYS

July 29, 1945
Tinian

In the predawn darkness on the edge of the North Field runway, most of the pilots, flight engineers, navigators, and bombardiers from the 509th stood listening while an intelligence officer barked out details of the day's mission: Japanese mainland military targets. Oil refineries. Factories. Antiaircraft fire would probably be "moderate to light," the officer said.

Robert Lewis opened his map and tipped it toward Van Kirk. Their target was an industrial complex in Koriyama. Van Kirk had bumped Lewis's regular navigator on today's mission. That must be Tibbets's doing, Lewis thought, with some resentment.

While Lewis tried to focus on the latest sortie, his thoughts always returned to the upcoming secret mission. Van Kirk and Ferebee no doubt would be on that crew, not his guys. Lewis didn't like it.

Like many military pilots, Lewis was superstitious and territorial. The B-29 with the number "82" stenciled under the fuselage was *his* plane. He loved the roar of the engines, the supercharged fuel injection system, the padded seat. He'd piloted that customized Superfortress since it rolled off the factory floor in Omaha. He'd flown it to Wendover and on to Tinian, and ever since on training and bombing missions, almost always with the same group of guys. *He broke it in—not Tibbets.* Some of his crew members felt the same way.

Lewis got along with just about everyone, but he felt most comfortable among enlisted men. He'd go to "unconventional lengths to be one of them," recalled Bob Caron, the tail gunner. Sometimes when Lewis was out with the men, he'd slip off his officer's jacket and put on another crew member's.

Lewis never connected with Van Kirk or Ferebee, Tibbets's old crewmen. Van Kirk acknowledged as much. When Lewis went out with them, they'd buy him "two or three stiff drinks to get rid of him." They felt he was too brash, that he might not make good command decisions.

Van Kirk thought Tibbets should have court-martialed Lewis after his AWOL flight home for Christmas. Lewis was a "good airplane driver," Van Kirk said, but what they needed for the secret mission was a commander.

While Van Kirk didn't get along with Lewis, he knew flight crews had to be flexible, no matter how they felt about one another. Number 82, Lewis's favorite, was in the shop for maintenance, so Lewis and Van Kirk would fly this long day's mission using Captain Charles Sweeney's airplane, dubbed the *Great Artiste*.

The briefing wound up. Trucks took the crews to their B-29s. Lewis's plane was fourth in line, right behind an aircraft called *Strange Cargo*, piloted by Major James Hopkins. Lewis sat in the cockpit and watched *Strange Cargo*'s four engines spin to life. As the plane taxied forward, Lewis heard the screech of metal grinding on metal. The bomb-bay door beneath *Strange Cargo* opened slowly. Hopkins brought the plane to a stop, and a five-ton bomb dropped onto the runway.

Lewis gasped. The huge bomb lay on the pavement a few feet in front of his B-29. If it exploded, everything within several hundred yards would be obliterated. This is bad, he thought.

Lewis didn't want his crew to panic. He quietly, calmly told them what was unfolding. He heard Hopkins over the radio calling the tower for help. Moments later, crash trucks and ambulances rushed in.

Firefighters blanketed the bomb with foam designed to deaden any explosion. Crews pushed a dolly and a winch crane under the belly of the plane. They placed shackles around the bomb and cranked it up, inch by inch, then slid the dolly under the bomb. A small tractor backed into position, then towed the bomb away.

A voice from the tower crackled over the radio. "All clear. Y'all can relax now." But Lewis bellowed a characteristic reply: "Like hell! We got a mission to fly!"

Within minutes, Lewis and his men were on their way to Koriyama. The mission was exhausting as ever, thirteen hours there and back, no losses, damage, or injuries. Tibbets was waiting on the runway when the planes came back, and he singled out Lewis for a greeting.

Tibbets was just back from Guam, where he and a cadre of top officers had congratulated General Carl Spaatz on assuming command of the U.S. Strategic Air Forces in the Pacific. Spaatz would supervise the ongoing bombing of Japan and, more important, the atomic bomb mission. Tibbets and Spaatz knew one another from the European campaign, when Tibbets had flown daylight bombing missions under Spaatz's command. It was Spaatz who first put Tibbets in the pilot's seat when top brass needed a safe ride into a combat zone.

Tibbets had heard about the morning's excitement at the airfield. He congratulated Lewis for keeping a level head with a live bomb on the ground so nearby. Lewis didn't waste any time on conversation. He had to lobby Tibbets, to ensure he and his men were included on the big upcoming operation. "My crew is the best you got," Lewis said. Tibbets said he knew that was true. He turned to Lewis and looked him in the face.

"You'll be flying the mission," Tibbets said.

It was the first time Tibbets had mentioned the possible makeup of his historic crew. Lewis flushed red. He assumed that Tibbets meant that *he*, Lewis, would pilot the fateful B-29. He was ecstatic. He thought he'd finally returned to Tibbets's good graces, as in the days of the B-29 test pilot program. Back then, they could joke around. According to Tibbets, Lewis was "young, rambunctious and unmarried," and whenever they stopped someplace new, he'd head to the "brightest lights in the neighborhood and start looking for girls." Back then, Tibbets playfully called Lewis a "young bull." Lewis had asked him to explain.

So Tibbets told a story about a young bull and an old bull who'd been shut up in a barn all winter. When spring came, the farmer turned them loose in a field with a whole herd of cows down on the far end. The young bull turned to the older one and said, "Come on! Let's run over there and make a cow!" But the wise old bull replied, "Son, let's take it easy and walk over there and make all of them." Lewis had laughed.

From that moment on, Lewis had called Tibbets "Old Bull." At least until they'd come to Tinian.

But that day on the runway, Lewis was wrong. He heard only what he wanted to hear. Tibbets had no intention of letting Lewis pilot the plane. Lewis would fly the mission all right, but as copilot. In Tibbets's mind, there was never any doubt who was going to be in the driver's seat.

COUNTDOWN:
6 DAYS

July 31, 1945
Potsdam, Germany

President Truman had now been away from Washington for twenty-five days. And at this point he wanted only one thing—to get out of Potsdam and go home. He wasn't sure which was worse, the emotional exhaustion or the political frustration.

He called his wife, Bess, by transatlantic telephone. Again, the conversation left him "terribly homesick." He wrote to his mother and sister back in Missouri. "Well, here another week has gone and I'm still in this godforsaken country."

One evening, after another frustrating day at the conference, Truman's motorcade was leaving the palace when an Army public relations officer asked if he could get in the president's car. Once the two men were by themselves in the backseat, the colonel said, "Listen, I know you're alone over here. If you need anything like, you know, I'll be glad to arrange it for you."

"Hold it, don't say anything more," the president interrupted. "I love my wife, my wife is my sweetheart. I don't want to do that kind of stuff. I don't want you ever to say that again to me." Truman and the colonel rode the rest of the way back to the Little White House in silence.

Developments around the world did little to improve his spirits. On July 26, with the Chinese finally sending their approval, the United States issued the Potsdam Declaration demanding Japan's "unconditional surrender." It stated, "The time has come for Japan to decide whether she will continue to be controlled by those self-willed militaristic advisers whose unintelligent calculations have brought the Empire of Japan to the threshold of annihilation, or whether she will follow the path of reason."

In addition to conventional methods, the United States got the message to the enemy in a more direct way. American warplanes dropped 600,000 leaflets across the Japanese homeland.

But, maddeningly, officials in Tokyo did not respond for two days. Finally, on July 28, Prime Minister Kantaro Suzuki announced that his government did not consider the declaration "of great importance. . . . We must *mokusatsu* it." That meant "to kill with silence." Without knowing it, Japan had rejected its last chance to avoid the fury of the atomic bomb.

And the enemy showed its determination to fight on. It soon launched a new wave of kamikaze suicide attacks against American ships. One of the planes hit the USS *Callaghan*, the last American destroyer to be sunk during the war. Forty-seven men on board lost their lives.

There was another development on the twenty-eighth. Britain's new prime minister, the unimpressive Clement Attlee, arrived back in Germany. Harry Truman and his team were shocked that the British people had rejected Churchill, the English bulldog who galvanized the resistance to Hitler and, ultimately, led his country to victory.

Truman was not impressed by Churchill's successor. He wrote his daughter, Margaret, "Mr. Attlee is not so keen as old fat Winston and Mr. [Ernest] Bevin looks rather rotund to be a Foreign Minister." He added for good measure, "I did like old Churchill . . . and these other two are sourpusses."

But now, on July 31, with the Potsdam Conference winding down, Truman was focused on what would happen in the Pacific. He woke that morning to another top-secret cable from Washington. It was 7:48 a.m. "The time schedule on Groves' project (S-1) is progressing so rapidly that it is now essential that statement for release by you be available not later than Wednesday, 1 August." This was the press statement the American team had worked on for weeks, the first official notice to be sent to the world that the United States had developed an atomic bomb—and had now used it for the first time as a weapon of war.

The president turned the pink cable over and grabbed a pencil. "Suggestions approved," he wrote, changing the schedule. "Release when ready but not sooner than August 2. HST." He wanted to be gone from Potsdam, and away from Stalin, before the bomb was dropped.

Truman was ready to go home. He wrote his beloved Bess about his plans to return through England. "I'll sure be glad to see you and the White House and be where I can at least go to bed without being watched. Kiss my baby [his daughter Margaret]. Lots and lots of love. Harry." Then he added this postscript: "I've got to lunch with the Limy King when I get to Plymouth."

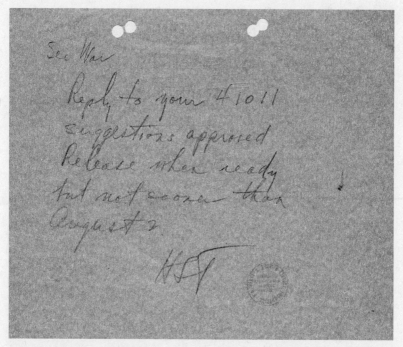

July 31 order by President Harry S Truman, signing off on atomic bomb statement.

COUNTDOWN:

5 DAYS

August 1, 1945

Tinian

After early chow, Tibbets headed back to his office, closed the door behind him, and sat down. The gadget or Little Boy or whatever they wanted to call it was all put together, minus the two small slugs of uranium that were being stored in the island's ordnance depot. They'd put the slugs inside the bomb just before it was loaded on the plane.

There was still no exact strike date, just sometime after August 3. But it was time to take the next step. Tibbets pulled out some paper, picked up a pen, and started drafting the document that had been kicking around in his head for weeks: a top-secret order for the first atomic bomb attack in history.

He drew on his experience as a combat pilot and as the commander of the elite squadron. He knew what his men could do. He'd pushed them hard, and it had brought out their best. While there were still so many unknowns—especially whether the bomb would work under combat conditions—he was confident his men would execute the mission flaw-lessly.

The mission called for seven B-29s. High command had ranked the targets in order: Hiroshima, Kokura, and Niigata. Tibbets would fly the strike plane and drop the bomb by visual sighting. Clear weather was a vital factor. Rather than rely on the long-distance voodoo of military meteorologists, three B-29s would fly out ahead to report on conditions over targets 1, 2, and 3. The information would be relayed back to Tibbets's plane. If the weather was bad in Hiroshima, he'd shift course and head to Kokura or Niigata.

A fifth B-29 would wait at Iwo Jima as backup. If the strike plane suffered mechanical problems, they'd land on Iwo Jima, load the bomb onto the new plane, then Tibbets would continue the mission.

Two more B-29s would accompany Tibbets to the target city. They wouldn't be there to protect, but to observe. One would carry scientific instruments to measure the intensity of the blast; the other would haul photographic equipment to make a pictorial record of the event. Before the bomb was dropped, the two other aircraft would drop back to allow Tibbets to complete his bomb run. So in the end, Tibbets's plane would be flying solo over Hiroshima, an attempt to catch the Japanese off guard. It would be risky, but Tibbets knew Japan now had a limited number of planes and pilots.

When he finished, Tibbets folded the report into an envelope. He'd send it by special courier to the high command on Guam.

The colonel then turned his attention to another important issue: selecting the planes that would fly with him. It didn't take long. The B-29s nicknamed *Straight Flush, Jabbitt III,* and *Full House* were assigned as the three weather planes. *The Big Stink* was the backup plane on Iwo Jima. The *Great Artiste* would carry the scientific instruments and *Necessary Evil* would be the camera plane. Each had their own fine crews. But now Tibbets had to pick the men who would fly with him on Number 82, the unnamed strike plane.

Again, it didn't take long. He already knew who he wanted. Most were regulars, guys who'd been flying together almost from the beginning in Wendover. Van Kirk and Ferebee, of course. In his mind, they were the best navigator and bombardier in the air force. Jacob Beser, the expert on detecting enemy radar and taking countermeasures, was finally going to get his combat mission. The same with Captain William "Deak" Parsons, the Navy weapons specialist and ordnance officer. The Evanston, Illinois, native had worked on the bomb at Los Alamos since the project began. His assistant, Second Lieutenant Morris Jeppson of Carson City, Nevada, would be on the flight, too. Like Parsons, he was an ordnance expert.

Sergeant Bob Caron, a tail gunner from Brooklyn, was one of Tibbets's favorites. They had known each other since the B-29 test program. Caron always wore his lucky Brooklyn Dodgers baseball cap on board the plane. He'd be their only line of defense over Hiroshima.

Tibbets selected the rest of his twelve-man crew—guys he knew would perform under pressure. Some were quiet. Others more outgoing. But they had one thing in common: they were all confident. For flight engineer, he chose Sergeant Wyatt Duzenbury of Lansing, Michigan, an ace poker player who seemed to know so much about B-29 engines the crew called them "Duze's engines." Robert Shumard of Detroit would be assistant flight engineer. At six feet four inches, he towered over everyone in the crew, including his best friends, Private Richard "Junior" Nelson, a radio operator from Los Angeles, and Sergeant Joseph Stiborik of Tyler, Texas, a radar operator who'd help watch for enemy aircraft. The crew represented every part of the United States—both coasts, the Midwest, and the South.

Tibbets sent messages to all of his officers, and asked to speak to each one, alone, about the plans. Charles Perry, the longtime mess officer, was the first to arrive. Tibbets told Perry to make sure he had a "goodly supply of pineapple fritters ready from August 3 onward." The fritters were Tibbets's favorite meal and he always had several helpings before he flew a mission. It was his version of a good luck ritual, and he didn't want to jinx the mission.

When Captain Charles Sweeney came in, Tibbets told him the *Great Artiste* would become a flying darkroom. Likewise, Captain Claude Eatherly learned the *Straight Flush* would be a flying science laboratory. Tibbets liked Eatherly—he was a terrific pilot, but a tad unpredictable. On a mission near Tokyo, Eatherly's assigned target was obscured by clouds. Instead of turning back, he decided instead to drop a bomb on Emperor Hirohito's palace. The weather wasn't great, and no one knew for sure where Hirohito's palace was, so the bomb missed its mark.

Had it worked, the bombing could have been a strategic disaster, as Hirohito was considered more moderate than his military leaders. He was worshipped by the Japanese people, and if he had been killed, they might never surrender, atomic bomb or not. When Tibbets learned about the escapade, he lit into Eatherly with one of the most "X-rated chewing-outs" he'd ever delivered.

By the end of the day, everyone knew his assignment. Tibbets chose Lewis as his copilot, despite their rocky relationship. He considered Lewis "competent and dependable." But unlike the others, Tibbets didn't tell Lewis right away. Tibbets assumed his decision was "self-evident," and he didn't need to call Lewis in for a conference.

But Lewis was living under his own presumptions. And when the reality dawned that he would sit in the second seat, not the first, the sting would stay with him for the rest of his life.

COUNTDOWN:
4 DAYS

August 2, 1945

Potsdam

Harry Truman awoke with a feeling of relief. It was time to go home. He had been in and around Berlin, which he called "that awful city," for seventeen days. The Potsdam Conference wrapped up the night before. It was a major disappointment.

Stalin stonewalled Truman and Churchill, and then Attlee, on almost every point. He would hold on to all of the gains the Red Army made in its sweep across Eastern Europe and into Germany. The authoritarian governments he'd established in those countries would stay in place. And Germany would stay divided, with the capital of Berlin deep inside the Soviet sector.

Years later, the president said he was "an innocent idealist" at Potsdam, and he called Stalin "an unconscionable Russian Dictator." Then he added this postscript: "And I liked the little son-of-a-bitch."

Truman's chief of staff, Admiral Leahy, assessed the new balance of power incisively. "The Soviet Union emerged at this time as the unquestioned all-powerful influence in Europe. . . . One effective factor was a decline of the power of the British Empire. . . . It was inescapable that the only two major powers remaining in the world were the Soviet Union and the United States."

Leahy concluded, "Potsdam had brought into sharp world focus the struggle of two great ideas—the Anglo-Saxon democratic principles of government and the aggressive and expansionist police-state tactics of Stalinist Russia. It was the beginning of the 'cold war.'"

Still, for all that, Truman got the one thing he wanted most from Potsdam before the conference even started: Stalin's commitment to enter the war against Japan in August. The president's satisfaction with that one pledge showed how much he still questioned whether the atomic bomb would work in a real-world situation—and even if it did, whether it would force the Japanese to surrender. Stalin's promise gave Truman an effective Plan B for the war in the Pacific.

At 7:15 on the morning of August 2, the president's motorcade left the Little White House in Babelsberg. By 8:05, the president's plane, *The Sacred Cow*, lifted off, bound for Plymouth, England. Eager to get home, Truman asked for no ceremonies at the airport. And by flying to England instead of sailing across the English Channel, he would cut two days off his trip back to the United States.

But before he could board the USS *Augusta* for the voyage back to the States, there was lunch with the "Limy King." "Welcome to my country," George VI greeted Truman as he boarded the battle cruiser HMS *Renown*. The president received full military honors, with thousands of British and American soldiers standing at attention.

Truman's first stop was the king's stateroom. George wanted to know all about the developments at the Potsdam Conference and "in our new terrific explosion," the status of the atom bomb.

The king brandished a weapon of his own, at one point showing Truman a sword that had been presented to Sir Francis Drake by Queen Elizabeth. "It was a powerful weapon," Truman noted, "but the King said it was not properly balanced."

The president recorded the menu at their lunch—"soup, fish, lamb chops, peas, potatoes, and ice cream with chocolate sauce." The two leaders "talked of most everything, and nothing much." But it was more serious than that. Truman found the king surprisingly well informed.

George brought up the atomic bomb, and discussed it in detail. He was especially interested in civilian use of atomic energy over the long term. Among the group at the lunch was Admiral Leahy, who once again expressed his doubt the bomb would work. "I do not think it will be as effective as expected," he said. "It sounds like a professor's dream to me."

The king disagreed. "Admiral, would you like to lay a little bet on that?"

After lunch, George escorted the president back to the *Augusta*. Truman reported the king inspected the guard, looked over the sailors, "took a snort of Haig & Haig, signed the ship's guest book, collected an autograph for each of his daughters and the Queen and, after some more formalities, went back for his ship."

The *Augusta* pushed off, and the president's thoughts returned to the bomb. Sometime during the trip, while he was in the middle of the Atlantic, the U.S. Army Air Forces would drop the new superweapon. With the *Augusta* at sea, and the few reporters on board cut off from any way to spread the news, the president called them into his cabin. He told them about the history of the Manhattan Project and the imminent use of the weapon. The impression he gave to legendary reporter Merriman Smith of the United Press was that Truman "was happy and thankful that we had a weapon in our hands which would speed the end of the war. But he was apprehensive over the development of such a monstrous weapon of destruction."

Smith felt excitement and frustration in equal measure. "Here was the greatest news story since the invention of gunpowder. And what could we do about it? Nothing. Just sit and wait."

Guam

Tibbets and Ferebee leaned over the huge aerial reconnaissance photo of Hiroshima that covered the map table. They could see every detail—the streets, rivers, landmarks. They'd studied city maps before, but this time they peered a little closer. They were looking for the perfect spot to drop the bomb.

Soon after Tibbets sent his battle plan to LeMay, he and Ferebee were summoned to the general's headquarters on Guam. There were too many targeting details to discuss on paper, LeMay said. Now, in the general's office, LeMay agreed that Hiroshima was the right choice. There were thousands of Japanese troops there, and its factories were still turning out weapons. While they discussed the remarkable detail offered by the photo, LeMay invited Colonel William Blanchard to join them.

Tibbets and Ferebee didn't like Blanchard. They knew he had tried to undermine the 509th and wrest the atomic bomb mission away for one of his squadrons to fly. But this was no time for wrangling. LeMay had an intriguing technical question.

The plan called for the bomb to fall from 31,000 feet above the city. That high up, couldn't crosswinds become an issue? A good gust could blow the bomb off course.

Blanchard evidently agreed. It might be better to fly downwind, Blanchard suggested, and with the wind pushing them along from behind they'd reduce their vulnerability over the target.

Tibbets thought otherwise. In his experience, he said, heading into the wind would reduce the effect of any crosswinds, and give his bombardier the best chance of accurately hitting the mark.

"Our primary purpose is to hit the target," Ferebee added. "We're going up there to bomb, not to play safe."

The men turned back to the map, and silence fell over the room. It was a remarkable image. The Ota River snaked through the city, homes and factories lining the banks. Bridges crossed the waterway and divided Hiroshima into several sections.

"Where's your aiming point?" LeMay asked Ferebee.

Without hesitation, Ferebee placed his finger on the Aioi Bridge, in the middle of the map. It stood out, as the center support made a T shape against the black water below. LeMay and Tibbets nodded their heads in agreement.

"It's the most perfect AP I've seen in this whole damn war," the bomber said.

The meeting ended and Tibbets and Ferebee returned to Tinian wondering when they'd get a firm date for the attack. They had their answer within the day.

Hiroshima "aiming" point.

COUNTDOWN:

3 DAYS

August 3, 1945
Washington, D.C.

Draper Kauffman sat in a Pentagon hallway and waited for his name to be called, picking at the buttons on his sleeves. They were snug again, newly re-sewn. He'd lost about fifty pounds in the last couple of months, and his wife had to get his too-loose uniform pants and shirts taken in a size or two.

Kauffman was here to deliver a sealed envelope to Admiral Randall Jacobs, head of the Bureau of Naval Personnel. Kauffman's commander, Admiral Richmond Turner, told Kauffman during a planning meeting in Manila that the letter was important, but nothing more. Kauffman didn't know what it said, or why he was chosen to be the deliveryman—but he was in Washington for a week of meetings anyway, so what the heck. Still, it was a little odd. If the message was so important, Turner would have phoned Jacobs, or sent a cable.

At this point, it didn't matter. Kauffman was here. He'd hand the envelope to Jacobs, make small talk with the admiral, then head to another meeting. It was nonstop at the Pentagon, where the forces were gearing up for the biggest military operation in U.S. history: Operation Olympic, the code name for the first phase of the invasion of Japan. Kauffman had heard details in June, in the Philippines. Since then, Kauffman had learned the role he'd play in the invasion.

The big push would start on November 1 on Kyushu, the southernmost of Japan's main islands, one of the few places in the island nation that could support an amphibious landing. The Kyushu invasion would begin with landings at three different beaches. Kauffman would lead one of them. Once beachheads were established, American troops would move inland and begin to build air bases and send in more forces for a second and larger invasion: Operation Coronet. That operation called for landing on Honshu, the largest island in Japan and the home of the capital, Tokyo. Operation Coronet was slated for March 1, 1946. It seemed the fighting would go on for a long time.

General MacArthur predicted the assault on Japan would be the greatest bloodletting in history. He figured the initial beachheads on Kyushu would cost 50,000 American lives. Predictions varied widely, but military planners thought up to 450,000 U.S. soldiers and sailors could die in Operation Olympic alone. The last years of fighting had proved that the closer they got to Japan, the fiercer and more fanatical the enemy became. Civilians might move into the countryside and fight as guerrillas for years after the war ended. How many American men would die in Japan? Kauffman wondered.

Kauffman was squeezing enjoyment out of every moment of this trip back to Washington. It was good being home with his wife, Peggy, and to visit with friends and family. He looked at them with new appreciation, and held them a little closer than he had before. For the first time, Kauffman felt pessimistic for himself and his men. This visit would probably be his last. He tried to shake the feeling, but it wasn't going away.

Kauffman heard his name, so he scurried into Admiral Jacobs's office, saluted, and handed him the envelope. Jacobs read Turner's letter, then glanced up at Kauffman. "You're taking two weeks leave. Now. That's an order," he said.

Kauffman was confused. He was already in Washington for a week. Why the extra time?

Then he realized: *Turner.* Kauffman had been incredibly busy. He was splitting his time between Oceanside, where he was training his men for the mission, and the Philippines, where he was helping commanders finalize plans for the massive invasion. Kauffman worked long hours, skipped meals, and lost track of his days. He didn't feel bad, but his weight had plunged to just 125 pounds.

Turner, the commander of U.S. amphibious forces in the Pacific, had noticed. When the whip-thin Kauffman arrived for a planning session a few weeks ago, Turner was stunned at his gaunt look. Kauffman was one of the most innovative commanders on his staff. Turner was going to need him in the coming months, so he had to do something.

Turner was tough. He'd never show softness or emotion, but Kauffman knew this "trick" was Turner's way of showing compassion. Kauffman had two free weeks to appreciate how much the admiral cared.

Kauffman felt a rush of gratitude. Now he could travel a little, tie up loose ends, and say good-bye to everyone.

He had to make the most of it, he thought. His time was coming. Once he left to take his place in the invasion, he wasn't going to make it back alive.

COUNTDOWN:
2 DAYS

August 4, 1945

Hiroshima

Hideko Tamura was a smart girl, and brave. And more than a little willful. But she got what she wanted. Hideko and her friend Miyoshi waited at the top of the long steps, scanning the street for the visitors who would save them.

"It's getting late," Miyoshi said.

"I know they're coming," Hideko said. "I know it. I can feel it."

"They should've been here by now," Miyoshi complained.

For months, Hideko and her friend had been stuck in this primitive temple and school in the middle of nowhere. Going back home to Hiroshima was dangerous, sure. The U.S. planes had firebombed other Japanese cities, and hundreds of thousands of regular people had been killed or injured in the attacks. She'd seen her mother crying over the newspaper photos of Tokyo burning. Everyone knew it was just a matter of time before their city was hit, too.

At ten years old, Hideko didn't fully grasp the danger. She'd taken part in air-raid drills. When she heard the sirens, she'd head to the closest bunker as instructed. But the planes never showed up.

Hideko shared the same longing as the American president on a ship half a world away: she wanted to go home.

She finally managed to get word to her parents that she was sick and miserable. The teachers at the school censored the children's letters home.

Hideko as a first grader at Seibi Academy in April 1940.
She was five years old.

They weren't allowed to talk about the lack of food and running water and the long days of forced labor. But one day Hideko came up with a plan. She and Miyoshi would write "real letters without censorship," then sneak down the long steps into the village and mail them at the post office.

It wasn't long before both girls got word that their mothers were on the way to collect them. Despite the war, they were going home! It was almost dinnertime, but the girls weren't hungry. No, they kept peeking, hoping they'd see their mothers. Suddenly, there they were. When two women finally rounded the corner, their daughters came running, squealing, down the stairs and into their arms. Hideko and Miyoshi hugged them close and cried with joy.

Once the celebration calmed a bit, the mothers gathered up their things and suggested they take a room and stay in the peaceful little town for a little while. "There are air raids every night in the city," Kimiko said. "We could have a good sleep here."

Hideko and Miyoshi hated the idea. They were eager to leave, so they protested and begged their mothers. "We can't stand being here," Hideko said. "We've got to go home now."

They agreed to leave the following morning, Sunday, August 5, for the long trip back to Hiroshima. For the first time in months, Hideko and Miyoshi were happy. They couldn't wait to see their families and friends. They didn't think about the danger. No, they only thought about sleeping in their own beds, playing in their own yards, picking up where they left off. All they had to do was wait until dawn.

Tinian

They'd just landed after a quick test run, and George Caron was sweating through his flight suit. The sun was high, humidity close to 100 percent. Caron knew he didn't smell too good, but nobody else did, either. It wasn't always a bad thing, working alone in the gun turret in the tail of the plane.

Caron pulled off his Dodgers ball cap and wiped his brow on his sleeve.

"Briefing 3 p.m.," someone told him. "Bring ID." Something important. Maybe today would be the *one.*

The scuttlebutt was that members of only seven flight crews were invited to the briefing. Caron felt privileged, and full of hope. Maybe today he'd get the facts about the big secret mission, the one they'd all been training for since they arrived ten months earlier at Wendover.

Caron walked fast across the tarmac and saw the 509th's briefing hut was sealed off. Marines carrying M1 Garand rifles surrounded the Quonset hut and barred the entrance. The MPs checked everyone's ID at the door before letting him inside. The hut was long and narrow, with a low ceiling, dim overhead lights, and benches. A big white screen was suspended above a platform with a lectern in front. Caron could feel a spark in the air. The place was packed and buzzing with quiet conversation.

Intelligence officers were pinning enlarged reconnaissance photographs of cities to two blackboards. The walls were covered with signs warning, "Careless talk costs lives."

Caron sat down at the end of the last row, hoping nobody was downwind. He shoved his baseball cap a little higher on his forehead, and then removed it when a ranking officer appeared—he was out of uniform, a punishable offense. He took a deep breath and rubbed the bill of his lucky cap. He wore it everywhere, even on missions when the crew was supposed to wear their flight caps. It had come in the mail in April, straight from the Brooklyn Dodgers' head office. Earlier in the year, Caron had written a letter to Branch Rickey, the team's president and general manager:

> *I heard that major league clubs will send their hats to combat crews and I wonder . . . if our crew could get some from the best club in the league, the Dodgers.*

Rickey didn't respond, but his assistant did. Bob Finch said they couldn't send any because they didn't have extras. Caron wrote Finch a thank-you note anyway.

> *I'm disappointed in not being able to get one, but I fully understand how difficult it is to meet all the similar requests you no doubt get. One of the boys suggested I make a similar request to another club, but I'll be damned if I will. Even if I haven't been home in three years to see a Dodgers' game, my kid sister is holding down my seat, rooting for me.*

Finch was so touched by the letter he sent Caron a cap and a note:

> *Anybody who can write that kind of letter in the midst of disappointment at not getting the right kind of answer to his first deserves everything*

in the world. I hope some day you wear it down the main street of
Tokyo.

Caron smiled at that last line. He didn't care about Tokyo. He'd rather wear it back home, walking up Flatbush Avenue with his wife, Kay, and their baby girl. He missed New York terribly. Maybe this briefing would be a step on the long journey home. He sure hoped so.

Lewis arrived just before 3:00 p.m., his face flushed. He'd gone on a demanding practice run with Van Kirk and Ferebee, just moments after telling his regular navigator and bombardier they wouldn't be going on the secret mission. It was painful. His throat and chest still ached for them. They'd been "superseded by rank," he'd told them: Van Kirk and Ferebee were "Tibbets' boys." Lewis understood how bad his guys were feeling. He'd just found out he wasn't piloting the strike plane after all. He'd only be the copilot.

Up on the dais were Captain Parsons and his assistant, Second Lieutenant Jeppson, along with a group of scientists. Parsons removed a reel of film from his briefcase and handed it to a technician, who laced it into a projector facing the big white screen.

Parsons had prepared this talk carefully. He'd disclose a little bit about the bomb, but not all the details. The important ones would come later. He would tell the men just enough to warn them of the danger.

At 3:00 p.m., Tibbets walked to the front of the room. The colonel's khaki uniform was neatly pressed, not a hair out of place. The murmuring ceased.

"The moment has arrived," he said. "Very recently, the weapon we are about to deliver was successfully tested in the States. We have received orders to drop it on the enemy."

Tibbets went over the mission orders and enumerated the intended targets. No one was surprised to learn that No. 82, Tibbets's B-29, would drop the secret weapon.

Navy captain William S. Parsons (left) and Colonel Paul W. Tibbets stand in a Quonset hut for a briefing before the Hiroshima mission.

Tibbets handed the meeting over to Parsons. The ordnance expert didn't waste any time.

"The bomb you are going to drop is something new in the history of warfare," he said. "It is the most destructive weapon ever produced. We think it will knock out almost everything within a three-mile area."

The crews were stunned. Caron wondered if he'd heard the man correctly. Parsons never used the words "atomic bomb," but he gave them the *Reader's Digest* version of the Manhattan Project. At times, it sounded part science fiction, part comic book. Parsons signaled to the technician to start the movie. The film started to roll, then sputtered, whirled, and stopped. The operator fiddled with the projector, but the celluloid tangled itself in the sprockets and the machine started to chew up the film. The room erupted in laughter. Here was an engineer for the world's most sophisti-cated weapon, undone by a simple film projector.

Parsons never missed a beat. He told the operator to stop the projector, that he'd describe everything that was on the film. It showed the only test they had ever performed with the new weapon.

"The flash of the explosion was seen for more than ten miles," Parsons said. "A soldier ten thousand feet away was knocked off his feet. A soldier more than five miles away was temporarily blinded. A girl in a town many miles away who had been blind her whole life saw the flash of light. The explosion was heard fifty miles away."

He had everyone's attention now.

"No one knows what will happen when the bomb is dropped from the air. This has never been done before," he said, turning to a blackboard. He drew a mushroom cloud, then turned to the men. He said they expected a cloud in the shape of a mushroom to rise at least 30,000 feet, "preceded by a flash of light much brighter than the sun."

The flight crews shifted on their benches. It didn't take a genius to fig-ure out that they would all be well within reach of the explosion, and the mushroom cloud.

One of the intelligence officers pulled out a pair of tinted goggles simi-lar to ones worn by welders. Parsons explained that every crew member on planes near the target would have to wear them at the time of the ex-plosion. The effects of the blast, shock waves, and radiation were still un-known, he said. To reduce the risk, Tibbets's plane would fly alone over the target. The shock waves might cripple or even destroy the plane. No one could say for sure.

And what will happen to the crew? Van Kirk couldn't help but won-der. Is this a suicide mission? He thought of his wife and son, waiting in rural Pennsylvania for him to return. He'd been away for so long. Van Kirk knew everyone in the room wanted to live. They had a purpose. They had families, jobs, futures. But they also had a duty, he told himself. He forced the negative thoughts out of his head. He had to have a clear mind for the mission.

Parsons went over a few more details, and the intelligence officers finished up. Tibbets stood up to end the briefing.

The room was quiet, all eyes focused on him.

Tibbets said he was proud of them, having worked so hard for so long on an unknown mission. Now, if things went according to plan, their work would cut short the war and save thousands of lives.

"Whatever work we've done up to now is small potatoes compared to what we are about to do," he said.

The men went silently out into the bright afternoon, wondering, worrying, and marveling.

COUNTDOWN:

1 DAY

August 5, 1945

Tinian

After a terrible Saturday plagued with plane crashes and multiple fatalities on Tinian, General Farrell was ready for a fresh start. He was up with the sun on Sunday morning, dressed in a crisp uniform, ready for a good weather report. Farrell was a by-the-book commander, handpicked by General Groves to be his deputy on the Manhattan Project. At fifty-three years old, Farrell had fought on the Western Front during World War I, taught civil engineering at West Point, studied the physics of the bomb at Los Alamos, and witnessed the Trinity test. Everything was ready to roll for the delivery mission. Everything except the weather.

For days they'd peered at weather maps and photos as a typhoon off Japan delayed the attack. Maybe today was the day. Farrell strode into headquarters. He had plenty of work to do, but nothing could really go forward until he had the weather report.

Just a few minutes before 9:00 a.m., an aide handed it over. The old soldier scanned it and smiled: clouds over Japan would clear within the next twenty-four hours. It was the news he'd been waiting for. Perfect conditions for dropping Little Boy.

Farrell quickly relayed the report to Groves, who in turn informed General George Marshall. Word came zipping back down the chain of command: The bomb would drop the next day, August 6. The planes would take off at 2:45 a.m. for the six-hour, 1,500-mile flight to Hiroshima.

Farrell scheduled a noon briefing with the "Tinian joint chiefs," the top military officers and scientists involved in the mission. They reviewed every detail of the delivery mission. Then ordnance specialist Parsons dropped a bomb of his own.

Few people knew more about the uranium bomb than "Deak" Parsons, a Naval Academy graduate who'd worked on the Manhattan Project since 1943. Parsons was organized, a natural leader, an explosives expert, and Oppenheimer's friend and neighbor at Los Alamos—Parsons's wife, Martha, often babysat the Oppenheimer children. He'd put his troubleshooting skills to work on the bomb-triggering challenge, and created the gun-type mechanism that would detonate Little Boy.

Parsons told the others that he was worried about taking off with a fully armed atomic bomb on board. In the few days since Parsons arrived on Tinian, he'd seen what happened when overloaded B-29s failed to lift off the airstrip in time. General Farrell was not the only person who'd lost sleep the night before after several B-29s crashed; thunderous explosions lit up the sky.

"If we crack up and the plane catches fire, there is danger of an atomic explosion that could wipe out half this island," Parsons told the other officers.

Farrell winced. "I pray that won't happen," he muttered.

Parsons suggested more than prayers. He volunteered to arm the weapon's trigger after takeoff, inserting one of the uranium slugs and the explosive charges into the bomb casing while the plane was en route to Hiroshima. If the plane crashed on takeoff, they'd lose only the crew and the airplane, not the bomb or the island.

"Can you do that?" Farrell asked.

"No," Parsons admitted. "But I've got all day to learn."

"That bomb bay is too small," Tibbets said.

"I'll do it," Parsons said. "Nobody else can."

If Parsons said he could do it, the commanders didn't doubt him. They agreed to say nothing to Groves about the change, as it would countermand the general's orders and create more delays.

Tibbets was at North Field by noon, watching as a trailer moved Little Boy from the assembly hut to the loading pit. Then the big silver plane was towed into position over the bomb.

He stared at the bomb and pondered its destructive power. It was incredible to think that ugly, twelve-foot object contained the explosive force of 20,000 tons of TNT. The bombs he'd dropped on Europe and North Africa in 1942 were sparklers compared to this thing—it was equal to 200,000 of them.

He thought about Oppenheimer and the other wizards at Los Alamos. He'd developed great respect for them. The fruit of all their labors was here before him, ready to be hoisted up into the belly of the airplane. Soon it would become Tibbets's responsibility. *Little Boy*. He chuckled. Why'd they call it that? It's not little by any standard, he thought. At 9,000 pounds it was a monster compared to any bomb he had ever dropped. Its flat gray paint and fins gave it a torpedo-like look, but it was much too broad in the beam for anything like grace. Caron called it "an elongated garbage can with fins."

A couple of crewmen stopped by and scrawled graffiti on the bomb, including a message for Japan's supreme leader: "Greetings to the Emperor from the men of the *Indianapolis*."

Tibbets watched them work. An idea began to form.

Things were getting hectic at the 509th's end of the base. All of the support sections—engineering, communications, radar, countermeasures, armament, photo, even the mess halls—were bustling with activity. Seven airplanes had to be fueled and greased. Guns were tested and reloaded. Radios and radar sets were tuned and checked. Bomb sights, autopilots, and compasses were calibrated.

The Little Boy atomic bomb.

Little Boy being loaded into the *Enola Gay*.

This was the busiest day of Beser's life. There was no time to fool around. He installed the proper radar-jamming antennas on Tibbets's plane, the two observation aircraft, and the plane being sent to Iwo Jima as a backup for the strike plane.

There was just one problem: the equipment needed to install each antenna array was unique to the set. If they had to land on Iwo Jima and switch airplanes, he'd need the tools to properly reinstall this equipment on the new plane. He had to ensure the flight engineer in the Iwo Jima plane had the proper tools for removing antenna bucket caps and replacing pressure gaskets. And he'd need the right gaskets, too. It all had to be done right now. His to-do list kept growing and growing.

Out on the flight line, Tibbets realized his plane was missing one thing: a name. All the other B-29s on the mission had flashy ones: *Straight Flush*, or pilot Frederick Bock's play on words, *Bock's Car*. The B-17 Tibbets flew over Europe was named *Red Gremlin*.

Tibbets knew the significance of this mission. If the bomb worked as advertised, his plane would go down in history. He had to give serious thought to the name. The world's first atomic bomb couldn't be dropped from "Aircraft 82."

He needed something dignified, poetic, but not too heavy.

"What would mother suggest?" he thought. Soon his mind turned to his mother, a courageous redhead whose quiet confidence had been a source of strength for him since he was a child. At the time when he left his medical studies, when his father thought he had lost his marbles, Enola Gay Tibbets had taken her son's side. "I know you will be all right, son," he heard her say.

Enola Gay. It had a nice ring. Tibbets had never heard of anyone else named Enola.

He jumped up from his desk and found Van Kirk and Ferebee playing cards in the next room. They had met the colonel's mother a few months earlier, when she visited Wendover. Name the plane for his mom? Why not?

they said. It might be good luck. Tibbets smiled, wrote his mom's name on a bit of paper, then headed to the airfield to find a maintenance man.

"Paint that on the strike ship, nice and big," Tibbets told him. And so he did.

Parsons was hot and sweaty, and his hands were filthy, but he was almost finished. Shortly after Little Boy was winched up into the plane, Parsons climbed up into the bomb bay. He stayed there for two hours, crammed into spaces not meant for man, dragging tools and bags of explosive cordite alongside. He practiced, over and over, removing the gun-breech plugs and inserting four bags of cordite as well as the uranium "bullet." His body pressed against the bomb, his hands blackened with graphite lubricant as he let the motions etch themselves into his muscles. It was close to 100 degrees inside the steel aircraft. Sweat stung his eyes. But Parsons didn't quit until he was sure he could do the job.

He emerged filthy, but confident he could pull it off while the B-29 was airborne. It would be risky. He'd need Jeppson, his assistant, to carry out the plan. They'd first have to navigate a narrow catwalk to get to the weapon. Then Parsons would have to squeeze into position, disconnect the primer wires, remove the gun-breech plug, insert the cordite powder bags, replace the breech plug, and reconnect all the wires.

Once the plane neared Hiroshima, the weapons men would switch on the trigger. Jeppson would replace the three green safety plugs on the internal battery with the red arming plugs. Only then would the nuclear weapon be ready to go.

As the hours passed, crew members without chores tried to relax amid the chaos. Some went to Sunday chapel services, others napped. Still others played ball or cards.

In the late afternoon, the officers started lining up outside the headquarters of the 509th. Tibbets, Lewis, Van Kirk, and Ferebee waited for the others. At 4:15, Caron, Stiborik, Shumard, Nelson, and Duzenbury finally showed up. Some were shirtless, fresh from a pickup softball game with the other crews. It was group photo time.

The photographer adjusted the lens and asked the enlisted men to kneel in front of the standing officers. It was to be the first of many mission photos. At that moment in front of the hut, the men smiled. They gave Caron grief for refusing to take off his Brooklyn Dodgers cap. Yes, they knew what was ahead. But for a moment, they weren't thinking about the danger.

The photographer got the shots he needed, and there was still time before dinner. Lewis and a few crew members jumped in a Jeep and drove to the airfield to inspect the plane. A military policeman stopped the vehicle before it got too close. Lewis jumped out of the Jeep and walked around to the front end to take in his silver bomber in the bright sun.

The guys on the other side heard Lewis scream.

"What the hell is *that* doing on *my* plane?" He had spotted the new "Enola Gay" paint job—bold black letters on the fuselage, right under the pilot's window.

Lewis was livid. He called the officer in charge of maintenance.

"Who put this name on here?"

The man refused to say, which only made Lewis angrier. He demanded the officer's men remove the name, but the man said he couldn't do it.

"What the hell are you talking about? Who authorized you to put it on?"

Finally the man gave up and told him.

This was it, the final indignity, Lewis raged. First, Tibbets bumps some of Lewis's regulars from the crew. Then Tibbets decides he's going to lead the mission. Now this? He rushed back to headquarters and barged into Tibbets's office.

He tried to steady his voice. "Did you authorize the maintenance men to put a name on *my* airplane?" he asked.

Tibbets didn't have time for this nonsense.

It was Tibbets who had gone to the Omaha factory and picked that

Group shot of the crew outside the 509th Composite Group's headquarters on Tinian. The photo was taken on the afternoon of August 5, 1945. Standing (from left to right): Major Thomas Ferebee, Captain Theodore J. Van Kirk, Colonel Paul W. Tibbets, and Captain Robert A. Lewis. Kneeling (from left to right): Sergeant George R. Caron, Sergeant Joe Stiborik, Sergeant Wyatt Duzenbury, Private Richard H. Nelson, and Sergeant Robert H. Shumard.

B-29 right off the production line. Yes, Lewis had piloted that plane a lot. But that was only because Tibbets was always in planning sessions in Washington, Los Alamos, and islands in the Pacific. Lewis was just borrowing the plane, like a kid borrowed a car from his parents. It was Tibbets's plane. If he wanted to put his mother's name on it, he'd do it, and he had. He didn't need Lewis's permission.

"It didn't occur to me you'd mind me naming the plane after my mother," Tibbets said.

His mother. It would be churlish to object to that, Lewis knew. He was still angry, but what could he do? Tibbets was his commanding officer. He took a deep breath, turned around, and left Tibbets's office. Years later,

Tibbets brushed off the encounter. "I wasn't concerned whether Bob cared or didn't care," he said.

Tibbets didn't tell Lewis why he chose the name, how his mother supported his decision to become a pilot. Or how, whenever Tibbets got into a tight spot—flying sorties over North Africa or Europe—he'd recall her soothing words. In getting ready for this top-secret mission, Tibbets rarely thought of what might happen if things went wrong. But when he did worry, his mother's voice always "put an end to it."

By 8:00 p.m., the entire air base was buzzing. A dozen ground officers were briefed on what to do and when. Scientists were escorted to safety, well away from the North Field. They would take no chances with the lives of irreplaceable atomic experts in case of an "unscheduled" nuclear explosion.

Fire trucks were stationed every fifty feet along the sides of Runway A, the North Field airstrip selected for takeoff. In case of a crash, a special unit would monitor the area for radioactive contamination.

Tibbets held a short preflight briefing in the assembly hut for the seven crews taking part in the mission. The commander went over the routes they'd follow, the altitudes for each segment of the flight, and the radio frequencies they'd use. There were two changes from the original plan: Tibbets changed their radio call signal from Victor to Dimples, just in case the enemy had found a way to monitor their calls. The other: during the first leg of their mission, they'd fly at an altitude of less than five thousand feet to give Parsons time to arm the weapon in the unpressurized bomb bay.

They had several hours to kill before they regrouped.

In the headquarters dining room, mess officer Charles Perry's cooks were preparing meals the combat crews would eat just after midnight, including Tibbets's pineapple fritters.

But for many, the idea of food was not tempting. Some lay quietly in their bunks, thinking of loved ones, writing letters. A few took shots of whiskey to calm their nerves. One went to a Catholic church to make a sacramental confession.

Beser hoped to get some sleep, but Tibbets intervened. Just before the preflight briefing, the colonel called Beser into his office and introduced him to William Laurence, the *New York Times* correspondent. "Bill has been loaned to the War Department to do all of the releases about our project," Tibbets told Beser. Then he turned to Laurence: "The two of you have a lot in common. Lieutenant Beser will be a good companion for you in the next few hours." Beser knew that was Tibbets's code for "Please keep him occupied and out of our hair."

Beser didn't get a nap. He got an education. The men talked for hours.

Beser quickly realized Laurence "had a mind that could comprehend the most complicated scientific theory and reduce it to simple layman's language." They were two of the few people on Tinian who had been at Los Alamos and knew what went on there. While no one had ever said the words "atomic bomb" to Beser, he knew all about the deadly payload they were carrying.

Laurence described the Trinity test to the keen young soldier, and expounded on the possibility of peaceful uses of the technology involved in their weapon, provided "they had the wisdom to harness it and channel it for mankind's benefit." He referred to the upcoming event as "the dawn of a new age," but warned, "We now have within our grasp the control of fundamental forces of the universe that could lead us to a millennium of good or to the destruction of civilization."

This was heavy stuff for the young lieutenant. When the call came for a final briefing at the 509th headquarters, Beser told Laurence he hoped they could talk again before the mission.

Scientist Ed Doll stopped Beser on his way into the building. They chatted for a minute, then Doll handed Beser a folded piece of rice paper with a line of numbers written on it. Beser recognized them: it was the radio frequency the bomb's radar would use as it fell, to measure the distance to the ground.

"Why the weird paper?" Beser asked.

"If something happens, if you think you might be captured, you ball this up and swallow it," Doll said.

First Laurence's apocalyptic visions, and now codes written on rice paper.

Beser wondered if he would make it back alive.

COUNTDOWN:
9 HOURS, 15 MINUTES

August 6, 1945

Tinian

This was it. No more practice, no more dry runs. This was the real deal. At midnight, Tibbets gathered the flight crews involved in the mission. It was time to tell them as much truth as they were allowed to hear.

"Our long months of training are about to be put to the test. We will soon know if we have been successful or failed. Upon our efforts tonight, it is possible that history will be made," Tibbets said. "We are going on a mission to drop a bomb different than any of you have ever seen or heard about. The bomb contains the destructive force equivalent to twenty thousand tons of dynamite."

Tibbets paused for a moment to wait for questions, but the crews were silent.

The colonel reviewed the plan—send one B-29 to Iwo Jima for backup, three planes to Japan to get real-time weather reports over the possible targets, then three planes to the target—a strike plane and two observers.

The final briefing was just for the crews of those final three: *Enola Gay*, *Great Artiste*, and *Necessary Evil*.

He repeated the same procedures and details, point by point. The men had already seen photos of the Trinity test and heard about the bomb's destructive power, but they were still struggling with the idea that one bomb could be so deadly. It was beyond comprehension—until Tibbets handed each man a pair of adjustable arc welders' lenses and warned them not to look at the flash with their naked eyes. Tibbets had commanded the unit for nearly a year, and not once had he used the words *atomic* or *nuclear*.

He spelled out the rules for a successful mission in a few crisp sentences: Do your jobs. Obey your orders. Don't cut corners or take chances.

Everyone knew the mission was mortally dangerous. Tibbets knew better than anyone. In his pocket was a cardboard pill box that contained twelve cyanide capsules. Flight surgeon Don Young had passed it across the colonel's desk earlier in the day. "I hope you don't have to use these," he said.

A few days earlier, Young and the crew discussed what to do if they had to bail out before or after they dropped the bomb. If they were captured, the Japanese would torture them.

"I'll be goddamned if I want to fall into their hands," Parsons said. Crewmen always carried pistols on missions. Yes, they could use the weapon to kill themselves. But as Young told them, "It would be easier to swallow a pill or capsule than to blow your brains out with a pistol shot."

And Tibbets knew there were other dangers. His B-29—and maybe the others—could be seriously damaged or destroyed by the shock waves after the atomic bomb was detonated. The weapon could blow up en route. There were all kinds of reasons they might not make it back alive. Tibbets asked for a chaplain to send his men on their way.

COUNTDOWN:

9 HOURS

The colonel introduced the men to Captain William Downey, a twenty-five-year-old Lutheran chaplain. Downey pulled out a scrap of paper and stared at the words he'd written. He knew the mission was something special, that it might somehow help shorten the war. Downey asked everyone in the room to bow his head. He read the formal prayer written on the back of an envelope.

> Almighty Father, who wilt hear the prayer of them that love thee, we pray thee to be with those who brave the heights of Thy heaven and who carry the battle to our enemies. Guard and protect them, we pray thee, as they fly their appointed rounds. May they, as well as we, know Thy strength and power, and armed with Thy might may they bring this war to a rapid end. We pray Thee that the end of the war may come soon, and that once more we may know peace on earth. May the men who fly this night be kept safe in Thy care, and may they be returned safely to us. We shall go forward trusting in Thee, knowing that we are in Thy care now and forever. In the name of Jesus Christ, Amen.

Beser stood respectfully by, thinking his own Jewish practice was more apt to give thanks after coming through "than to ask a special favor beforehand." Still, he knew prayers couldn't hurt.

After the "amen," the crews headed to the mess hall for the breakfast. Mess Sergeant Elliot Easterly tried to make the room feel festive, with paper pumpkin decorations on the walls in honor of the 509th's pumpkin bombs. Each item on the menu included a wisecrack: rolled oats ("Why?"), sausage ("We think it's pork"), and apple butter ("Looks like axle grease"). There were more than thirty dishes, including bacon, eggs, steak, and pineapple fritters. Many of the men were too nervous to eat. Others picked at their food. Tibbets drank several cups of black coffee, tried to make small talk with the others, and pretended to feel perfectly calm.

But he wasn't. He was tense, almost afraid. He'd have to fight off the feeling.

Beser took the opposite approach. He heaped his tray with oatmeal, eggs, and a mutton chop. A quart of milk and several slices of GI bread and butter sufficed for his dessert. If he was going to die, he would at least go out on a full stomach.

COUNTDOWN:

8 HOURS

After breakfast, Tibbets and his crew went back to quarters to pick up their flying gear and personal items they'd need on the six-hour flight to Hiroshima. Tibbets scooped up his smoking equipment—cigarettes, cigars, pipe tobacco, and pipes. Tibbets, Van Kirk, and Ferebee drove their Jeep to the flight line.

Waiting there for their ride to the plane, Van Kirk thought over all the work they'd done on board in the last couple of days. He was a perfectionist. Everything had to be in place, especially for this flight. He and Ferebee had deep-cleaned the cockpit and work areas on the plane, fishing from the nooks and crannies crumpled candy wrappers, gum, and a pair of ladies' panties that dated back to Omaha.

Van Kirk had their trip mapped out in his mind already and would use the stars in the night sky to navigate the plane most of the way. He felt celestial navigation was the most accurate and natural method of traveling from A to B. They needed perfect accuracy on this mission. In Europe and North Africa, he could see the ground. Here, over the vast Pacific, it was a different story. Van Kirk's work area was neatly organized: maps, charts, pencils, paper, a drift meter, and an old-fashioned sextant for measuring the angular distance between visible objects.

Ferebee made sure there were no glitches with his Norden bomb sight. The bombardier spent most of a mission staying out of the way. But when the moment arrived, if everything went right, he'd step up to deliver the goods. The bomb bays would open, he'd fix the target in his sights, then take over flying the plane for a moment, holding it steady as he synchronized the sight's tracking speed with the plane's ground speed. At the right moment, near the target, he'd release the bomb, then step back offstage while the pilots reengaged the controls.

Now the two friends stood silently in the warm night, feeling the August heat radiating from the pavement. They'd feel better when they were on their way.

Their troop truck finally pulled up and they climbed aboard in their pale green combat overalls. The only identification they carried were dog tags. They didn't say much on the short ride to the plane. They didn't have to.

Most of the crew members of the *Enola Gay* just before takeoff to Hiroshima. Standing (from left to right): Lieutenant Colonel John Porter, ground maintenance crew (he was not on the flight); Captain Theodore J. Van Kirk, navigator; Major Thomas Ferebee, the bombardier; Colonel Paul W. Tibbets, pilot; Captain Robert A. Lewis, copilot; and Lieutenant Jacob Beser, the radar countermeasure officer. Kneeling (from left to right): Sergeant Joe A. Stiborik, radar operator; Sergeant George R. Caron, tail gunner; Private Richard H. Nelson, radio operator; Sergeant Robert H. Shumard, assistant flight engineer; and Sergeant Wyatt Duzenbury, flight engineer. Missing from picture: Navy captain William S. Parsons and Army Air Forces lieutenant Morris Jeppson.

COUNTDOWN:

7 HOURS, 38 MINUTES

The three weather planes took off, followed by the *Big Stink*, headed to Iwo Jima to stand by in case the strike plane faltered.

COUNTDOWN:

7 HOURS, 10 MINUTES

Enola Gay's crew rolled up ready to board their plane, but found their B-29 bathed in floodlights, the runway crowded with more than one hundred photographers, filmmakers, and well-wishers. It was like a Hollywood premiere. It was General Groves's idea. He wanted a record of the *Enola Gay*'s departure.

Tibbets was stunned. He knew there would be some picture taking, but all this? For a single plane? He was unprepared for the attention. He realized his crew looked pretty motley. Tibbets wasn't big on dress codes— as long as the men did their jobs and did them well. He certainly wasn't going to demand full uniform tonight. Some of their civilian gear had become good-luck charms: there was Caron in his Dodgers hat, and Stiborik in his knit ski cap, not to mention pockets full of rosaries and rabbits' feet.

The crew was asked to pose for pictures, to say a few words on camera. Beser singled out Laurence in the crowd and went to shake his hand. The reporter was filled with envy. He was originally slated to fly on the strike plane, but logistics got in the way. He would be on the second atomic bomb mission, if there was one. He wished his young friend all the luck in the world.

Amid the fanfare, Lewis rounded up the crewmen. He had calmed down and resigned himself to the fact that Tibbets was the pilot. He was glad to be going on the mission, at least. He wanted to have a word with the men. Laurence interrupted. He handed Lewis a notebook and pen, and asked him if he would keep a log of the *Enola Gay*'s flight for the *New York Times* to publish later. Lewis agreed. Lewis then turned to the enlisted men:

"You guys, this bomb costs more than an aircraft carrier. We've got it made, we're going to win the war, just don't screw it up. Let's do this really great."

Time was getting short, but the 509th's photographic officer needed to get the official crew shot. As usual, the officers stood over the kneeling enlisted men. As he squatted—and as the photographer called for them to squeeze closer together—Caron could feel someone's boot on his ass. He looked up and saw Van Kirk grinning. Both men guffawed.

With the last photo taken, Tibbets turned to his crew. "Okay. Let's go to work," he said.

Colonel Paul W. Tibbets waves good-bye before
his B-29 leaves for Hiroshima on August 6, 1945.

COUNTDOWN:

7 HOURS, 5 MINUTES

Enola Gay was towed to its takeoff position. Tibbets went through his pre-flight checklist, then signaled for Duzenbury to start testing the engines. Everything started up smoothly. Oil pressure, fuel pressure, gauges—all at "full efficiency." When he finished, Tibbets waved to the crowd from the window of his cockpit—a moment captured by a photographer—and taxied more than a mile to the southwest end of the runway.

General Farrell joined the *New York Times* journalist and Chaplain Downey in the control tower to watch the takeoff.

Tibbets stared straight down nearly two miles of runway. On one side stood the blackened skeletons of the four burned-out B-29s that had crashed the night before.

During her life as Aircraft 82, his plane carried 135,000 pounds max. Today, *Enola Gay* weighed 150,000 pounds. It wasn't all bomb—they were carrying extra fuel in the back, to offset the weight of Little Boy in the front bay. The balance of a plane is critical, especially on takeoff. If the B-29 didn't get up enough speed by the end of the runway, it wouldn't lift off the ground. And on Tinian, the ocean began where the runway ended.

Tibbets was known for keeping cool under fire. But here he was, gripping the controls with a nervous tension he hadn't felt since his first combat mission in 1942. *This is just another takeoff. You've done it so many times before. No sweat*, he thought. But his palms were wet. On his first combat mission, his B-17 carried a total of 2,200 pounds in bombs. Now he had a single 9,000-pound bomb cradled in the aircraft's belly. This was it. He had to fight through the nerves. So many people were depending on him.

Tibbets turned his attention to his crew. Everyone was in position. He called the tower: "Dimples Eight Two to North Tinian Tower. Ready for Takeoff on Runway Able." The tower cleared him for takeoff.

Tibbets turned to Lewis. "Let's go."

Tibbets pushed all of the throttles forward and the craft rolled forward at full speed. He would wait until the very last moment, to build up every possible knot of speed, before lifting the plane's nose into the air. As the *Enola Gay* roared down the runway, some of the crew braced themselves for the worst. Lewis gripped his controls like he was the one piloting the aircraft. He wasn't the only one wondering if the *Enola Gay* would fly. In the tower, Downey whispered to himself as he watched the B-29 labor down the runway. He wasn't sure if they'd make it.

The plane neared the end of the pavement, but the RPM counter was still below 2,550 RPM—the figure Tibbets calculated he'd need to get airborne. Lewis stared nervously at the instrument panel. "Too heavy. Too slow," he said.

Tibbets ignored him. He wasn't going to abort. At the last possible moment, he eased the wheel back and the *Enola Gay* leaped into the air. Van Kirk exhaled and scribbled an entry in his navigator's log: "I looked out and could see the water, so we must have got off the ground."

A roar went up from the control tower. A sigh of relief passed over the crewmen inside the plane.

COUNTDOWN:
6 HOURS, 30 MINUTES

The engines moaned their steady song. The instruments were harmonized. Caron fired a few rounds of his .50-caliber machine gun out the tail of the plane, to make sure it worked. It did.

Parsons tapped Tibbets on the shoulder and pointed downward. Time to arm Little Boy.

Tibbets held the plane steady at 5,500 feet, just above the clouds. Parsons and Jeppson opened the bomb-bay hatch and lowered themselves down to the catwalk. They crept along to the cradle that held the bomb above the closed doors below. It was noisy, drafty, and dark. Jeppson held a flashlight and a kit of tools. Parsons wedged himself into the cramped space and went to work. They followed a checklist, with Jeppson handing Parsons the right tools at the right moment, like a nurse and a surgeon. Parsons had practiced and his battered hands worked skillfully, but it was nerve-racking. It wasn't only the danger of the bomb exploding. If one of the men slipped and fell, there was nothing between them and the open sky and ocean but thin aluminum doors not designed to bear a man's weight.

Parsons carefully removed wires and the rear plate of the gun breech, inserted the uranium and four bags of cordite, reconnected the wires, and reinstalled the plate. Parsons kept Tibbets advised of every step, speaking through an intercom system they had extended into the bomb bay. In twenty minutes, he finished the delicate task.

"The bomb is armed," Parsons told Tibbets. The colonel sent word by radio up the chain of command, then climbed to cruising altitude.

COUNTDOWN:

3 HOURS, 30 MINUTES

The *Great Artiste* and *Necessary Evil* met up with the *Enola Gay* over Iwo Jima. The planes set their courses for Japan. With the bomb armed, the crew settled in for the long flight. Many of the men hadn't slept in twenty-four hours. Some took catnaps. Tibbets decided to make the rounds of the plane and check on his crew. He started from the back with Caron, the tail gunner.

With the gun duly tested and hours of darkness ahead, Caron had tucked into his folding chair welded to the bulkhead, smoking Lucky Strikes, fingering the rosary his mother had given him. He'd stuck a snapshot of his wife and daughter into an angle of the window glass.

Caron was glad for the colonel's company. They talked about the mission, the mushroom cloud pictures of the Trinity test, the incomprehensible physics behind it all. As Tibbets rose to leave, Caron asked one last question.

"Colonel, are we splitting atoms?"

"That's about it," he said.

Tibbets knew that some of the men had probably figured it out. But no one was allowed to talk about it.

Tibbets returned to the cockpit and asked Lewis to keep an eye on the autopilot for a while. He was ready for a nap. Yes, the bomb was armed, but everything was under control. Lewis was writing his observations in the log for Laurence. Parsons and Jeppson were hovering over the custom-installed console that monitored the bomb's circuitry. Van Kirk looked at it over their shoulders, then looked at Jeppson. "What happens if those green lights go out and the red lights go on?" he asked.

Jeppson shook his head. "Then we are in a hell of a lot of trouble," he said.

Tibbets leaned back in his seat, closed his eyes, and slept. Lewis noted it in his log: "Tibbets 'Old Bull' caught a few winks while Lewis looked after the autopilot, nicknamed 'George.'"

COUNTDOWN:
2 HOURS, 15 MINUTES

Jeppson headed back into the bomb bay, alone this time. He clambered down alongside the bomb, removed three green safety plugs, and replaced them with red ones, activating the bomb's internal batteries. "It's live," he said to the intercom.

It was time to share the secret with the crew. Tibbets keyed the intercom. "We are carrying the world's first atomic bomb," he announced.

Several of the crew members gasped. Lewis gave a long, low whistle and thought, Now it all makes sense.

He felt uneasy. "The bomb is now alive," he wrote in his log. "It's a funny feeling knowing it is right in back of you. Knock on wood."

Beser had brought along an awkward audio recording apparatus. Tibbets told them, "When the bomb is dropped, Lieutenant Beser will record our reactions to what we see. This recording is being made for history. Watch your language and don't clutter up the intercom."

Meanwhile, Beser carefully monitored radio frequencies. The bomb had three fuses. The radar proximity fuse, responsible for detonating the nuclear weapon above the ground, was the most worrisome. Beser didn't want to scare anyone, but he knew that fuse operated on a very obscure frequency. If the Japanese appeared on that frequency right now, they could trigger the bomb.

COUNTDOWN:
51 MINUTES

The weather planes flew over the target cities. The pilot of the *Straight Flush* sent a coded message: "Cloud cover less than 3/10ths at all altitudes. Advice: bomb primary." Tibbets turned on the intercom. "It's Hiroshima," he said.

Tibbets turned his head and asked Richard Nelson, the radio operator, to send a one-word message to William Uanna, the squadron security chief on Iwo Jima: "Primary."

COUNTDOWN:
25 MINUTES

Flying at 31,000 feet, the *Enola Gay* crossed over Shikoku, due east of Hiroshima. The skies were clear. Bombing conditions were good. The crew recognized the roads and rivers below from studying the maps and reconnaissance photos.

COUNTDOWN:
10 MINUTES

The *Enola Gay* was at an altitude of 31,060 feet with an airspeed of 200 miles per hour when Hiroshima came into view. Van Kirk and Ferebee spotted the T-shaped Aioi Bridge. "Ten minutes to the AP," Van Kirk announced.

COUNTDOWN:
3 MINUTES

The bomb run commenced. Tibbets handed control of the *Enola Gay* over to Ferebee. "It's all yours," he said. Ferebee pressed his left eye against the viewfinder of the bomb sight. "We're on target," he said. Lewis made another entry in his log: "We'll have a short intermission while we bomb our target."

COUNTDOWN:
1 MINUTE

"On glasses," Tibbets told the crew. This was it. No turning back.

COUNTDOWN:
58 SECONDS

The T-shaped Aioi Bridge was in clear range.

COUNTDOWN:

43 SECONDS

The bomb-bay doors opened. Ferebee pushed the button to release the bomb. Little Boy dropped clear of its restraining hook and fell free from the plane, 31,060 feet above the bridge.

"Bomb away!" Ferebee shouted.

The nose of the *Enola Gay* suddenly rose ten feet upward as Tibbets pulled the B-29 into a sharp 155-degree turn to the right.

Ferebee saw the bomb wobble before it picked up speed. "It's clear," he said to the intercom.

"Can you see anything?" Tibbets asked Caron.

The tail gunner was spread-eagled in his turret with g-forces draining the blood from his head. "Nothing," Caron gasped.

Beser was also plastered against a bulkhead by the force of the turn. For a moment he was unable to lift his hand to activate the tape recorder. The bomb continued to drop toward the Aioi Bridge. Still, nothing. Was it a dud?

Tibbets called Caron again. "You see anything?" Again, no. But then a flash—brighter than the midday sun—lit up the plane in white light.

In that moment, everything changed.

COUNTDOWN:
FIRESTORM

Little Boy plummeted almost six miles in forty-three seconds. It exploded 1,890 feet above Hiroshima, about 550 feet southeast of directly over the Aioi Bridge. By then, the *Enola Gay* was six miles away, flying as fast as her engines could take her.

The craft was still far from safety. Tibbets braced for shock waves, wondering if the plane would withstand the impact. Were these their final moments? With his back to the city, Tibbets couldn't see the destruction, but he knew it had to be bad—he could taste it. His teeth tingled, his mouth filled with a leaden flavor. This must be what radioactive forces taste like, he thought.

From his seat in the tail of the plane Caron could see the shock wave coming, approaching at the speed of sound. It looked like shimmering heat rising from blacktop on a hot summer day. Holy Moses, here it comes, he thought. He triggered his microphone. "Colonel, it's coming toward us," he said.

The shock wave smashed into the plane nine miles east of Hiroshima. The B-29 shuddered and groaned. The crew shouted, wondering if the *Enola Gay* would break apart in midair. The racket the plane was making reminded Tibbets of antiaircraft shells that exploded near his plane during combat missions in Europe and North Africa. Parsons thought the same thing. "It's flak!" he shouted, before realizing it was the shock wave. For Lewis, it felt like a giant was beating the plane with a telephone pole.

Then, as quickly as it started, the violent shaking stopped.

Caron was the only one on the B-29 with a view of the destruction. Now that the shock wave passed, he tried to describe the scene to the rest of the crew. Words failed him. Tibbets turned the plane around so everyone could see. As Hiroshima came into view, a feeling of astonishment and sorrow swept over the men.

A purplish mushroom cloud rose to a height of 45,000 feet, towering over the shattered landscape. Robert Shumard, the assistant flight engineer, knew there was nothing but death in that cloud, maybe all the souls of the victims rising to heaven. Below, the city was covered in black smoke.

Van Kirk said it resembled a "cauldron of burning black oil." For Tibbets the smoke was an image from Dante's *Inferno*, "boiling upward like something terribly alive." Fires sprang up everywhere below the roiling smoke, "bubbling like hot tar."

Caron focused on the cloud. With its red core, it "looked like lava or molasses covering the whole city," he recalled.

Ferebee, the bombardier, could see "parts of things actually moving up in the cloud—parts of buildings, rubbish, boiling dirt."

For Richard Nelson, the cloud was "so huge and so high" it threatened to swallow the plane.

Beser took out his recording device. Everyone made a statement for the record, but no one said anything profound. They were transfixed. Beser put away the machine.

Lewis was stunned. Moments ago he'd seen a lively city, with boats in little channels, trolley cars, schools, houses, factories, stores. Now it all was obliterated. It disappeared before his eyes. It was "just a huge mass of clouds and debris and smoke and fire all mixed together." So he turned to his log, the one he was keeping for the *New York Times* reporter, and wrote: "My God, what have we done?"

They had seen enough. Tibbets turned the plane back to Tinian. The

The mushroom cloud rising after the atomic bomb was dropped over Hiroshima.

world will never be the same, he thought. "War, the scourge of human race since time began, now held terrors beyond belief," he later wrote.

At the same time, they felt relief. They had accomplished their mission. "I think this is the end of the war," Tibbets told Lewis. He tamped tobacco into the bowl of his pipe and lit up a smoke. He jotted down a few notes for Nelson to transmit back to the base. The primary target had been bombed visually with good results, and there had been no fighter plane opposition or antiaircraft fire.

At the same time, Parsons dictated his own message back to the base: "Visual effects were greater than the New Mexico test."

Hiroshima, Japan

Little Hideko Tamura lay beneath the collapsed ceiling of her bedroom and screamed. She'd returned home to her grandfather's estate just the day before, but her room, her books, her parents' embraces, the sunny morning, and knowing she'd never have to return to the horrible children's camp, all of it was blown away in an instant. Blown away like the house around her.

Hideko thought of her mother, out in the neighborhood somewhere tearing down abandoned houses in a "compulsory volunteer" project. Kimiko almost didn't go to work that morning. She was still tired from the long journey to collect her daughter and wanted to spend some time with Hideko, but in the end she'd decided to go.

Shortly after her mother left, Hideko heard an air-raid siren and turned on the radio. Three enemy planes were headed toward Hiroshima. A few minutes later, the announcer said the planes had turned around. The warning signal was canceled.

Hideko picked up a book her cousin had given her the night before and was soon absorbed in the story.

Suddenly a blinding flash lit up the page. She looked to the window and saw a "huge band of white light plummeting past the trees" and heard a roaring sound like a massive waterfall. Then she passed out.

Hideko awoke to a thunderous explosion. It jolted the air and the earth shook, knocking down everything in the house that was upright. And that's when she heard her mother's voice in her mind, and the instructions on how to save her life in case of a bombing. "Find something strong to hold on to."

The girl braced herself between two sturdy beams and a cupboard. A

lamp smashed to the floor, her father's glasses, a basket of winter clothing; the cupboard emptied itself onto the floor, then threw its shelves onto
the pile. The room suddenly became dark, as if the sun had disappeared.
Hideko was trapped beneath something. She could no longer see. She was
overcome by terror. She was going to die, and she was resigned to let it happen without protest.

Suddenly the roar and shaking stopped. The thick dusty air began to
clear. Hideko realized she was alive, saved by the beams she had held on to,
but trapped beneath the rubble. "Help me, someone, please help me!" she
shouted.

Her aunt Fumiko heard her and pulled away the plaster and beams.
Hideko emerged with only bruises and a deep gash on the heel of her right
foot. Fumiko was hurt, too, but her baby daughter was all right. The pair
searched the remains of the house and freed other family members. Everyone was injured somehow, stunned or crying. Hideko realized she'd have
to take care of herself.

She dug out a pair of pants and slip-on sneakers from her traveling bag.
She placed a few pieces of paper on her wound and inside her shoes. She
was ready to continue following her mother's warnings about bombings:
the next step was to get out of the house, or she would be surrounded by
fire. The point was illustrated time and again in the massive incendiary
bombings of Tokyo and other major cities. People were incinerated because they were trapped inside their homes.

"We can't stay in here," Hideko told her family. "The fires are coming
next. Please, let's go. Let's go to the river!" But they didn't respond to what
she was saying.

Just then her fear was realized. A huge ball of fire exploded from a
factory across the street and grew into an engulfing orange wave. Hideko
screamed in terror, "Fire! Fire!" The relatives sat, listless. Kimiko's instructions came back to Hideko. *Get out. Go to the river.* Hideko left the house.
She headed to the water, the Ota River, almost a mile away. The water
would protect her. Maybe there were people at the river who could help.

Hideko took a deep breath and started her journey by herself through an apocalyptic landscape populated by the dead and those who would surely die soon. She saw people, people who were still alive, whose skin was falling off their bodies. On another street the howling victims were blind, their eyes sucked from the sockets by the thermal wind. Others, old and young, crawled on the ground, begging for help. Hideko thought of her mother—could one of these grotesques be her?

"Mama, where are you?" she called out. "I can't help you. I don't know where you are!" She fought back panic, tried not to cry. She prayed to God, asking for help to find and comfort her mother. As she walked among the fire and rubble and bodies, the frightened ten-year-old started humming a tune her mother used to sing to her, a song of spring. She thought, God, there's nothing I can do. But can you please carry this song on the wind and deliver the sound to my mother? Please comfort Kimiko. You know where she is.

Hideko didn't cry much as a child, but that day, as she hummed, she also wept. She wept as she walked past the living and the dead to the river.

The child could not know it, but the city and countryside around her were a chaos. Military bases outside Hiroshima suddenly lost radio and telephone contact with the city. When rescuers finally arrived, they were shocked by the devastation. Japanese radio reports said, "Practically all living things—human and animal—were literally seared to death."

But by the time Hideko made it to the river, she knew that. Now she'd have to find a way to survive.

In the Atlantic Ocean

Half a world away, the USS *Augusta* was four days into its voyage, now south of Newfoundland, just a day from home. The Advance Map Room, set up in the first lieutenant's office, received a top-secret message from the Navy Department in Washington. The staff on board used special cryptographic equipment to decode the alert.

Truman was having lunch in the aft mess hall with six enlisted men. At 11:45 a.m., Navy captain Frank Graham rushed into the room. He handed the president the note and a map of Japan, on which Graham had drawn a circle around Hiroshima with a red pencil.

"Following info regarding Manhattan received," the message said. "Results clear cut and successful in all respects. Visible effects greater than in any test." The president shook hands with the captain. "This is the greatest thing in history," Truman said.

Ten minutes later, Graham returned with a second message, this time from Secretary Stimson, who had returned to Washington ahead of the president. "Big bomb dropped on Hiroshima. . . . First reports indicate complete success which was even more conspicuous than earlier test." Now Truman jumped to his feet and called across the table to Secretary of State Byrnes, "It's time for us to get on home."

The president started banging on his glass with a piece of silverware. The mess hall went silent. Truman announced he had just received two messages reporting on the "first assault on Japan with a terrifically powerful new weapon." It used an explosive 15,000 times as powerful as a ton of TNT. The room erupted in cheers.

With Byrnes in tow, the president rushed to the wardroom to give the news to the ship's officers. He declared, "We won the gamble." As word spread across the *Augusta*, the crew shared the same thought. Maybe the war would end soon. Maybe they would get to go home.

Washington, D.C.

Back in Washington, assistant White House press secretary Eben Ayers summoned reporters to come in for an "important" press announcement. The White House beat was usually pretty dead when the president was away, so some newspapers sent junior reporters.

Ayers stood in the front of the room, holding copies of the president's statement. "I have got here what I think is a darned good story. It's a statement by the president, which starts off this way." Ayers then read the first paragraph to reporters. "Sixteen hours ago, an American airplane dropped one bomb on Hiroshima and destroyed its usefulness to the enemy. That bomb had more power than 20,000 tons of T.N.T. It had more than two thousand times the blast power of the British 'Grand Slam,' which is the largest bomb ever yet used in the history of warfare."

Ayers continued in his own words. "Now, the statement explains the whole thing. It is an atomic bomb, releasing atomic energy. This is the first time it has ever been done." But by then, reporters were rushing to the front of the room to grab the statement and call their editors. One of them yelled, "It's a hell of a story."

Los Alamos, New Mexico

Oppenheimer was waiting for the phone to ring. He had sent physicist John Manley to Washington with instructions: he was to call Oppenheimer as soon as he heard any news about the bombing. But so far, nothing. Then Oppenheimer turned on the radio. And to his surprise, he heard Truman's voice.

The president was announcing to the nation that an atomic bomb had been dropped. Moments later, Oppenheimer's phone finally rang. It was Manley. He told Oppie that Captain Parsons, the weaponeer, had sent a teletype from the *Enola Gay* that all had gone to plan. But Manley said Groves stopped him from calling until after Truman's radio address.

Oppenheimer was annoyed. "Why the hell did you think I sent you to Washington in the first place?" he snapped.

When Oppenheimer hung up the phone, it rang again. This time it was Groves.

"I'm very proud of you and all your people," the general said.

"It went all right?" Oppenheimer asked.

"Apparently it went with a tremendous bang."

"Everybody is feeling reasonably good about it, and I extend my heartiest congratulations. It's been a long road," Oppenheimer said.

"Yes," Groves said. "It's been a long road and I think one of the wisest things I ever did was when I selected you as the director of Los Alamos."

"Well, I have my doubts, General Groves."

"Well, you know I've never concurred with those doubts at any time."

Just then, an announcement crackled over the public address loud-speakers throughout the Los Alamos facility. "Attention please. Attention please. One of our units has been successfully dropped on Japan." The place erupted in cheers. Many of the scientists in the Tech Area began celebrating. Otto Frisch, a physicist, heard people running up the hallway shouting, "Hiroshima has been destroyed!"

The phones lit up as workers booked tables at hangouts in Santa Fe. Frisch thought it was "ghoulish" to celebrate the deaths of so many people—even if they were America's enemies. Others felt the same way. They still couldn't reconcile the fact they helped create a weapon that could kill so many people. No one knew yet how many people had died, or what remained of the ill-fated city in Japan.

They celebrated that night in the Los Alamos auditorium, the same platform where Oppenheimer eulogized President Roosevelt a few months before. The place was packed, and Oppie, as usual, made a grand entrance, walking from the rear up the center aisle until he reached the stage.

As the assembly cheered and applauded, he raised his arms over his head and pumped his fists like a victorious prizefighter at Madison Square Garden. When the crowd quieted, he told them it was their hard work that made this happen. It was too early to judge the results of the bomb, but he was sure the Japanese "didn't like it." His only regret was not finishing the bomb soon enough to drop it on the Nazis.

Donald and Lilli Hornig missed the celebration at Los Alamos. They were back in Milwaukee, visiting family. Donald's brother was in the Navy, on leave with orders to head to the Pacific. Everyone assumed he'd take part in the invasion of Japan.

The Hornigs saw the newspapers downtown, the special edition head-lines: ATOMIC BOMB DROPPED.

Donald Hornig knew right away his brother was safe. He felt joy and relief. But he and Lilli agreed, theirs was a dark sort of happiness. Reports of the destruction were "just so incredible." They would be haunted by a vague guilt for years to come.

Oak Ridge, Tennessee

Ruth Sisson struggled to stay awake. The work was tedious, the cubicle overly warm and getting a little shabby. She knew the stool she sat on was designed to keep her upright and focused—if she dozed too deeply, she'd fall right on the floor. Her shift was finally winding up. Down the passageway she heard whistles and shouts, sounds of people "whooping it up."

One of her supervisors came into the room and addressed the women. America had dropped an atomic bomb on Japan, he said—a bomb so powerful it had killed tens of thousands of people. He said he couldn't disclose the details, but the end of the conflict was now closer. "You all helped make that bomb," he told them proudly. The workers cheered.

Ruth was elated, too, but didn't want to celebrate. Not yet. The war still wasn't over. She wouldn't celebrate until the Japanese gave up and Lawrence came back.

On the way home, everyone on the bus said the war would be done in no time. The driver told them five square miles of the city of Hiroshima was burnt black, with no survivors.

When Ruth got home, her mother greeted her from the kitchen, "Have you heard the news?" Ruth nodded. "Maybe Lawrence will be home soon," her mother gushed.

Ruth felt hopeful, but mostly just tired. Her mother fixed her a plate of eggs, but she only picked at them. She pushed herself away from the table and went to her room. She lay down on her bed and closed her eyes. She thought about Lawrence. She didn't know where he was. She was tired of thinking about him.

Something else was bothering her. Something she couldn't say out loud.

Ruth had been a participant in killing all those people. Part of her felt angry and betrayed. They'd put her to work on such a terrible weapon without her knowing, and now she had blood on her hands. She tried to sleep, but couldn't.

Every time she closed her eyes she saw five square miles of blackened city.

Washington, D.C.

Draper Kauffman was home when he heard about Hiroshima on the radio. At first, he couldn't believe it. Then he told his wife, Peggy, and they went to the Washington National Cathedral to offer prayers. They prayed the war would end, that no more lives on either side would be lost.

Tinian

With Tinian in sight, Tibbets and his crew braced for some kind of celebration. They were happy to have accomplished the mission, but the mood on the Enola Gay had changed. The adrenaline and awe had left them feeling drained. The mushroom cloud had been visible for four hundred miles.

The crew looked for words to describe what they witnessed. They weren't novices. They had dropped bombs many times, seen them explode and smoke rise from targets below. But this? This was beyond comprehension.

The crew asked a lot of questions on the long journey back to Tinian, and finally Tibbets was able to answer most of them. He told them about the Manhattan Project, how scientists had worked for years to turn an obscure theory into a weapon of mass destruction.

Ferebee was worried. He hadn't put his goggles on before the big flash of light, and he wondered if his vision would be all right. He worried about that mushroom cloud, and the radiation inside the bomb itself. Might it make them all sterile? They'd been so close to it. Parsons assured Ferebee they'd be okay, that he personally would never have cuddled up to Little Boy in that bomb bay if he thought it was dangerous.

Everyone laughed with relief. The rest of the trip was like a "slumber party." As the excitement died down, many crew members dozed. There would be a big fuss when they got back, and who could say when they'd get to sleep again.

They landed at 2:58 p.m. Waiting on the runway were two hundred military leaders, including General Spaatz and General Farrell. It was a ceremonial occasion, so Tibbets was the first to descend from the plane. He saluted Spaatz, but when he tried to shake the general's hand, Spaatz stopped him. Instead, he pinned the Distinguished Service Cross to Tibbets's rumpled flight coveralls. Silver Stars would later be presented to his crew and the men who took part in the mission.

They headed in Jeeps to a Quonset hut where James Nolan, the physician and radiologist who delivered babies at Los Alamos and that shipment of uranium on the USS *Indianapolis*, gave them all a going-over, looking for radiation damage. He checked Ferebee's eyes, gave them all a clean bill of health. When commanders heard their description of the mushroom cloud and fire and smoke and death at their debriefing, it seemed unbelievable. But as everyone would soon find out, it was even worse than they thought.

Washington, D.C.

Just past 11:00 p.m. on August 7, President Truman arrived back at the White House. He invited a small group of Cabinet secretaries and staffers who had not been on the trip to Germany up to his second-floor study. He played the piano, then called Bess to say he was safely home. She said she would leave Independence the next day to come back to the White House.

Drinks were poured as Truman filled the group in on Potsdam—the diplomacy, the personalities, the gossip. But one thing was never mentioned: the dropping of the bomb on Hiroshima. The event was too shocking, the carnage too immense, to discuss over drinks.

But in an official statement, the president laid out the stark choice Japanese officials faced after Hiroshima. "If they do not now accept our terms they may expect a rain of ruin from the air, the like of which has never been seen on this earth." And that is just what happened.

The following day, August 8, the Soviet Union declared war on Japan. Soviet infantry tanks and aircraft invaded Manchuria. Skeptics called the timing "convenient," and suspected the Soviets were more interested in expanding their empire to the Far East than defeating Japan.

Meanwhile, U.S. planes dropped leaflets over Japanese cities warning of a second nuclear attack. "We are in possession of the most destructive explosive ever devised by man. . . . We have just begun to use this weapon against your homeland. If you have any doubt, make inquiry as to what happened in Hiroshima."

Japanese leaders remained silent.

Tinian

A day later, August 9, the 509th delivered Fat Man, the nuclear weapon with the plutonium core, to Nagasaki. The mission was a nightmare of second-guessing and near misses, and almost failed before it began.

General LeMay assumed Tibbets would fly the second mission, too, but he refused, saying he'd taken the Hiroshima run just to prove it could be done. He wanted to give others on his team the chance to be a part of history. But he was still in charge of planning.

Tibbets originally assigned Captain Charles Sweeney to pilot *Great Artiste* as the strike plane. Sweeney was supposed to bomb Kokura, a center for Japanese munitions manufacture, on August 11. But after reviewing the meteorological reports, Tibbets changed the plans. Several days of bad

Fat Man.

weather were forecast, so Tibbets moved up the attack from August 11 to
August 9. But that didn't leave enough time to get the *Great Artiste* ready.
It was still carrying scientific equipment from the Hiroshima mission. So
Sweeney was assigned to fly *Bock's Car* as the strike plane. Pilot Frederick
Bock would fly the *Great Artiste* and its payload of monitors and measure-
ments.

And this time, the *New York Times* reporter, William Laurence, flew
along on the strike plane to write the story for the world.

"I watched the assembly of this man-made meteor during the past two
days," Laurence wrote, "and was among the small group of scientists and
Army and Navy representatives privileged to be present at the ritual of its
loading in the 'Superfort' last night, against a background of threatening
black skies torn open at intervals by great lightning flashes. It is a thing of
beauty to behold, this 'gadget.' In its design went millions of man-hours of
what is without doubt the most concentrated intellectual effort in history.
Never before had so much brain power been focused on a single problem."

Trouble started on the runway. Just before takeoff, Sweeney's crew discovered that a fuel pump in the plane's reserve tanks was broken. They
wouldn't be able to use 640 gallons of fuel in the airplane's tail. There was

no time to replace the pump. Sweeney stopped the engines right there, as regulations required, and ordered everyone off the plane.

Tibbets and General Thomas Farrell and other military leaders met them on the tarmac for a heated discussion. Sweeney said they wouldn't be able to unload the extra fuel, and that might spell trouble. But Tibbets wouldn't hear of it.

"You don't need the damn fuel," Tibbets snapped. "It's only in there to offset some of the bomb weight in the front." They hadn't used any reserve fuel on the Hiroshima mission. Stay or go. It was his call. "I say go," he said.

Sweeney hesitated, then decided. "The hell with it. I want to do this. We're going." The men on the runway looked at each other and then climbed back into the plane.

Sweeney left Tinian more than an hour behind schedule.

On the long flight to Japan, Laurence mused over the people on the ground below. "Does one not feel any pity for the poor devils about to die? Not when one thinks of Pearl Harbor or the death march on Bataan," he wrote.

Navy commander Frederick Ashworth was the weaponeer. Since Fat Man was a plutonium bomb, he didn't have to assemble it after takeoff, but he still had to crawl into the bomb bay to remove the green safety plugs and replace them with red arming plugs. He did the job, then settled in for a nap. He was startled awake by a terrified crew member. A red light on a console monitor was blinking. The bomb was alive—and ticking. Unlike Parsons, Ashworth wasn't familiar with the bomb's inner workings. He scrambled to find the blueprints while everyone on board braced for the worst. Ashworth and Lieutenant Philip Barnes, the assistant weaponeer, climbed down into the bomb bay, took off the casing, and scrutinized the switches: two had been reversed during the arming process. Barnes flipped each into its proper position. The red light stopped blinking.

But the problems didn't end there. *Bock's Car* was supposed to meet up with the two observation planes, but when it arrived at the rendezvous point, only one was there. Sweeney kept circling, waiting for the third plane, burning fuel. Meanwhile, Ashworth was getting antsy. He urged Sweeney to fly on to Kokura.

But the sky over that target was overcast, and Japanese gunners on the ground were sending up flak. *Bock's Car* had no guns to defend itself. Sweeney wanted to circle the city again, to see if bombardier Kermit Beahan could find an opening in the clouds. With the flak and low fuel, the mission should have been scrubbed, but Sweeney felt they'd come too far to turn back. He decided to fly to the alternate target: Nagasaki.

"Destiny chose Nagasaki as the ultimate target," Laurence noted.

A seaside city, Nagasaki was home to 253,000 people. When *Bock's Car* arrived over the city's aiming point, Beahan could not see through the overcast well enough for a visual bomb drop. Suddenly the clouds parted. "I have a hole!" he shouted. At 11:20 a.m., the crew donned their welders' lenses and released Fat Man.

It exploded 1,890 feet above the city. The plutonium core generated the force of 21,000 tons of TNT—one and a half times greater than Little Boy. The weapon missed the aiming point by nearly two miles, but the damage was catastrophic. Some 40,000 people perished instantly. Another 70,000 would die from radiation-related injuries and illness. The bomb destroyed a three-mile area and more than a third of the city's 50,000 buildings. In a stroke of poetic justice, the munitions plant that manufactured the torpedoes used at Pearl Harbor was obliterated.

"Despite the fact that it was broad daylight in our cabin, all of us became aware of a giant flash that broke through the dark barrier of our arc-welder's lenses and flooded our cabin with intense light," Laurence wrote. "We removed our glasses after the first flash, but the light still lingered on, a bluish-green light that illuminated the entire sky all around. A tremendous blast wave struck our ship and made it tremble from nose to tail. This was followed by four more blasts in rapid succession, each resounding like the boom of cannon fire hitting our plane from all directions.

A mushroom cloud rising over Nagasaki after an atomic bomb
was dropped on August 9, 1945.

"Observers in the tail of our ship saw a giant ball of fire rise as though from the bowels of the earth, belching forth enormous white smoke rings. Next they saw a giant pillar of purple fire, 10,000 feet high, shooting skyward with enormous speed.

"By the time our ship had made another turn in the direction of the atomic explosion the pillar of purple fire had reached the level of our altitude. Only about forty-five seconds had passed. Awestruck, we watched it shoot upward like a meteor coming from the earth instead of from outer space, becoming ever more alive as it climbed skyward through the white clouds. It was no longer smoke, or dust, or even a cloud of fire. It was a living thing, a new species of being, born right before our incredulous eyes."

Bock's Car headed for safety. They'd used too much fuel. The plane couldn't make it back to Tinian, so they set a heading for Okinawa. By "blind luck and fuel vapors," as Tibbets later said, Sweeney managed to land on the island. Even that was dicey. The plane touched down at 140 miles per hour, about 30 mph too fast. It bounced twenty-five feet in the air past rows of armed B-24 bombers until it skidded to a stop at the end of the runway.

When the planes finally returned to Tinian, there was no fanfare. The mission debrief felt like a court-martial as each disturbing detail was dissected. It could have been a disaster in several ways, several times. General LeMay turned to Sweeney, stared him straight in the eye, and said, "You fucked up, didn't you, Chuck?"

LeMay said he wouldn't launch an investigation, as it would serve no purpose. They were safely home. The bomb was dropped, although far off target. They all hoped the Japanese would finally come to their senses and surrender, so they would never have to fly another of these hellishly complicated missions.

Washington, D.C.

While Nagasaki burned, the world waited for the Japanese to respond. The night of August 9, Truman delivered a radio address to the American people, ostensibly about the Potsdam Conference. But he turned to the bombings of Hiroshima and Nagasaki, urging the Japanese people to leave industrial cities that were potential targets immediately.

"I realize the tragic significance of the atomic bomb," the president said. "We have used it against those who attacked us without warning at Pearl Harbor, against those who have starved and beaten and executed American prisoners of war, against those who have abandoned all pretense of obeying international laws of warfare."

Once again, Truman said, the choice was up to Tokyo. "We shall continue to use it until we completely destroy Japan's power to make war. Only a Japanese surrender will stop us." Truman had been told by the people running the Manhattan Project that they could have another atomic bomb ready within eight days.

Emperor Hirohito had little doubt the United States would continue dropping atomic bombs if his country did not surrender. His military leaders opposed capitulation fiercely, so the emperor began negotiating a surrender on his own.

In his first radio address ever, Hirohito spoke to his nation. His announcement marked the first time ordinary citizens in Japan had heard his voice. "The enemy now possesses a new and terrible weapon with the power to destroy many innocent lives and do incalculable damage. Should we continue to fight, not only would it result in ultimate collapse and obliteration of the Japanese nation, but also would lead to the total extinction of human civilization," he told his people.

The Japanese had long believed the emperor was the spiritual embodiment of their homeland, and an unconditional surrender would end his rule and erase their cultural identity. On August 10, the Japanese presented a surrender offer to the United States, with a provision the emperor would remain as the ceremonial head of state.

Truman wrote in his diary, "Our terms are 'unconditional.' They wanted to keep the Emperor [and] we told 'em we'd tell 'em how to keep him, but we'd make the terms."

The Allied powers accepted Japan's proposal, making it clear the United States would dictate the conflict's resolution. Hirohito would answer to the U.S. commander in Japan, Douglas MacArthur.

At 4:05 p.m. on Tuesday, August 14, Truman received Japan's formal surrender. Three hours later, he called reporters into the Oval Office. Standing behind his desk, he was flanked by Byrnes and Leahy on one side, and FDR's longtime secretary of state Cordell Hull on the other.

Sue Gentry of the Independence, Missouri, *Examiner* was also there. Earlier that afternoon, the reporter from back home had tea with the first lady. Truman told her to stick around because she "might get a story."

The president was wearing a double-breasted navy blue suit, a blue shirt, and a silver-and-blue-striped tie and handkerchief. With bright lights on for the newsreel cameras, he started reading from a statement. "I have received this afternoon a message from the Japanese Government," he announced. "I deem this reply a full acceptance of the Potsdam Declaration which specifies the unconditional surrender of Japan." General MacArthur would become the supreme Allied commander over Japan and would receive the enemy's formal surrender.

The news—and jubilation—spread quickly across the nation. After almost four years of bloody conflict, the Second World War was finally over. The cost to America was unthinkable: 405,799 dead, 670,864 wounded. Based on the population of the United States at the time, one of every 136 Americans was either killed or wounded.

The price was much steeper around the globe. Seventy-two million people were dead, including 47 million civilians.

And now it was over. Thousands began to gather in Lafayette Square, across from the White House. The crowd grew to some seventy-five thousand. People stood on top of cars. Horns blared. A conga line formed. And they began to chant, "We want Harry! We want Harry!"

Finally, around 7:00 p.m., the president and first lady came out on the North Lawn of the White House. He gave the V-for-victory sign, and the crowd erupted in cheers. Then, according to one person who was there, Truman started "pumping his arms like an orchestra conductor at tens of thousands of cheering Americans who suddenly had materialized in front of the mansion."

The Trumans went inside, and the president called his mother back in Missouri. "That was Harry," his mama told her guests after the call. "He always calls me after something that happens is over."

Truman also phoned Eleanor Roosevelt. He told her, "In this hour of triumph, I wished that it had been President Roosevelt, and not I, who had given the message to our people."

Now the president went out to see the crowd again, and this time he had a microphone. "This is a great day," he said, "the day we've been waiting for. This is the day for free governments in the world. This is the day that fascism and police government ceases in the world."

That night, half a million people filled the streets of Washington. And there were joyous celebrations in big cities and small towns across America, and around the world.

For Truman and his country, it was the end of a terrible struggle. But it was the start of a new era—and dealing with a world that had changed forever.

EPILOGUE

While the vast majority of Americans celebrated the end of war in the Pacific—and the new superweapon that forced the Japanese to surrender—there were some who sounded an immediate alarm.

The *New York Times* ran six triumphant front-page stories the day after the Hiroshima attack. But its editorial page struck a very different note. "Yesterday man unleashed the atom to destroy man, and another chapter in human history opened. . . . We clinched the victory in the Pacific, but sowed the whirlwind."

Hanson Baldwin, military editor of the *Times*, spelled out his concerns. "Americans have become a synonym for destruction. And now we have been the first to introduce a new weapon of unknowable effects which may bring us victory more quickly, but will sow the seeds of hate more widely than ever."

The warnings came from across the country and the political spectrum. The conservative *Chicago Tribune* wrote, "It is not impossible that whole cities and all the people in them will be obliterated in a fraction of a second by a single bomb."

Bruce Bliven, writing in the liberal *New Republic*: "There is no doubt that [the atomic bomb] is, in its potentialities, the most significant event in the history of mankind for many generations. At least it seems literally true that humanity as a whole must either learn to live at peace or face destruction on a grotesquely vast scale."

But it was the scientists, who had sounded the first alarm even before Hiroshima, who now continued the fight after the dropping of the bomb. In November 1945, almost a thousand people working at Los Alamos, Oak Ridge, Hanford, and Chicago formed the Federation of Atomic Scientists. With their "crew cuts, bow ties, and tab collars," they lobbied Congress, opposing military control of nuclear technology. In 1946, the Atomic Energy Commission was created, with civilians in charge.

That same year, Leo Szilard, who led the petition drive before the devastation of Hiroshima, joined with Albert Einstein and others to create the Emergency Committee of Atomic Scientists. Their mission was to encourage the peaceful use of atomic energy. But in the growing Cold War between the United States and Soviet Union, the group soon dissolved.

Szilard tried again in the 1960s, founding the Council for a Livable World. He warned of the dangers of an arms race. But the nuclear competition between East and West rolled on.

Einstein also regretted his role in the creation of the atomic bomb. He was not part of the S-1 project, after being denied a security clearance in 1940 because of his pacifist beliefs. But he later said of the part he played in bringing the issue to FDR's attention, "Had I known that the Germans would not succeed in producing an atomic bomb, I never would have lifted a finger."

In 1954, just five months before his death, Einstein declared, "I made one great mistake in my life, when I signed the letter to President Roosevelt recommending that atom bombs be made." His only excuse, he said, was his worry the Germans had their own program.

But all of this—all the petitions from scientists, all the cautionary editorials—didn't matter. The war was over. And after close to four years of bitter, bloody battle, the American people were thankful.

A Gallup poll just days after the destruction of Hiroshima and

Nagasaki found 85 percent of Americans approved of the decision to drop the atomic bomb. Following the attack on Pearl Harbor, and then years of reported atrocities committed by the Japanese military, there was little sympathy for the enemy.

Dr. George Gallup wrote in September 1945, "Even though such bombs with their destructive power contain a threat to the security of mankind, in the public's mind the atomic bomb hastened the end of the war and pointed the way to useful development of atomic energy in the future."

There was another element in the shaping of American opinion. The government conducted a skillful public relations campaign. Part of it was what they shared. In a blizzard of press releases, "the public received selected background information on the Trinity test, atomic processes, production plants, communities, significant personalities, and the prospects of harnessing nuclear energy. The well-orchestrated program of public releases revealed the drama of the atomic story in surprisingly detailed episodes."

But Americans learned as little as possible about the devastating effect of the atomic explosions on the people of Hiroshima and Nagasaki. This was no accident. General MacArthur, supreme commander of occupying forces in Japan, enforced a strict blackout on all information about the devastation from the bombings.

A thirty-two-man Japanese film crew shot documentary footage of the utter destruction of Hiroshima and Nagasaki. It was confiscated by U.S. authorities. Some of the first images Americans saw were not photographs, but drawings. A Japanese couple, Toshi and Iri Maruki, went to Hiroshima shortly after the bombing to look for their relatives. They published their drawings in a book called *Pika-don*—"Flash-bang"—in 1950.

But there were breaches in the cloak of silence. Australian reporter Wilfred Burchett, the first foreign journalist to visit Hiroshima, sent a dispatch by Morse code to London to avoid censorship. The *Daily Express* published his article on September 5, 1945, and it was distributed around the world.

"Hiroshima," he wrote, "does not look like a bombed city. It looks as if a monster steamroller had passed over it and squashed it out of existence. I write these facts as dispassionately as I can in the hope that they will act as a warning to the world. In this first testing ground of the atomic bomb I have seen the most terrible and frightening desolation in four years of war. It makes a blitzed Pacific island seem like an Eden. The damage is far greater than photographs can show."

But most Americans did not get a true understanding of what their government had done until a full year after the bombings. William Shawn, the legendary editor of the *New Yorker*, felt there was a vital story that had not yet been told. He commissioned war correspondent John Hersey to travel through China and spend a month in Hiroshima interviewing survivors, before returning to the United States to write his report. That way, he would avoid MacArthur's censors.

It is impossible to overstate the impact of Hersey's work. He reported the firsthand accounts of six survivors of the explosion and the terrible aftereffects of the bomb. He introduced Americans to a new term—*hibakusha*—literally "explosion-affected persons." For the first time, Americans learned what really happened in Hiroshima.

Shawn knew what he had. He persuaded the publisher to print the article in its 31,000-word entirety in a single issue on August 31, 1946, without the *New Yorker*'s trademark cartoons. The full story was read over the radio. Advance copies were sent to newspapers across the country. Many wrote editorials urging people to read the magazine. All 300,000 copies sold out immediately. Later that year, three million copies of Hersey's story were sold in book form.

Hersey told the story of six *hibakusha*—two women, two doctors, a Methodist clergyman, and a German Jesuit priest. It was a trip into Dante's *Inferno*—horrifying accounts of instant death, unimaginable suffering, radiation poisoning. Hersey wrote of twenty men "in exactly the same nightmarish state: their faces were wholly burned, their eye sockets were hollow, the fluid of their melted eyes had run down their cheeks." For anyone who read it, there was no escaping the images, or the responsibility. "They were the objects of the first great experiment in the use of atomic power."

One of Hersey's survivors made his own statement. In the early 1950s, the minister, Kiyoshi Tanimoto, started touring America, in one trip visiting 256 cities. He raised money to create a World Peace Center in Hiroshima that would serve as a laboratory for peace initiatives.

But in an update to his book, John Hersey told of a surreal experience Tanimoto had on another trip to America. On May 11, 1955, he was brought into a television studio for what he was told would be a local interview to help him raise funds for the antinuclear movement.

Instead, it turned out to be an episode of *This Is Your Life*, a popular live national show on which the host, Ralph Edwards, surprised guests with key figures from their past. A missionary who taught Tanimoto about Christ showed up. Also, a friend from divinity school. And then, the shocker.

In walked a stocky man Edwards introduced as Captain Robert Lewis, copilot of the *Enola Gay* mission that destroyed Hiroshima. Lewis talked about that terrible day. "Tanimoto sat there with a face of wood," Hersey wrote.

Lewis presented Tanimoto with a check on behalf of the crew of the *Enola Gay*.

But if all of this was unsettling, even deeply disturbing, most Americans still supported the decision to drop the bomb. In Gallup polling, public approval never fell below 53 percent. After all, the atomic bomb ended the war, likely a year before an invasion would have. And it spared the lives of hundreds of thousands of American soldiers.

As the decades passed, the debate over the bomb tracked the changing currents of American politics. In 1958, an article in the *National Review* said the real target of the bomb was not Japan. Harry Elmer Barnes wrote that enemy was already defeated. "The tens of thousands of Japanese who were roasted at Hiroshima and Nagasaki were sacrificed not to end the war or save American and Japanese lives, but to strengthen American diplomacy vis a vis Russia."

In the 1960s and '70s, "New Left" historians like Gar Alperovitz made a similar point: the bomb was an early warning to the Soviets at the start of the Cold War. And Truman was ready to play that card. During the Berlin Blockade of 1948–49, he moved B-29 bombers like the *Enola Gay* within striking distance of Germany's capital. During the Korean War, Truman deployed B-29s to that region.

The debate echoed through the decades, along with a terrifying arms race. In 1949, Russia tested a nuclear device. A new national security doctrine took hold—Mutual Assured Destruction, or MAD. Neither the United States nor the Soviet Union would launch a nuclear strike to wipe out the enemy, because they could not prevent a retaliatory strike that would wipe them out.

The United States and Russia negotiated arms control treaties, starting with the Limited Test Ban in 1963. But all they did was limit the number of missiles and multiple warheads, not eliminate them.

And with nuclear technology now available, it spread to some of the most dangerous hot spots on earth. India and Pakistan have fought for decades over their border, each armed with a nuclear arsenal. Israel is thought to have the only nuclear weapons in the Middle East. But Iran gets ever closer to the breakout capacity to develop its own. And North Korea continues to build its capability, as well as the long-range ballistic missiles required to hit the United States.

Meanwhile, the argument over Hiroshima continues. In 1995, the Smithsonian's National Air and Space Museum in Washington planned an exhibit to mark the fiftieth anniversary. The concept was to encourage visitors to reconsider the decision to drop the bomb, with full knowledge of what happened on the ground and the continuing arms race.

But veterans groups and politicians protested the exhibit was too sympathetic to the Japanese, an insult to the U.S. soldiers who died in the Pacific. One of the crew members on the *Enola Gay*, Dutch Van Kirk, complained about scripts for the exhibit. "One line said something to the effect that for the Japanese, the bombing was primarily a campaign of vengeance and alleged American racism. Another stated that we all went crazy."

Van Kirk noted, "You know, we all did not go crazy."

In the end, the project was scaled back dramatically, and featured the *Enola Gay*'s fuselage. Even the plane was drawn into the debate. For years, it was stored at Andrews Air Force Base outside Washington, its wings gone to rust, and vandalized by souvenir hunters. In 2003, the plane was fully restored, wings and all, and is now part of the collection at the Smithsonian's Udvar-Hazy Center, near Dulles Airport in northern Virginia.

Some historians argue Japan would have surrendered in 1945—without the United States either dropping the bomb or invading the homeland. Russia declared war on Japan on August 8, sending one million Soviet troops into Japanese-occupied Manchuria. There is also the question of whether Truman could have made it clearer to leaders in Tokyo that he would accept a role for the emperor as part of "unconditional surrender." But all this has the enormous benefit of hindsight, in many cases decades after decisions were made.

Remember Admiral Leahy, Truman's chief of staff, who repeatedly said the bomb would never work? In his memoir after the war, he wrote, "The Japanese were already defeated and ready to surrender. . . . My own feeling was that in being the first to use it, we had adopted an ethical standard common to the barbarians of the Dark Ages." There is no record of Leahy ever sharing that sentiment with Truman before Hiroshima.

If public approval of the decision to drop the bomb never returned to the 85 percent from the days after the attack, it stayed steady and strong. In 2005, on the sixtieth anniversary of Hiroshima, 57 percent supported using the bomb, while 38 percent disapproved. There was a sharp generational divide. Seven in ten Americans over age sixty-five said use of atomic weapons was justified. Less than half of those under thirty agreed.

Which takes us back to the man who made the decision. Through the years and changes in political debate, Harry Truman never wavered. Two months after Hiroshima, on October 25, 1945, the president met Robert

Oppenheimer for the first time. Truman wanted his support for legislation that would give the government control over atomic energy. But the man most responsible for developing the bomb now had terrible second thoughts.

"Mr. President," Oppenheimer said, "I feel I have blood on my hands." An angry Truman recounted his response: "I told him the blood was on my hands—to let me worry about it." The president later told his final Secretary of State Dean Acheson, "I don't want to see that son of a bitch in this office ever again."

In 1948, Truman finally met Paul Tibbets, the man at the controls when the bomb was dropped. "What do you think?" the president asked.

Tibbets replied, "Mr. President, I did what I was told."

Truman slapped his hand on the desk. "You're damn right you did. And I'm the guy who sent you."

For the rest of his life, Truman was asked about his decision. And he always defended it. In a 1948 letter to his sister Mary, he wrote, "It was a terrible decision. But I made it to save 250,000 boys from the United States, and I'd make it again under similar circumstances. It stopped the Jap War."

In the early 1960s, a television producer came up with the idea for Truman to travel to Hiroshima for a town hall with survivors of the bomb. "I'll go to Japan if that's what you want," he said. "But I won't kiss their ass." The project never came off.

In a 1965 lecture, the former president talked again about saving American lives. "I couldn't worry about what history would say about my personal morality. I made the only decision I ever knew how to make. I did what I thought was right."

But leave the final word to an interview Truman did with famed *New York Times* obituary writer Alden Whitman in 1966, for an article that appeared after his death in December 1972. "I did not like the weapon, but I had no qualms, if in the long run millions of lives could be saved."

In the end, for all the questions about the morality of dropping the atomic bomb, it is unrealistic to think Harry Truman would make any other choice. He came to the presidency without any warning about a project FDR approved three years before. More than 100,000 people were recruited, and $2 billion was spent. And just three months later, the atomic bomb was tested successfully.

Truman's top generals estimated a conventional war against Japan would take a fearsome toll: at least 250,000 Americans killed and 500,000 wounded. The fighting would continue for more than another year. And now Truman had a way to save those lives and end the conflict.

For those who still question his decision, remember that Truman consulted widely, listening to advisers like Eisenhower, who argued against using the bomb. He struggled with the decision through sleepless nights and fierce headaches in the heat of the German summer. And in his apocalyptic writings about "the fire destruction prophesied in the Euphrates Valley Era," it is clear that he fully understood the stakes.

In just 116 days, a new, untested leader made one of history's most consequential decisions. He ushered in the nuclear age, creating a world where the future of mankind now rests on a hair trigger.

The stockpile of nuclear bombs and warheads on our planet—each one vastly more powerful than Little Boy and Fat Man—is now almost 50,000—equivalent to several million Hiroshima explosions. But seventy-five years later, only one nation has ever used the weapon in war. The United States.

POSTSCRIPT

Life went on, and America boomed. Soldiers, sailors, Marines, and airmen returned home, started families, built homes, businesses, and communities. They went to college on the GI Bill, or returned to the jobs they held before the war. Women who'd labored on farms and in factories gave up their jobs so men could step in and run the country again. Factories retooled to once again manufacture cars, appliances, and consumer goods. "Bedroom communities" sprang up on the outskirts of cities. An Interstate Highway System was built to connect all those new communities that stretched from coast to coast.

But for many, the war never faded.

WOMEN AND CHILDREN

Ruth Sisson

The day she heard the Japanese surrendered, Ruth Sisson finally allowed herself to celebrate. Lawrence, her sweet man, landed in New York and phoned her from there, breathless. He couldn't wait to get home, he said. He'd be discharged soon, he didn't know when, and while he was in the Big Apple he had "something important to buy." He didn't say what.

He showed up on her doorstep a week later, still in uniform, smiling.

Stunned, Ruth threw her arms around him. They embraced and kissed while family members gathered on the porch to join in the joy. He finally broke free.

"Put out your hand," he said, grinning.

She shrugged and said, "Okay."

He pulled a small box from his pocket, opened it, and slipped a diamond ring on her finger, the "important thing" he'd bought in New York.

"I've waited a long time for this," he said.

The next few days were a whirlwind. She showed her ring to everyone, gave her notice at the plant, and went along on visits to Lawrence's sisters. They brought flowers to his mother's grave. When the time came to set a wedding date, Lawrence said he had an important, difficult errand to fulfill beforehand.

During the war, he'd befriended a young man from Lake City, Tennessee, not too far from his hometown. In France, in the thick of battle, Lawrence found his friend bleeding on the ground. A round had pierced his stomach. Lawrence could see the kid was beyond saving, but he knelt alongside and eased his pain with morphine and reassurance. The boy wasn't fooled. He pulled Lawrence close, pulled a ring off his finger, and removed a billfold from his pants pocket.

"Please make sure my parents get these. Let them know how I died," he whispered. Lawrence nodded his head and took the items. He carried the ring and billfold with him for the rest of the war. Now it was time for Lawrence to keep his promise.

"Will you go with me?" he asked Ruth.

She didn't hesitate. "Yes, of course." A few days later, as the leaves began changing colors in the mountains, they drove to Lake City. "He didn't talk about anything the whole ride," Ruth recalled. "He dreaded it."

Lawrence didn't know the name of the boy's parents, but he knew they'd attended the First Baptist Church. They found the church. The pastor took them to the boy's house, where Lawrence sat in their living room and told the parents what he knew of their son's final days. "He

Ruth Sisson and her fiancé, Lawrence Huddleston, after the war.

was a brave soldier," Lawrence said, handing over the wallet and ring. Lawrence, Ruth, and the pastor sobbed along with the stricken mother and father.

On the drive home, Lawrence opened up a little more about what he'd seen in the war and the work he'd done, but he didn't want to scare Ruth with gruesome details.

On November 9, 1945, the couple drove to Rossville, Georgia, and were married at the county courthouse. As they walked down the courthouse steps, the radio in a nearby car played their song: "Oh, What a Beautiful Morning."

After leaving the defense plant, Ruth took night classes at the University of Tennessee and became a first-grade teacher. She later got a master's degree in education and worked as a guidance counselor.

Lawrence never got over the war. He woke up in the night screaming, tortured by nightmares. Like many men of his generation, he kept everything inside. Today, we call these symptoms "post-traumatic stress disorder," or PTSD. The condition afflicted thousands of World War II veterans, but it was decades away from being identified or treated. The trauma they experienced had no acceptable outlet, so servicemen like Lawrence suffered silently.

He developed ulcers and died in 1971. Ruth never remarried. At the end of February 2020, at age ninety-four, she still enjoys telling her six grandchildren stories of growing up in the mountains and working at the secret defense plant that helped win the war. "I've lived a good life. I've been happy," she recalled. But every now and then, when she thinks back, she still feels guilt about the role she played in building the bomb.

Hideko Tamura

Hideko Tamura prayed the day the bomb destroyed her home. On the edge of the Ota River, she found adults and children gathered with their hands clasped in prayer while an older man, the head of the family, prayed aloud for the safety of others left behind. Hideko bowed her head, too, and prayed for her mother and her father, who was stationed by the harbor. "Please, God, please keep them safe," she whispered.

The next few hours blurred as Hideko wandered: She rode in a truck out to the countryside. She knocked on doors, ate dried soybeans that strangers handed out to victims. Hideko and hundreds of others wandered, stunned and aimless.

A man on a bicycle finally took the injured girl home to his family, who fed and clothed her while he combed Hiroshima for Hideko's relatives. Hours later, she learned her father, grandmother, and uncle Hisao survived, but her mother was still missing.

Hiroshima after the bomb.

Hideko's father took the girl to a small village where family members had a home to share. Every day, Jiro, Hideko, and others would go back to Hiroshima to look for Kimiko. They went to rescue stations, schools, police yards, and temples to examine the dead and dying. The once-bustling city was gone. Hiroshima was now filled with "horrifying places drenched in the smell of rotting flesh and death," she recalled. It was unbearable. Singed, bloated bodies lay in the streets, their faces unrecognizable.

People near the epicenter of the blast were vaporized; Hideko could see their shadows imprinted on the walls and pavement. Her friend Miyoshi was also dead. To cope, she again hummed the songs her mother sang to her, her favorite lullabies and melodies.

Finally, in September, they found a neighbor who had been with Kimiko the moment the bomb exploded. They'd been taking a break by an abandoned concrete building. The flash of light almost blinded them. Kimiko pulled her straw hat down over her ears and ran inside the building, just as the structure collapsed, trapping her and several others inside.

The woman took Jiro to the building. He found several burned bodies in the rubble, one with his old army canteen alongside—the one he had given his wife. Distraught, Jiro knelt and collected Kimiko's ashes in his handkerchief.

Hideko begged her father to take her to the building, but he refused. Time passed, but it was difficult for Hideko to deal with the guilt of pushing her mother to bring her back from the countryside to Hiroshima on August 5. If she hadn't, they would have been in that faraway village when the bomb was dropped. Her mother and her friend Miyoshi would still be alive.

Estimates for the number of people killed and injured in the bombing have varied widely over the years. A summary report by the U.S. Strategic Bombing Survey issued on July 1, 1946, estimated 60,000 to 70,000 people were killed and 50,000 injured. But the final death toll—including the thousands who died from radiation sickness in the weeks and months to come—was estimated at 135,000, including some 20,000 military personnel.

After the war, Hideko's father built a house along the Ota River near Hiroshima. Hideko found solace in "the sunsets that would shine over the moving water of the river flowing into the bay."

Survivors were not celebrated as heroes, she said. "We tended to be very discreet about being survivors. You were very undesirable. You tired easily, so you were an employment risk. You gave birth to deformed children, so you were a marriage risk. In a country where arranged marriage was predominant, anybody hearing about you being a survivor, well, there was no good to come of it."

At age seventeen, Hideko worked up the courage to end her own life.

She stood on the platform at the train station, waiting to leap in front of the incoming locomotive, but it shrieked to a stop just before it reached her. An elderly man had thrown himself in front of the same train several yards ahead.

A teacher at her Methodist missionary school convinced Hideko to keep living, to join the new world that was born August 6, 1945, even as the old one died.

Hideko touching the Memorial Dome one last time
before leaving Hiroshima in August 1952.

Hideko traveled to the United States and earned a degree in sociology from Ohio's College of Wooster in 1953. She married an American, had healthy children, and continued her education at the University of Chicago—the same place where Manhattan Project scientists in 1942 produced the first controlled nuclear chain reaction. She became a psychotherapist and a social worker in the radiation oncology department at the University of Chicago Hospitals.

Dr. Hideko Tamura Snider says she knows she can't change the past. She came to the United States because of the educational opportunities at the time. And although the memories are still raw, she tries not to be bitter about what happened. That's why she's become a peace activist. She never wants anyone to experience her pain.

On August 6, 2007—exactly sixty-two years after the bomb destroyed Hiroshima—Hideko's granddaughter was born. "It was the most amazing birth of hope," she said. "It changed the tone and feeling of my grief. I could focus on the birth of a new life."

THE SCIENTISTS AND THE GENERALS

J. Robert Oppenheimer

Oppenheimer and many other scientists believed that in the wake of Hiroshima and Nagasaki, nuclear weapons and technology must be tightly controlled by the international scientific community.

He suddenly found himself the most famous scientist in the world. As his celebrity grew, so did his depression. Reports about the extent of human suffering in Japan were difficult for Oppenheimer to hear. He worried politicians and generals would reach for nuclear bombs too readily when future conflicts arose.

So Oppenheimer was finished with bomb building. The government planned to continue its nuclear research and development program at Los Alamos, but Oppie wanted no part of it. In October 1945, he resigned as the program's scientific director. At a special ceremony, he expressed his feelings about nuclear weapons. "If atomic bombs are to be added as new weapons to arsenals of a warring world, or to arsenals of nations preparing for war, then the time will come when mankind will curse the names of Los Alamos and Hiroshima."

After the war, Oppenheimer returned to teaching, taking a position at Princeton's Institute for Advanced Study, an independent postdoctoral research center for theoretical research and an academic home for Albert Einstein and other leading scientists. And he decided to promote the safe use of atomic energy. In 1947, he was unanimously elected chairman of the general advisory committee of the newly formed Atomic Energy Commission—a civilian agency overseeing U.S. atomic affairs.

But when the Soviet Union developed nuclear weapons, America was plunged into a new era of fear and suspicion. And Oppenheimer was dragged into the mire. He was no longer hailed as the father of the atomic bomb. Instead, he was labeled a security risk.

For years, Americans heard about "the Red Menace," the threat that communists would overrun America and the world. Any security Americans felt because the United States was the only nation with a nuclear arsenal was blown away on August 29, 1949, when the Soviets detonated their first atomic weapon. The Soviet nuclear bomb created tremendous pressure for the United States to develop an even larger fusion weapon, a "hydrogen bomb." Oppenheimer's opposition to more advanced nuclear weapons was tantamount to treason in some quarters. The Atomic Energy Commission in 1954 held a public hearing on Oppenheimer's security clearance. His early communist sympathies were trotted out. He denied any ties to the Communist Party, but said he had known communists in the late 1930s and early 1940s. "I did not regard them as dangerous and some of their declared objectives seemed to me desirable," he said.

The AEC found that although Oppenheimer was loyal, he was a security risk in part because his association with known communists "extended far beyond the tolerable limits of prudence and self-restraint."

Oppenheimer was denied access to atomic secrets. One of the most famous men in the world, the man who made science cool, "the living symbol of the new atomic age," was exiled from his field of expertise, replaced by scientists like Edward Teller, "the father of the hydrogen bomb."

But a strange thing happened. Many Americans came to see Oppenheimer as a scientist-martyr, a man who paid too dearly for his integrity. He rarely talked in public about Hiroshima, but when he did, he expressed regret. In June 1956, he called the bombing a "tragic mistake."

In 1963, nine years after the AEC stripped away Oppenheimer's security clearance, it awarded him its highest honor: the $50,000 Enrico Fermi Award for "his outstanding contributions to theoretical physics and scientific and administrative leadership." President Lyndon Johnson presented the award.

In early 1966, doctors discovered Oppenheimer had throat cancer; he died the following year. By then, his public image had been restored. On the U.S. Senate floor, J. William Fulbright, a Democrat from Arkansas, eulogized Oppenheimer. "Let us remember not only what his special genius did for us. Let us also remember what we did to him."

Donald and Lilli Hornig

For many scientists and academics, Japan's surrender signaled the end of their time at Los Alamos. Many had started already planning their next steps when the bomb fell on Hiroshima.

Donald Hornig, the physicist who spent that stormy night with the bomb before the New Mexico test, became an assistant professor at Brown University, was later chairman of Princeton's chemistry department, and in 1964 became President Lyndon Johnson's science adviser. Six years later, he was named president of Brown University.

His wife, Lilli, completed her PhD in chemistry at Brown and later became a fierce advocate for women in higher education, founding Higher

Education Resource Services, a nonprofit dedicated to the cause. They both signed Leo Szilard's petition, but said later they had no regrets about the roles they played in the Manhattan Project. They had mixed feelings about using nuclear power as a weapon of war.

"I think we were all very elated that it worked," Lilli said late in her life. "But we all carry around some guilt. A lot of people were killed. It's all difficult in a way. You do feel guilt for all those lives, but of course, the real trouble is war. It isn't the weapons you use."

For many scientists, that was the conundrum. Some were so consumed during the Manhattan Project with the challenge of turning theory into a working bomb that they didn't consider the moral or physical consequences. Afterward many were haunted by the weapon's destructive power. Some became depressed about the role they played in developing the atomic bomb.

General Leslie Groves

After the war ended, Groves was promoted to lieutenant general. He retired in 1948 and took a job with the Sperry Rand Corporation, a defense contractor. Over the years, Groves remained one of Oppenheimer's biggest supporters. And he shared many of Oppenheimer's concerns about nuclear weapons.

"When it finally came, V-J Day was a sober and thoughtful occasion for most of us who had labored so hard and so long to help bring it about," Groves wrote. "We had solved the immediate problem of ending the war, but in so doing we had raised up many unknowns." He later said, "This weapon must be kept under the control of the United States until all of the nations of the world are as anxious for peace as we are."

Groves died in 1970, a month short of his seventy-fourth birthday. In his obituary, Groves was praised as the "hard-driving Army engineer who headed the Manhattan Project." As one columnist put it, "Groves had the guts the job needed."

THE JOURNALIST

For William Laurence, the bomb was the story of a lifetime. But like many others involved in the Manhattan Project, his work would be sharply criticized by later generations.

The *Times* published Laurence's exclusive stories, ten in all, in late 1945. The following year, he was awarded the Pulitzer Prize for reporting for his eyewitness account of the bombing of Nagasaki and subsequent articles on the development, production, and significance of the atomic bomb.

The Pulitzer was only the start. People began to call him "Atomic Bill." Credited with coining the phrase "atomic age," Laurence continued as a science reporter for the *Times*. In 1946, his book *Dawn Over Zero: The Story of the Atomic Bomb* was published.

Laurence was a member of the *Times* staff for thirty-four years as a reporter and editor. He retired in 1964, and died in 1977 at the age of eighty-nine. His *Times* obituary called Laurence one of the country's first full-time science reporters, and his biggest exclusive was the dawn of the nuclear age. He wrote with a "style that often relied on vivid but simple imagery" that a "man could understand."

But in 2004, twenty-seven years after he died, a group of journalists called for the Pulitzer Board to strip Laurence of his prize. They argued the stories were produced while Laurence "was on the payroll of War Department" and that after the atomic bombings, he wrote a front-page story in the *Times* disputing the notion that "radiation sickness was killing people." They added, "His faithful parroting of the government line was crucial in launching a half-century of silence about the deadly lingering effects of the bomb."

The *New York Times* didn't give back his Pulitzer.

THE FLIGHT CREW

The crew of the *Enola Gay* were celebrated as heroes when they returned to Tinian and later when they came back to the United States. Parades, news stories, and accolades came first, and were followed by magazine articles, books and movies about the mission.

A few years after the war, NBC produced a radio show called *The Story of the Atomic Bomb: The Quick and the Dead.* Celebrities like Bob Hope and military leaders like General Dwight Eisenhower read from a script about key moments in the bomb's history. Robert Lewis read from his flight log, including the line "There will be a short intermission now while we bomb our target."

Some crew members stayed in the military while others returned to civilian life. Robert Shumard became a sales manager for a plumbing and heating supply company in Detroit. George "Bob" Caron, the tail gunner with the Brooklyn Dodgers cap, became a design engineer for Sundstrand Corporation in Denver.

As time passed, the onetime heroes were sometimes swept up in questions about the morality of the bomb. The debate intensified as nuclear weapons proliferated.

Robert A. Lewis

Over the years, Captain Robert A. Lewis explained repeatedly what he meant when he wrote in his log, "My God, what have we done?" In a 1960 interview for a military project honoring the fifteenth anniversary of Hiroshima, Lewis said he didn't regret the mission, and that his log entry had been misinterpreted. "What has mankind done in designing and developing a bomb like this to destroy mankind?" he explained.

If he could volunteer again for the mission, would he go? Lewis didn't flinch. "There would be no hesitancy on my part to defend my country.

None whatsoever. If it meant the dropping of an atomic bomb, or of a hydrogen bomb, this would be something that I would readily do."

Lewis took a job as an airline pilot, then became plant manager for the New Jersey candy company where he worked before the war. He married, had five children, and spent his lifetime reflecting on the mission.

He met with Hiroshima survivors and became friends with one, Reverend Hubert Schiffler. On the morning the bomb fell, Schiffler was eight blocks away from ground zero. Later in life, Lewis became a stone sculptor. One of his works was titled *God's Wind at Hiroshima*.

In 1971, Lewis's manuscript log from the Hiroshima mission was sold to David Kirschenbaum, a dealer in rare books and manuscripts, for $37,000. The manuscript was later resold to entrepreneur Malcolm Forbes. Lewis made six handwritten copies of the log for his family. In 2015, one of them sold for $50,000.

Years later, Lewis still felt bitter about how Tibbets treated him. In letters and conversations with 509th historian Joseph Papalia, Lewis said books and movies hadn't accurately portrayed the mission. He was particularly angry about an NBC made-for-TV movie that lionized the top brass. "The enlisted men have always gotten the dirty end of the stick," Lewis said in a 1981 letter. "What an interesting story if it could be put together, a story just about the enlisted men, their training, experience and feelings."

Still, he was philosophical about it all.

"Five hundred years from now, if there is still an earth, August 6, 1945, will be remembered as the day the world witnessed the birth of a new and terrible weapon, not if a Jones or Smith was the pilot or bombardier. Pope John Paul put it best when he visited Hiroshima the other day and said, 'To remember Hiroshima is to commit oneself to peace or to remember Hiroshima is to abhor war.'"

Lewis died in 1983. He was sixty-five years old. He was haunted to the end by the images of the burning city. As he wrote in his log: "If I live a hundred years, I'll never quite get these few minutes out of my mind."

Thomas Ferebee

Ferebee stayed in the military after World War II. He spent most of his career in the Strategic Air Command, serving through the Korea, Cold War, and Vietnam eras. He retired in 1970 as a colonel.

Ferebee married and had four sons. He never expressed regret for his role in the bombing, saying "it was a job that had to be done."

In late 1999, Ferebee told his friends he had pancreatic cancer, and only six months to live. Ferebee asked his friends to "say something nice at my funeral."

"If I can think of anything," Van Kirk quipped.

Ferebee died in March 2000. He was eighty-one years old. Van Kirk and Tibbets attended the funeral in a chapel in rural Mocksville, North Carolina. He found peace as he grew older—tending roses in his garden, bass fishing with his boys, and playing catch with his grandchildren. His wife, Mary Ann, said Ferebee had a life beyond the atomic bomb. "Tom was a kind, caring and generous man," she recalled.

Hanging above the living room fireplace in his home was a picture of a B-29 soaring across the sky. The print was signed by Tibbets, Van Kirk, and two other crew members.

At the funeral, Van Kirk said Ferebee was a magician with the bomb sight, but he was also really good at poker. "I will bet money there is a big poker game going on in heaven" with other friends who had passed away. "All I can do is hope that they save a place for me if I go there, too."

Theodore "Dutch" Van Kirk

The last surviving *Enola Gay* crew member, Van Kirk, died in 2014. He was ninety-three years old. After the war, Van Kirk returned to his wife and son in Northumberland, Pennsylvania. He got his master's degree in chemical engineering at Bucknell University, then spent a long career working for DuPont.

Like his colleagues, Van Kirk defended using atomic bombs. "We were fighting an enemy that had a reputation for never surrendering, never accepting defeat," he said. "It's really hard to talk about morality and war in the same sentence."

Jacob Beser

Jacob Beser had the distinction of being the only person to fly on both atomic bomb missions. He stayed in the military until 1946, then began a long career working on defense projects for Westinghouse. He returned to Baltimore, got married, and had four boys.

Beser died in June 1992. He left behind a speech he wrote for presentation at a science conference. In it, Beser was pragmatic about why the United States used the bomb.

"In America," he wrote, "nothing is more natural in the time of war then for our leaders, whom we elected, to attempt to ensure victory with a minimum loss of life. For our armed forces, the extravagant use of firepower was the approach to achieve the desired effect and had been employed from day one. Fire-bombing raids on the Empire are good examples. Using the atomic bombs against Japan was simply the ultimate step in this approach."

Beser said he believed dropping the bombs ended the war in the Pacific.

"I have often been asked if I had any remorse for what we did in 1945. I assure you that I have no remorse whatsoever and I will never apologize for what we did to end World War II. Humane warfare is an oxymoron. War by definition is barbaric. To try and distinguish between an acceptable method of killing and an unacceptable method is ludicrous."

With fifty thousand atomic weapons in the world, a nuclear war would mean the end of mankind, he said.

Maybe that is what haunted everyone associated with the Manhattan Project. They unlocked the secrets of the atom, and brought civilization to the brink of destruction.

Toward the end of his life, Beser said, "The solution to the problem is not being sorry for what has already happened, but individually and collectively dedicating ourselves to the eradication of the causes of wars and of war itself."

And he warned, "Deterrence, up until now, has worked. It cannot continue forever."

Paul W. Tibbets

Tibbets's service didn't end with the Hiroshima mission. He remained in the Air Force, and in 1959 was promoted to brigadier general. He served as commander of two Strategic Air Command bomber wings before retiring from the military in 1966. He settled in Columbus, Ohio, and eventually became the chairman of the board of Executive Jet Aviation. He remained one of the most famous pilots in history, and was enshrined in the National Aviation Hall of Fame. He died in 2007 at age ninety-two.

Like his crew, Tibbets never wavered in defense of his mission. In a little-known interview on the fifteenth anniversary of Hiroshima, Tibbets, who had just been promoted to general, talked about the mission.

"I believe this weapon prevented the United States and allied forces from invading Japan," he recalled. "And because of the prevention of such an invasion, I'm sure that we've saved many, many lives. I couldn't hazard a guess to how many, but I think it brought a quick end to the war. . . . The lives lost as a result of the explosions were war casualties and these are things that you have to expect in war."

When pressed about how he felt about the morality of weapons of mass destruction, Tibbets tried to explain his position.

"If wars are going to be fought, I believe the object is to win the war. You're going to win it with all resources at your disposal. And if you're fortunate enough to possess powerful weapons or weapons more powerful than those of your enemies, there's only one thing to do and that's to use them," he said.

When he was asked if he had any regrets, he was blunt. "I've been asked that question before, and I can assure you I have absolutely no feeling of guilt. . . . I have no remorse whatsoever. It was an assignment, a military assignment in time of war," he said.

Over the years, Tibbets kept in close contact with Van Kirk and Ferebee. For Tibbets, their year together in Europe, in 1942, was the best time of his life. Every mission was an encounter with death as the *Red Gremlin* took antiaircraft fire and rained bombs on German cities. They lived for the moment, carousing at London's nightspots, drinking, playing cards, gambling, staying up all night and watching the sun rise. They were in their twenties, fighting for America, democracy, freedom.

Tibbets's friendship with Van Kirk and Ferebee grew stronger with time. In a 1989 inscription in a book to Van Kirk, Tibbets wrote: "This inscription will be inadequate in expressing my feelings toward you (I told Tom the same) because you as well as Tom have always been special as far as I am concerned. During the war I considered us as a three-legged stool; sometimes against big odds. Post war you took a different path, but I did and I know Tom felt that you were 'not that far away.' Since our retirements, I think we may be even closer and that's the way it will remain."

When Tibbets died, he asked for no funeral or headstone. He feared opponents of the bombing might use it as a place of protest. Instead, his body was cremated and his ashes were scattered over the English Channel, where he had flown so many missions during the war.

THE PRESIDENT

Harry S Truman

In the weeks following the end of World War II, the president's job approval rating was at 87 percent. But as he faced a series of postwar challenges, his numbers began to drop.

Although the Soviet Union was a powerful ally during the conflict, relations deteriorated quickly when it became clear the Soviets intended to hold on to their control of Eastern Europe. This was the beginning of the Cold War. But Truman was also beset with troubles at home as the American economy shifted from war to peace.

He had to deal with the often-clashing interests of consumers, labor, and business. There was inflation and union unrest. The political landscape for Truman's election looked bleak. In 1946, the Republicans gained control of both houses of Congress. Pundits predicted Truman would lose the 1948 presidential election to Republican New York governor Thomas Dewey.

But Truman confounded the conventional wisdom. He campaigned relentlessly and effectively, often making speeches from the back of trains as he barnstormed across America. At almost every juncture he was greeted by enthusiastic crowds shouting: "Give 'em hell, Harry!" In one of the biggest comeback victories in American political history, Truman defeated Dewey in November 1948.

While Truman had notable achievements—he issued executive orders banning racial discrimination in the military and the government—he continued to face problems at home and overseas. He introduced what he called his "Fair Deal" program, designed to build on FDR's New Deal. It included proposals for universal health care and more funding for education. He couldn't get it through Congress.

The Korean War broke out in 1950 and Truman swiftly committed U.S. troops to the conflict. Thousands of Americans were killed and wounded in a war that many Americans didn't understand. He also had to deal with the anticommunist "red-baiting" of Wisconsin senator Joseph McCarthy and his allies. All of it contributed to Truman's declining popularity. Truman decided not to seek reelection in 1952. When he left office in January 1953, his job approval rating was just 31 percent.

Truman returned home to Independence, Missouri, no longer protected by the Secret Service. He moved into his mother-in-law's old home at 219 North Delaware Street. When a reporter asked him what he intended to do first, he quipped, "Take the grips [suitcases] up to the attic."

He built his presidential library in Independence. He spent his days taking brisk morning walks around town, greeting old friends and important guests, and working in his office at the library. Visitors there could come in and shake his hand. He told a friend, "You don't need an appointment to see me now."

But over the years, something interesting happened to Truman's reputation. Presidential historians and the public began to judge him differently. They saw how Truman responded to the Soviet threat with political, diplomatic, and military initiatives designed to contain Russian aggression. There was the Marshall Plan, which gave more than $12 billion in economic assistance to help rebuild Western Europe after the ravages of World War II. And Truman helped form the North Atlantic Treaty Organization (NATO), the United States and Canada joining with ten European nations in a mutual defense pact based on the principle that an attack on one country was an attack on all.

With time, Truman's stature grew. Historians now look favorably on his time in the White House. They view Truman as the straight shooter from middle America. And they appreciate his accomplishments.

Today it's common to find him ranked high on the list of the top American presidents, just behind Abraham Lincoln, George Washington, and Truman's old boss, FDR.

The day after Christmas in 1972, Truman passed away at the age of eighty-eight. He was buried in the courtyard of the Truman Library. The only inscription on his gravestone are the dates he held his official positions—from Jackson County judge to president of the United States.

Bess Truman lived another ten years. In 1982, she was buried alongside him, on his right side. The story goes that's the way he wanted it, because she had always been his right-hand man.

ACKNOWLEDGMENTS

It turns out that writing a book involves thousands of decisions. I was fortunate to make so many that brought in the right people to turn my initial idea into the book you've just read.

First, I need to thank House Speaker Nancy Pelosi for giving me my subject. In February 2019, she invited several news anchors to Sam Rayburn's famous "Board of Education" hideaway in the Capitol. She wanted to give a prebuttal to the State of the Union speech President Donald Trump would deliver that night. But in the course of the meeting, she told the story of Vice President Harry Truman's call to the White House. She said that after he hung up, he exclaimed, "Jesus Christ and General Jackson." For the rest of the day, I kept thinking about our 33rd president, not our 45th.

How to turn what I thought was a good idea into a book? My longtime manager Larry Kramer introduced me to Claudia Cross, of Folio Literary Management. They were my Sherpa guides in what turned out to be the long, complicated process of climbing my version of Mount Everest.

They also introduced me to Mitch Weiss, my invaluable cowriter. Mitch is a Pulitzer Prize–winning investigative reporter for the Associated Press. In his spare time, he also writes riveting books that put you in the moment. As soon as I read his work and then met him, I knew I had the colleague I needed to take this on. But I also needed a researcher, and that was the easiest decision I had to make. For the past ten years, Lori Crim has been my researcher on *Fox News Sunday*. Together we have taken on everything from presidential debates to Vladimir Putin. I only half-jokingly call her "Chris's brain."

And then, the publisher. We were lucky to attract a lot of attention for this project. But as soon as I met Jofie Ferrari-Adler, editor and publisher of Avid Reader Press, and his boss, Jonathan Karp of Simon & Schuster, I was certain I had the team for this expedition. And it was a team. I want to thank Carolyn Reidy, Ben Loehnen, Meredith Vilarello, Jordan Rodman, Alison Forner, Amanda Mulholland, Brigid Black, Jessica Chin, Ruth Lee-Mui, Richard Ljoenes, Morgan Hoit, Carolyn Kelly, Elizabeth Hubbard, and Allie Lawrence.

Now we were ready to get to work and dig into those 116 days that changed the world. The first stop was the Harry S Truman Library in Independence, Missouri. I spent several days there looking through documents. The treasure trove was Truman's letters to his beloved Bess, his mother, and his sister, as well as the revealing diary he kept during these four tumultuous months. Library director Kurt Graham opened the files to me at a time when the building was being renovated. And he asked archivist Randy Sowell to help me make my way through thousands of documents. I also want to thank Samuel Rushay, Laurie Austin, and David Clark for their assistance in research, locating and providing the best images to capture this period in Truman's presidency, and overall guidance.

Historians opened other doors for us. Joseph Papalia is an expert on the 509th Composite Group, and helped us tell the story of those colorful flight crews. John Coster-Mullen is an expert on Los Alamos and the development of the atomic bomb. Special thanks to both.

One of the great revelations in researching this book was that seventy-five years later, some key figures are still alive. Ruth Huddleston told fascinating stories about her experience as one of the "Calutron Girls" at the Oak Ridge facility. She also put a face on the concern of so many Americans that after surviving the war in Europe, their loved ones were about to be sent to an even bloodier conflict in the Pacific.

And then there is Hideko Tamura Snider, that brave little ten-year-old girl who survived the atomic blast at Hiroshima and told us what she and her family went through. Seventy-five years later, she lives in the United States and looks back on her life with remarkable wisdom and not a trace of bitterness.

The archivists at the National Archives provided many of the images that captured the crew of the *Enola Gay* and the team of scientists through various stages of training and preparation. Assistance from Michelle Brown, Holly Reed, and Kaitlyn Crain Enriquez of the National Archives textual and still pictures departments was instrumental in letting us show—not just tell you about—these larger-than-life characters.

Thank you to Pamela Ives with the United States Air Force for her help in locating the operation orders of the 509th, the team that trained to make up the flight crew of the *Enola Gay* and all of its support.

And thanks to Olivia Garrison at the Iowa State University Library, for locating some of the first radio interviews of the two atomic bomb flight crews after their missions, conducted by journalist Jack Shelley on the island of Tinian during those August days in 1945.

The story of the U.S. decision to deploy the world's first atomic bomb cannot be told without showing its devastating impact on Hiroshima. The stunning pictures of that city's "atomic bomb dome," which was located almost directly underneath the explosion, yet somehow escaped complete destruction, helps show what happened there. Thank you to Rie Nakanishi of the Hiroshima Peace Memorial Museum for allowing us to use those images in telling this important part of the story. The museum, which opened on August 24, 1955, holds some of the personal belongings of the victims, and hopes to encourage its visitors to advance nuclear disarmament and peace in the world.

Many thanks to Gary Younger of the U.S. Department of Energy for providing images of key players in the Truman Administration, who were an integral part of the chain of events throughout the life of the atomic program

Historian Alan Brady Carr of the Los Alamos National Laboratory and Archivist Rebecca Collinsworth of the Los Alamos Historical Society Archives were helpful in providing information to recreate the look and feel of the tight community of scientists at Los Alamos, who worked under tight deadlines to meet the Truman Administration's timetable.

I want to express my gratitude to the executives at Fox News who not only allowed me to write this book, but encouraged me along the way. I thank Fox News Chief Executive Officer Suzanne Scott, President Jay Wallace, Senior Executive Vice President of Corporate Communications Irena Briganti, and Vice President Carly Shanahan, and my team at *Fox News Sunday*, especially executive producer Jessica Loker and producer Andrea DeVito.

Finally, Mitch and I want to thank our families for their love and support during early mornings and late nights as well as countless lost weekends, when in addition to our day jobs, we took on this project during what should have been family time. We promise to make it up to you.

I want to conclude by expressing my gratitude to two members of my family. My daughter Catherine Wallace gave me valuable advice from her years in publishing. When I would complain about how hard it is to write a book, she would roll her eyes at my "discovery."

Most of all, I thank my wife Lorraine. You are the beginning and end of everything in my life. And you always will be.

NOTES

COUNTDOWN: 116 DAYS

1   "a windy Senator from Wisconsin": Harry Truman Library, Truman letter, dated April 15, 1945.

2   "Board of Education": U.S. Capitol Historical Society.

2   "got a little paler": Baime, *The Accidental President*, p. 25.

4   he was the first one there: Harry Truman Library, Truman letter, dated April 16, 1945.

4   "waiting in a huge leather chair": Baime, *The Accidental President*, p. 30.

6   would brief Truman about it fully: *Memoirs by Harry S Truman*, vol. 1, p. 10.

6   "world fell in on me": Harry Truman Library, Truman letter to May Wallace, dated April 12, 1945.

6   "and face the music": Truman diary, dated April 12, 1945.

COUNTDOWN: 113 DAYS

8   "a date that will live in infamy": *Public Papers*, Franklin D. Roosevelt, December 7, 1941.

9   "Now, there was no one": Smith and Weiner, *Robert Oppenheimer: Letters and Collections*, p. 287.

12 "magnetic personality": Thomas O. Jones, interview, *Voices of the Manhattan Project*, August 9, 2002.

13 "I am sure we can": Franklin D. Roosevelt letter, dated June 29, 1943.

13 "gesture of consolation": Smith and Weiner, *Robert Oppenheimer: Letters and Collections*, p. 287.

15 "When, three days ago": Ibid., p. 288.

16 "Roosevelt was a great architect": Palevsky, *Atomic Fragments: A Daughter's Questions*, p. 116.

COUNTDOWN: 105 DAYS

19   "given an exhilarating sample": Paul Tibbets, interview, *Airport Journals*, 2002.

20   "Do you want to learn": Ibid.

22   "They're building an airplane": Ibid.

23   "Have you ever been arrested?": Tibbets, *The Return of the Enola Gay*, p. 159.

25   "Is that you, Bob?": Caron, *Fire of a Thousand Suns*, p. 151.

25   "Bob, I need": Thomas and Witts, *Enola Gay: The Bombing of Hiroshima*, p. 27.

26   "You don't discuss": Widowsky, interview, Atomic Heritage Foundation, 2016.

27   "Dammit, you've got": Tibbets, *The Return of the Enola Gay*, p. 186.

COUNTDOWN: 104 DAYS

28   "Kamikazes": Kauffman, U.S. Naval Institute, interviews, vol. 1.

29   "enemy is stronger": Stilwell, *Stars and Stripes*, April 9, 1945.

29   "largest armed force": Roosevelt, *Stars and Stripes*, March 24, 1945.

33   "We became naked warriors": Cunningham, *The Frogmen of World War II: An Oral History of the U.S. Navy's Underwater Demolition Teams*, p. 106.

34   "Let me put it this way": Kauffman, U.S. Naval Institute, interviews, vol. 1.

34   "That's as poor a reason": Bush, *America's First Frogman: The Draper Kauffman Story*, p. 183.

COUNTDOWN: 103 DAYS

36   "eager to decide in advance of thinking": Baime, *The Accidental President*, p. 204.

37   broke and out of work: Miller, *Plain Speaking: An Oral Biography of Harry S. Truman*, ebook.

39   Bess for approval: McCullough, *Truman*, p. 579.

39   "get him to say 'manure'": "Remembering Bess," *Washington Post*, October 19, 1982.

39   "if he wants to break up the Democratic Party": Baime, *The Accidental President*, p. 101.

42   preferred to be called "Colonel Stimson": Dobbs, *Six Months in 1945: From World War to Cold War*, p. 166.

42   "that led to very vigorous control": Leslie Groves interview, Part 1, Atomic Heritage Foundation, January 5, 1965.

42   "a little alarm bell rang 'Caution' in your brain": Vogel, *The Pentagon: A History*, p. 26.

44   "A single bomb of this type": Albert Einstein, letter, dated August 2, 1939.

48   "I am the impresario": Groves, *The A-Bomb Program in Science, Technology and Management*, p. 40.

49   "This is a big project": Dobbs, *Six Months in 1945: From World War to Cold War*, p. 172.

COUNTDOWN: 90 DAYS

50   "You needn't be uneasy": *Public Papers*, Harry S. Truman, May 8, 1945, p. 44.

51   "This is a solemn": Ibid.

52   "V-E Day Proclaimed. Japan Next": *Pittsburgh Press*, May 7, 1945.

52   "Japs Being Measured for Burial Kimono": *Hattiesburg (Mississippi) American*, May 7, 1945.

52   "It's Over": New York *Daily News*, May 7, 1945.

COUNTDOWN: 70 DAYS

63   *Kyoto:* The former capital: *Summary of Target Committee Meetings*, May 10 and 11, 1945.

63   "Many people and industries": Ibid.

63   "It is such a size": Ibid.

64   "An important urban industrial area": Ibid.

64   "The arsenal is important": Ibid.

64   "Its importance is increasing": Ibid.

64   "all *that* top brass": Thomas and Witts, *Enola Gay: The Bombing of Hiroshima*, p. 133.

66   "copious quantities of Arrow Beer": Jacob Beser, *Last Lecture*, presentation, 1992.

66   "The United States has been attacked": H. V. Kaltenborn, transcript, radio broadcast, December 7, 1941.

68   "There's a full-scale war": Jacob Beser, *Last Lecture*, presentation, 1992.

68   "If the United States ever": Ibid.

68   "Lieutenant, you are": Beser, *Hiroshima and Nagasaki Revisited*, p. 35.

68   "How do you feel": Beser, *The Rising Sun Sets: The Complete Story of the Bombing of Nagasaki*, p. 62.

70   "fundamental forces of the universe": Jacob Beser, *Last Lecture*, presentation, 1992.

72   "And in no way can a submarine": Ibid.

COUNTDOWN: 66 DAYS

82   "There is no easy way to win": *Public Papers*, Harry S. Truman, June 1, 1945.

82   "No matter how you slice it": Smith, *Fire in the Sky*, p. 54.

82   international law and: Stimson, *Active Service in Peace and War*, p. 632.

82   "legitimate military targets": Ibid.

83   "a Frankenstein": Stimson, notes, Interim Committee, May 9, 1945.

83   the reputation of the United States: Stimson, diary, quoted in Rhodes, *The Making of the Atomic Bomb*, p. 640.

83   "revolutionary change in the relations": Stimson, notes, Interim Committee, May 9, 1945.

84   "wisdom of testing bombs": Rhodes, *The Making of the Atomic Bomb*, p. 635.

84   "Perhaps the greatest": Szilard, *Perspectives in American History*, vol. 2, 1968, p. 146.

85   "would be tremendous": Oppenheimer, notes of Interim Committee meeting, May 31, 1945, p. 13.

85   "a brilliant luminescence": Ibid.

86   "Nothing would have been": Stimson, "The Decision to Use the Atomic Bomb," *Harper's Magazine*, February 1947.

86   "It was vital": Ibid.

86   "The opinions of our scientific": Oppenheimer, *Recommendations on the Immediate Use of Nuclear Weapons, by the Scientific Panel of the Interim Committee*, June 16, 1945.

86   "Such an effective": Stimson, "The Decision to Use the Atomic Bomb."

COUNTDOWN: 53 DAYS

90   "Today was typical": Thomas and Witts, *Enola Gay: The Bombing of Hiroshima*, p. 52.

COUNTDOWN: 49 DAYS

93   "Dear Bess," he wrote: Truman letter to Bess, June 12, 1945.

95   "for preparation of defenses": *Minutes of White House meeting*, June 18, 1945.

96   "Go ahead": Baime, *The Accidental President*, p. 251.

98   "The idea of someone literally throwing himself": Bush, *America's First Frogman: The Draper Kauffman Story*, p. 184.

99   "The whole thing is incomprehensible": Admiral James Kauffman letter to Draper Kauffman, 1940.

COUNTDOWN: 36 DAYS

105   "That's interesting," Hornig said. "Who requested me?": Donald Hornig, interview, Lyndon Baines Johnson Library, December 4, 1968.

105   "Everyone's mad that you": Ibid.

105   "Remember, Hornig, Uncle Sam": Ibid.

106   "I don't type": Lilli Hornig, interview, Atomic Heritage Foundation, 2003.

COUNTDOWN: 34 DAYS

113   "not for the lay public": Laurence, *New York Times*, obituary, March 19, 1977.

113   "I never thought of it": Ibid.

115   "They won't believe": Laurence, "Drama of Atomic Bomb Found Climax in July 16 Test," *New York Times*, September 26, 1945.

115   "They'll believe it": Ibid.

115   "The key to atomic": Ibid.

116   "impossibles of yesterday": Ibid.

COUNTDOWN: 21 DAYS

117 "hammer on those boys": Moffett, "Truman's Atom-Bomb Dilemma," *Christian Science Monitor*, July 31, 1995.

118 "and we must win": Walker, *Prompt and Utter Destruction: Truman and the Use of the Atomic Bombs on Japan*, pp. 52–53.

118 Russians would enter the fight: *Memoirs by Harry S Truman*, vol. 1, p. 314.

119 play poker in his room: Baime, *The Accidental President*, p. 275.

119 "It is dirty yellow and red": Truman diary, dated July 16, 1945.

119 "working over": Potsdam Log, Harry S. Truman Library and Museum.

121 "delighted" with the president: Baime, *The Accidental President*, p. 280.

121 "too much soft soap": McCullough, *Truman*, ebook.

121 reviewed the troops: Dobbs, *Six Months in 1945: From World War to Cold War*, p. 289.

121 "Nobody has stopped them yet": Ibid.

122 "never saw such destruction": Potsdam Log, Harry S. Truman Library and Museum.

129 "miles away from nowhere": Laurence, "Drama of Atomic Bomb Found Climax in July 16 Test," *New York Times*, September 26, 1945.

130 "Do not watch": Ibid.

130 "Lord, these affairs": Lamont, *Day of Trinity*, p. 226.

132 "awesome roar, which": Farrell, Trinity test report to Truman, July 21, 1945.

132 "I no longer consider": Groves, memo to Stimson, July 18, 1945.

132 "whole world has": Hershberg, *James B. Conant: Harvard to Hiroshima and the Making of the Nuclear Age*, p. 232.

132 "opening the heavy": Teller and Brown, *The Legacy of Hiroshima*, p. 17.

132 "I am sure that": Laurence, "Drama of Atomic Bomb Found Climax in July 16 Test," *New York Times*, September 26, 1945.

133 "Several inquiries have been": Groves, *Now It Can Be Told*, p. 301.

134 "The Atomic Age began": Laurence, "Drama of Atomic Bomb Found Climax in July 16 Test," *New York Times*, September 26, 1945.

134 "foul and awesome": *Bulletin of the Atomic Scientists* 32 (May 5, 1975).

135 "Now we're all sons of bitches": Lamont, *Day of Trinity*, p. 242.

COUNTDOWN: 20 DAYS

136 "overexertion": Beschloss, *The Conquerors: Roosevelt, Truman and the Destruction of Hitler's Germany, 1941–1945*, p. 244.

137 His eyes were yellow: Baime, *The Accidental President*, p. 289.

137 "Kremlin complexion": McCullough, *Truman*, p. 417.

139 felt comfortable with the setup: Baime, *The Accidental President*, p. 291.

140 "I was so scared": Truman letter to Bess, June 12, 1945.

COUNTDOWN: 19 DAYS

142 "one or two violent shocks": Baime, *The Accidental President*, p. 300.

142 "over their homeland": Truman diary, dated July 18, 1945.

143 "crisp and to the point": Baime, *The Accidental President*, ebook.

143 "Stalin just grunts": Truman letter to his mother, quoted in Truman, *Harry Truman*, ebook.

143 "home to the Senate for that": Truman diary, dated July 18, 1945.

COUNTDOWN: 18 DAYS

145 "I think he'll be coming home": Ruth Sisson, interview, July 21, 2019.

COUNTDOWN: 17 DAYS

148 "I want 'em both in it": Dobbs, *Six Months in 1942: From World War to Cold War*, p. 301.

150 "feeling of depression": Ambrose, *Eisenhower: Soldier, General of the Army, President-Elect, 1890–1952*, ebook.

COUNTDOWN: 16 DAYS

155 "Are all of your crews": Tibbets, *The Return of the Enola Gay*, p. 189.

156 "It's bad news": Ibid., p. 192.

158 "Goddamit, Lieutenant Beser": Thomas and Witts, *Enola Gay: The Bombing of Hiroshima*, p. 182.

158 "The Old Man": Ibid.

COUNTDOWN: 13 DAYS

160 an hour to get through it: Baime, *The Accidental President*, p. 311.

160 "an entirely new confidence": Stimson diary, dated July 21, 1945.

161 "prosecute the war against Japan until she ceases to resist": McCullough, *Truman*, p. 436.

162 "We have discovered the most": Truman diary, dated July 25, 1945.

162 "This weapon is to be used": Ibid.

163 "to shock [the Japanese] into action": Marshall interview, February 11, 1957.

163 "worth a couple of Japanese cities": McCullough, *Truman*, p. 439.

165 "began at the Cecilienhof Palace at 7:30 pm, on July 24, 1945": Baime, *The Accidental President*, p. 317.

COUNTDOWN: 12 DAYS

167 "It's a terrible thing": Badash, Hirshfelder, and Brioda, *Reminiscences of Los Alamos 1943–1945*, p. 132.

167 "Those poor little": Bird and Sherwin, *American Prometheus: The Triumph and Tragedy of J. Robert Oppenheimer*, p. 313.

167 "Don't let them bomb": Moynahan, *Atomic Diary*, p. 15.

168 "Kiss the Baby": Truman letter to Bess, cited in "Excerpts from Truman's 1911 and Potsdam Letters to Bess Wallace Truman," *New York Times*, March 14, 1983.

169 "We will issue a warning": Truman diary, dated July 25, 1945.

170 "Perhaps this is the end": Dobbs, *Six Months in 1942: From World War to Cold War*, p. 333.

170 "bear thinking over": Baime, *The Accidental President*, p. 319.

COUNTDOWN: 8 DAYS

176 "two or three": Van Kirk, *My True Course: Northumberland to Hiroshima*, p. 433.

177 "You'll be flying": Thomas and Witts, *Enola Gay: The Bombing of Hiroshima*, p. 208.

178 "young bull": Tibbets, *The Return of the Enola Gay*, p. 221.

COUNTDOWN: 6 DAYS

179 "this godforsaken country": Baime, *The Accidental President*, p. 323.

COUNTDOWN: 5 DAYS

184 "goodly supply of": Thomas and Witts, *Enola Gay: The Bombing of Hiroshima*, p. 218.

185 "competent and dependable": Tibbets, *The Return of the Enola Gay*, p. 203.

COUNTDOWN: 4 DAYS

186 "little son-of-a-bitch": Truman letter to Dean Acheson, dated March 13, 1957.

188 "like to lay a little bet on that?": Baime, *The Accidental President*, p. 330.

188 "monstrous weapon of destruction": McCullough, *Truman*, p. 548.

189 "Our primary purpose": Thomas and Witts, *Enola Gay: The Bombing of Hiroshima*, p. 219.

190 "It's the most perfect AP": Ibid.

COUNTDOWN: 3 DAYS

192 "You're taking two": Kauffman, U.S. Naval Institute, interviews, vol. 1.

COUNTDOWN: 2 DAYS

194 "It's getting late": Hideko Tamura, interview, July 2019.

196 "There are air raids": Ibid.

197 "I heard that": Caron, *Fire of a Thousand Suns*, p. 175.

197 "I'm disappointed in": Ibid.

197 "Anybody who can": Ibid., p. 176.

198 "The moment has arrived": Thomas and Witts, *Enola Gay: The Bombing of Hiroshima*, p. 227.

200 "The flash of": Ibid., p. 229.

200   "No one knows": Caron, *Fire of a Thousand Suns*, p. 229.

201   "Whatever work we've": Ibid., p. 230.

COUNTDOWN: 1 DAY

203   "If we crack up": Laurence, *Dawn Over Zero*, p. 171.

203   "I pray that": Ibid.

203   "Can you do that?": Ibid., p. 173.

203   "No," Parsons admitted. "But I've": Ibid.

206   a courageous redhead: Tibbets, *The Return of the Enola Gay*, p. 203.

208   "What the hell": Thomas and Witts, *Enola Gay: The Bombing of Hiroshima*, p. 233.

210   "I wasn't concerned": Ibid.

211   "Please keep him:" Beser, *Hiroshima and Nagasaki Revisited*, p. 89.

212   "Why the weird paper?": Ibid., p. 114 .

COUNTDOWN: 9 HOURS, 15 MINUTES

214   "I'll be goddamned": Tibbets, *The Return of the Enola Gay*, p. 211.

214   "It would be easier": Ibid.

COUNTDOWN: 9 HOURS

215   "Almighty Father, who": Laurence, *Dawn Over Zero*, p. 173.

COUNTDOWN: 7 HOURS, 10 MINUTES

219   "You guys, this": Thomas and Witts, *Enola Gay: The Bombing of Hiroshima*, p. 240.

COUNTDOWN: 6 HOURS, 30 MINUTES

222   "The bomb is": Van Kirk, *My True Course: From Northumberland to Hiroshima*, p. 462.

COUNTDOWN: 3 HOURS, 30 MINUTES

223   "Colonel, are we": Tibbets, *The Return of the Enola Gay*, p. 219.

223   "That's about it:" Ibid.

223   "What happens if": Van Kirk, *My True Course: From Northumberland to Hiroshima*, p. 465.

223   "Then we are in": Ibid.

COUNTDOWN: 2 HOURS, 15 MINUTES

224   "The bomb is": Lewis, copilot log, August 1945.

COUNTDOWN: 10 MINUTES

225   "Ten minutes to": Tibbets, *The Return of the Enola Gay*, p. 228.

COUNTDOWN: 43 SECONDS

226 "Bomb away!": Caron, *Fire of a Thousand Suns*, p. 247.

226 "It's clear": Ibid.

226 "Can you see": Ibid.

COUNTDOWN: FIRESTORM

227 "Colonel, it's coming": Caron, *Fire of a Thousand Suns*, p. 250.

228 "boiling upward like": Van Kirk, interview, February 1960.

228 "looked like lava": Caron, *Fire of a Thousand Suns*, p. 250.

228 "parts of things": Ferebee, interview, February 1960.

228 "so huge and": Nelson, interview, February 1960.

228 "My God, what": Lewis, interview, February 1960.

229 "I think this": Tibbets, *The Return of the Enola Gay*, p. 234.

231 "We can't stay": Hideko Tamura, interview, July 2019.

233 as a ton of TNT: Truman Library, Log of President Harry S. Truman's Trip to the Berlin Conference, dated August 6, 1945.

234 "It's a hell of a story": Baime, *The Accidental President*, p. 340.

234 "Why the hell": Badash, Hirshfelder, and Brioda, *Reminiscences of Los Alamos 1943–1945*, p. 37.

234 "I'm very proud": Groves, transcript of telephone call to Oppenheimer, August 6, 1945.

235 "Attention please": Else, *The Day After Trinity*, p. 58.

235 "Hiroshima has been": Rhodes, *The Making of the Atomic Bomb*, p. 735.

240 "I watched the": Laurence, "Atomic Bombing of Nagasaki," *New York Times*, September 9, 1945.

241 "The hell with it": Tibbets, *The Return of the Enola Gay*, p. 247.

241 "Does one not": Laurence, "Atomic Bombing of Nagasaki," *New York Times*, September 9, 1945.

242 "Destiny chose Nagasaki": Ibid.

242 "Despite the fact": Ibid.

244 "blind luck and": Tibbets, *The Return of the Enola Gay*, p. 250.

244 "You fucked up": Ibid.

245 "The enemy now": Text of Hirohito's address, *New York Times*, August 15, 1945.

246 "might get a story": McCullough, *Truman*, p. 461.

247 "had given the message to our people," Baime, *The Accidental President*, p. 353.

EPILOGUE

248 "seeds of hate more widely than ever": O'Reilly, *Killing the Rising Sun*, p. 209.

248 "in a fraction of a second by a single bomb": McCullough, *Truman*, p. 456.

249 "crew cuts, bow ties, and tab collars": Federation of American Scientists, *President's Message: Reinvention and Renewal*, May 10, 2016.

249 "recommending that atom bombs be made": Linus Pauling and the International Peace Movement.

250 "in surprisingly detailed episodes": U.S. Department of Energy, *Informing the Public.*

250 called *Pika-don*—"Flash-bang"—in 1950: Atomic Heritage, *Survivors of Hiroshima and Nagasaki,* July 27, 2017.

252 "American diplomacy vis a vis Russia": Mohan and Tree, "Hiroshima, American Media and the Construction of Conventional Wisdom," *Journal of American-East Asian Relations* 4, no. 2 (Summer 1995): 159.

255 "son of a bitch in this office ever again": Bird and Sherwin, *American Prometheus: The Triumph and Tragedy of J. Robert Oppenheimer,* ebook.

255 "I'm the guy who sent you": O'Reilly, *Killing the Rising Sun,* p. 278.

255 "It stopped the Jap War": Truman, *Harry Truman,* ebook.

255 "I did what I thought was right": Truman, *Harry Truman,* ebook.

POSTSCRIPT

258 "Put out your hand": Ruth Huddleston, interview, July 2019.

260 "I've lived a": Ibid.

262 "We tended to": Hideko Tamura Snider, interview, July 2019.

264 "It was the": Ibid.

265 "If atomic bombs": Bird and Sherwin, *American Prometheus. The Triumph and Tragedy of J. Robert Oppenheimer,* p. 329.

267 "I think we": Lilli Hornig, *Providence Journal,* August 9, 2015.

267 "When it finally": Groves, *Now it Can Be Told: The Story of the Manhattan Project,* p. 354.

269 "What has mankind": Lewis, interview, February 1960.

270 "The enlisted men": Lewis, in March 10, 1981, letter to Joseph Papalia, historian for the 509th Composite Group.

270 "Five hundred years": Ibid.

271 "say something nice": Van Kirk, *My True Course: From Northumberland to Hiroshima,* p. 535.

271 "I will bet": Ibid., p. 536.

272 "We were fighting": Van Kirk, interview, February 1960.

272 "In America": Jacob Beser, *Last Lecture,* presentation, 1992.

272 "I have often": Ibid.

273 "The solution to": Ibid.

273 "I believe this weapon": Tibbets, interview, February, 1960.

274 "This inscription will": Van Kirk, *My True Course: From Northumberland to Hiroshima,* p. 530.

276 "appointment to see me now": McCullough, *Truman,* p. 932.

BIBLIOGRAPHY

BOOKS

Ambrose, Stephen E. *Eisenhower: Soldier, General of the Army, President-Elect 1890–1952.* New York: Simon & Schuster, 2014.

Badash, Hirshfelder, and Brioda, *Reminiscences of Los Alamos 1943–1945.* Boston, Massachusetts: D. Reidel Publishing Company, 1980.

Baime, A. J. *The Accidental President: Harry S. Truman and the Four Months That Changed the World.* Boston: Houghton Mifflin Harcourt, 2017.

Beschloss, Michael. *The Conquerors: Roosevelt, Truman, and the Destruction of Hitler's Germany, 1941–1945.* New York: Simon & Schuster, 2002.

Beser, Jacob. *Hiroshima and Nagasaki Revisited.* Memphis, Tennessee: Global Press, 1988.

Beser, Jerome, and Jack Spangler. *The Rising Sun Sets: The Complete Story of the Bombing of Nagasaki.* Baltimore: Jacob Beser Foundation, 2007.

Bird, Kai, and Martin J. Sherwin. *American Prometheus: The Triumph and Tragedy of J. Robert Oppenheimer.* New York: Vintage Books, 2005.

Blassingame, Wyatt. *The Frogmen of World War II.* New York: Random House, 1964.

Bundy, McGeorge. *Danger and Survival: Choices About the Bomb in the First Fifty Years.* New York: Random House, 1988.

Bush, Elizabeth Kauffman. *America's First Frogmen: The Draper Kauffman Story.* Annapolis, MD: Naval Institute Press, 2004.

Cantelon, Philip L., and Robert C. Williams, eds. *The American Atom: A Documentary History of Fission to the Present, 1939–1984.* Philadelphia: University of Pennsylvania Press, 1984.

Caron, George R. *Fire of a Thousand Suns: The George R. "Bob" Caron Story—Tail Gunner of the Enola Gay.* Westminster, CO: Web Publishing, 1995.

Conant, Jennet. *109 East Palace: Robert Oppenheimer and the Secret City of Los Alamos.* New York: Simon & Schuster, 2005.

Dietz, Suzanne Simon. *My True Course: Dutch Van Kirk, Northumberland to Hiroshima.* Lawrenceville, GA: Red Gremlin Press, 2012.

Dobbs, Michael. *Six Months in 1945: FDR, Stalin, Churchill, and Truman—from World War to Cold War.* New York: Vintage, 2013.

Edgerton, Robert B. *Warriors of the Rising Sun: A History of the Japanese Military.* New York: Norton, 1997.

Farrell, Robert H. *Off the Record: The Private Papers of Harry S. Truman.* New York: Harper & Row, 1980.

Giovannitti, Len, and Fred Freed. *The Decision to Drop the Bomb: A Political History.* New York: Coward-McCann, 1965.

Groves, Leslie M. *Now It Can Be Told. The Story of the Manhattan Project.* New York: Da Capo Press, 1962.

Harder, Robert O. *The Three Musketeers of the Army Air Forces: From Hitler's Fortress Europa to Hiroshima and Nagasaki.* Annapolis, MD: Naval Institute Press, 2015.

Hersey, John. *Hiroshima.* London: Penguin Books, 1946.

Hershberg, James. *James B. Conant: Harvard to Hiroshima and the Making of the Nuclear Age.* New York: Knopf, 1993.

Hewlett, Richard G., and Oscar Anderson Jr. *The New World, 1939–1946.* Vol. 1 of *A History of the United States Atomic Energy Commission.* University Park: Pennsylvania State University Press, 1962.

Isley, Jeter A., and Philip Crowl. *The U.S. Marines and Amphibious War: Its Theory and Its Practice in the Pacific.* Princeton, NJ: Princeton University Press, 1951.

Jones, Vincent. *Manhattan: The Army and the Atomic Bomb.* Center of Military History, U.S. Army, 1985.

Kelly, Cynthia. *Manhattan Project: The Birth of the Atomic Bomb in the Words of Its Creators, Eyewitnesses, and Historians.* New York: Black Dog & Leventhal, 2017.

Kiernan, Denise. *The Girls of Atomic City: The Untold Story of the Women Who Helped Win World War II.* New York: Touchstone, 2013.

Krauss, Robert, and Amelia Krauss. *The 509th Remembered: A History of the 509th Composite Group as Told by the Veterans That Dropped the Atomic Bombs on Japan.* Buchanan, MI: First Atomic Bombardment, 2005.

Kunetka, James. *City of Fire: Los Alamos and the Atomic Age, 1943–1945.* Albuquerque: University of New Mexico Press, 1978.

Lamont, Lansing. *Day of Trinity.* New York: Atheneum, 1985.

Laurence, William L. *Dawn Over Zero: The Story of the Atomic Bomb.* New York: Knopf, 1946.

McCullough, David. *Truman.* New York: Simon & Schuster, 1993.

Miller, Merle. *Plain Speaking: An Oral Biography of Harry S. Truman.* New York: Rosetta Books, 2018.

Morrison, Samuel Eliot. *Victory in the Pacific.* Boston: Little, Brown, 1960.

Moynahan, John F. *Atomic Diary.* Newark, N.J.: Barton Publishing Company, 1946.

Norris, Robert. *Racing for the Bomb: The True Story of General Leslie R. Groves, the Man Behind the Birth of the Atomic Age.* New York: Skyhorse, 2014.

O'Reilly, Bill, and Martin Dugard. *Killing the Rising Sun: How America Vanquished World War II Japan.* New York: Henry Holt, 2016.

Oppenheimer, Robert, Alice Kimball Smith, and Charles Weiner. *Robert Oppenheimer: Letters and Recollections.* Cambridge, MA: Harvard University Press, 1980.

Palevsky, Mary. *Atomic Fragments: A Daughter's Questions.* Berkeley: University of California Press, 2000.

Polnberg, Richard. *In the Matter of J. Robert Oppenheimer: The Security Clearance Hearing.* Ithaca, NY: Cornell University Press, 2002.

Rhodes, Richard. *The Making of the Atomic Bomb.* New York: Touchstone, 1986.

Smith, Jeffrey. *Fire in the Sky: The Story of the Atomic Bomb.* Bloomington, IN: Author-House, 2010.

Smyth, Henry D. *Atomic Energy for Military Purposes: The Official Report on the Development of the Atomic Bomb Under the Auspice of the United States Government 1940–1945.* Washington, DC: U.S. Government Printing Office, 1945.

Snider, Hideko Tamura. *One Sunny Day. A Child's Memories of Hiroshima.* Peru, IL: Carus, 1996.

Stimson, Henry, and McGeorge Bundy. *On Active Service in Peace and War.* New York: Hippocrene Books, 1971.

Szasz, Ferenc. *The Day the Sun Rose Twice.* Albuquerque: University of New Mexico Press, 1984.

Teller, Edward, and Allen Brown. *The Legacy of Hiroshima.* New York: Doubleday, 1962.

Thomas, Gordon, and Max Morgan Witts. *Enola Gay: The Bombing of Hiroshima.* Old Saybrook, CT: Konecky & Konecky, 1977.

Tibbets, Paul W. *Return of the Enola Gay.* Columbus, OH: Mid Coast Marketing, 1998.

Truman, Harry S. *Memoirs by Harry S Truman.* Vol. 1, *Year of Decisions.* New York: Doubleday, 1955.

———. *Where the Buck Stops: The Personal and Private Writings of Harry S. Truman.* New Word City, February 4, 2015.

Truman, Margaret S. *Harry Truman.* New Word City, 2015.

Truslow, Edith C. *Manhattan District History: Nonscientific Aspects of Los Alamos Project Y: 1942 Through 1946.* Los Alamos, NM: Los Alamos Historical Society, 1997.

United States Atomic Energy Commission. *In the Matter of J. Robert Oppenheimer: Transcript of Hearing Before Personnel Security Board Washington, D.C., April 12, 1954, Through May 6, 1954.* Washington, DC: U.S. Government Printing Office, 1954.

VanDeMark, Brian. *Pandora's Keepers: Nine Men and the Atomic Bomb.* New York: Little, Brown, 2003.

Vogel, Steve. *The Pentagon: A History.* New York: Random House, 2008.

Walker, J. Samuel. *Prompt and Utter Destruction: Truman and the Use of the Atomic Bombs on Japan.* Chapel Hill: University of North Carolina Press, 1997.

Wyden, Peter. *Day One.* New York: Simon & Schuster, 1984.

ARCHIVES AND DOCUMENTS

Beser Foundation, Baltimore, Maryland. The archive includes records, documents, and other materials related to the Hiroshima and Nagasaki missions. The materials include personal records donated by Jacob Beser, the only man to fly on both atomic bomb missions, flight logs, transcripts of interviews with crew members, maps, and correspondence.

Federation of American Scientists.

Frank, James. *Report of the Committee on Social and Political Implications.* June 1945.

George C. Marshall Foundation. *George C. Marshall: Interviews and Reminiscences for Forrest C. Pogue.* February 11, 1957.

Harry S. Truman Library and Museum.

History of the 509th Composite Group from activation to August 15, 1945.

Hornig, Donald. *Lyndon Baines Johnson—Library.* December 4, 1968.

Linus Pauling and the International Peace Movement. Oregon State University.

National Archives and Record Administration, Washington, D.C. This archive includes U.S. Navy, U.S. Army, and other military files related to World War II, the War in the Pacific, and the Manhattan Project. They include declassified memos about the atomic bomb missions, including minutes of Interim Committee and Target Committee meetings, flight logs, navigation track charts, and orders.

Public Papers, Franklin D. Roosevelt.

Public Papers, Harry S. Truman.

U.S. Department of Energy. Office of History and Heritage Resources. Manhattan Project.

U.S. Naval Institute, Annapolis, Maryland. A series of taped interviews with Rear Admiral Draper L. Kauffman, Volume I and Volume II. It contains more than 1,300 pages of transcripts from interviews with Kauffman in which he reflects on his time in the U.S. Navy and the Underwater Demolition Teams during World War II.

U.S. State Department. *Foreign Relations of the United States: Diplomatic Papers, The Conference of Berlin (The Potsdam Conference),* 1945, vol. 2. Stimson diary dated July 24, 1945.

U.S. State Department. Office of Historian. Atomic Diplomacy.

PERIODICALS

Bainbridge, Kenneth T. "A Foul and Awesome Display." *Bulletin of the Atomic Scientists,* May 31, 1975.

Groves, Leslie R. "The Atom General Answers His Critics." *Saturday Evening Post,* May 19, 1948.

Isaacson, Walter. "Chain Reaction: From Einstein to the Atomic Bomb." *Discover Magazine*, March 18, 2008.

Kistiakowsky, George B. "Trinity—A Reminiscence." *Bulletin of the Atomic Scientists*, June 1980.

Laurence, William L. "The Atom Gives Up." *Saturday Evening Post*, September 7, 1940.

Lewis, Robert A. "How We Dropped the A-Bomb." *Popular Science*, August 1957.

Michaud, John. "Double Take Eighty-Five from the Archive: John Hersey." *New Yorker*, June 8, 2010.

Moffett, George. "Truman's Atom-Bomb Dilemma." *Christian Science Monitor*, July 31, 1995.

Mohan, Uday, and Sahno Tree. "Hiroshima, American Media, and the Construction of Conventional Wisdom." *Journal of American-East Asian Relations* 4, no. 2 (summer 1995).

Moore, David W. "Majority Supports Use of Atomic Bomb on Japan in WWII." Gallup News Service, August 5, 2005.

Stimson, Henry J. "The Decision to Use the Atomic Bomb." *Harper's Magazine* 194 (February 1947).

Stokes, Bruce. "70 Years after Hiroshima, Opinions Have Shifted on Use of Atomic Bomb." Pew Research, August 4, 2015.

Szilard, Leo. "Perspectives in American History, Volume II." 1968.

Tibbets, Paul. "How to Drop an Atom Bomb." *Saturday Evening Post*, June 8, 1946.

"The War Ends: Burst of Atomic Bomb Brings Swift Surrender of Japanese." *Life*, August 20, 1945.

Wellerstein, Alex. "What Presidents Talk About When They Talk About Hiroshima." *New Yorker*, May 27, 2016.

NEWSPAPERS AND WIRE SERVICES

Asbury Park Press. "A-Bomb Pilot Carves New Career." August 2, 1970.

Associated Press. "Old Pals Differ on Using Bomb." August 7, 1957.

Chicago Tribune. "40 Years Later, John Hersey Revisits Hiroshima." July 17, 1985.

Hattiesburg American. May 7, 1945.

New York Daily News. May 7, 1945.

New York Times. "Atomic Bombing of Nagasaki Told by Flight Members." September 9, 1945.

———. "Drama of the Atomic Bomb Found Climax in July 16 Test." September 26, 1943.

———. "Lightning Blew Up Dummy Atom Bomb." September 27, 1945.

———. "Atom Bomb Based on Einstein Theory." September 28, 1945.

———. "Atomic Factories Incredible Sight." September 29, 1945.

———. "Engineering Vision in Atomic Project." October 1, 1945.

———. "Gases Explain Size of Atomic Plants." October 3, 1945.

———. "Scientists 'Create' in Atomic Project." October 4, 1945.

———. "Element 94 Key to Atomic Puzzle." October 5, 1945.

———. "Plutonium Lifted by New Chemistry." October 8, 1945.

———. "Atomic Key to Life Is Feasible Now." October 9, 1945.

Parsons, Louella O. "Ralph Edwards Show." Column, May 14, 1955.

Pittsburgh Press. May 7, 1945.

Providence Journal. August 9, 2015.

St. Louis Post-Dispatch.

Stars and Stripes. March 24, 1945.

———. April 9, 1945.

United Press International.

Washington Post. "Remembering Bess." October 19, 1982.

INTERVIEWS

Voices of the Manhattan Project Oral Histories, including Lilli Hornig, Thomas O. Jones, and George Caron.

The Harry S. Truman Library and Museum: Oral history interview with George M. Elsey.

Ruth Huddleston, interview, July 21, 2019.

Hideko Tamura Snider, interviews, July and August 2019.

INDEX

NOTE: **Bold** page numbers refer to images.

Acheson, Dean, 255
Advisory Committee on Uranium, 45–46
Alamogordo, New Mexico
    testing of atomic bomb at, 117, 122–35, **124, 127,**
      131, 133, 135, 136–37, 152, 166
    testing of B-29s at, 22
Alcoa, 146
Alperovitz, Gar, 253
Alvarez, Luis, 132, **133**
American Baptist Foreign Mission, 82
American Volunteer Motor Ambulance Corps, 30,
    98
amphibious operations, 32, 192. *See also* frogmen;
    Underwater Demolition Teams; *specific person*
Army Air Force, U.S.: and dropping of atomic bomb,
    188
Army Corps of Engineers, U.S.: in Belgian Congo,
    47
Army, U.S.
    on Okinawa, 34
    and testing of atomic bomb, 126, 133–34
Arnold, Henry "Hap," 22, 94
Ashworth, Frederick, 241, 242
Associated Press: and testing of atomic bomb, 133
atomic bomb—target for, determination of, 62,
    63–73, 87, 162, 169, 175–78, 182–83
atomic bomb—testing of
    at Alamogordo, 117, 122–35, **124, 127, 131, 133,**
      135, 136–37, 152, 156, 166
    and briefing about Hiroshima mission, 200
    and debate about atomic/nuclear weapons,
      166–67
    and description of explosion, 131–32, **131,** 141,
      160, 166, 200, 211
    and development of bomb, 62, 63, 83, 98,
      101–2

Groves report about, 160–61
    and Potsdam Conference, 62, 117, 122–23,
      136–37, 140, 141
    press releases about, 250
Atomic Energy Commission, 249, 265–66
atomic/nuclear age
    arms race in, 85, 165
    beginning of, 116, 134, 150, 151, 211, 247,
      256
    debate about, 248–56
    government control in, 255
    military control in, 249
    peaceful/civilian uses in, 188, 211, 249
atomic/nuclear weapons
    assembling of, 47–48
    backups of, 86, 169
    complexity of, 43
    debate about, 13, 81–87, 94–98, 102, 106, 149,
      150–51, 166–67, 235–36, 248–56, 267,
      269–74
    espionage concerning, 172
    firing system for, 70, 171–73
    funding for development of, **46**
    importance/significance of, 48, 49, 63, 83, 84,
      134–35, 160, 211, 248–56, 273
    method for delivery of, 23
    power of, 48, 204, 213–14, 233, 234, 242,
      256
    public reaction to use of, 246–47, 249–50,
      252, 254
    readiness of, 159–60
    security concerning, 107–10, **108**
    spread of, 253
    stockpile of, 256
    triggering of, 67, 71–72, 116, 126, 127, 130–31,
      173

atomic/nuclear weapons (*cont.*)
    See also atomic bomb—target for; atomic
        bomb—testing of; atomic/nuclear age; Fat
        Man; Hiroshima—bombing of; Little Boy;
        Los Alamos, New Mexico; Manhattan Project;
        specific person or topic
Attlee, Clement, 139, 170, 174, 180, 186
Atwood, Julius, 3
Ayers, Eben, 233–34

B-17 Flying Fortress airplanes, 21, 22
B-29 Superfortress airplanes
    as backup at Iwo Jima, 206, 213, 218
    and Berlin Blockade, 253
    crash of, 203
    Ferebee picture of, 271
    and Korean War, 253
    modifications on, 91–92
    overloading of, 203
    and preparations for dropping atomic bomb, 173,
        182, 183, 203, 204
    production of, 88–89, 91–92
    testing of, 22, 89
    and Tibbets-LeMay Rota training flight, 157
    on Tinian Island, 26, 155–56, 157
    training school for, 22
    See also specific airplane or person
B-29 Superfortress (No. 82). *See Enola Gay*
Baby Ruth candy bars: and Tibbets as pilot, 19
Bainbridge, Kenneth, 125, 134, 135
Baldwin, Hanson, 248
Barkley, Alben, 37
Barnes, Harry Elmer, 252
Barnes, Philip, 241
Battle of the Bulge, 53
Beahan, Kermit, 242
Belgian Congo, as source of uranium, 47
Berlin, Germany
    destruction in, 121, 122–23, **122**
    and division of Germany, 186
    Truman tour of, 121–23, **122**
Beser, Jacob
    appearance of, 65
    and bombing of Hiroshima, **65**, 218, 224, 226,
        228
    dangers facing, 215–16
    death of, 272
    and debate about atomic/nuclear weapons,
        272–73
    family of, 272
    importance of, 152–53
    and Laurence, 211, 218
    Los Alamos visit of, 69–71
    personal/professional background of, 24–25,
        66, 68
    personality of, 65
    photograph of, **65, 217**

post-war life of, 272–73
    and preparations for dropping atomic bomb, 206,
        211–12, 215–16
    as radar specialist, 25, 66, 67–68, 152–53
    recording equipment of, 224, 226, 228
    recruited for Manhattan Project, 24–25,
        68–69
    responsibilities of, 70
    rice paper for, 211–12
    as strike crew member, 183–84
    and Target Committee, 62, 64–65, 72–73
    and Tibbets, 64, 65, 68–69, 72, 73, 152–53,
        157–58
    at Wendover Airfield, 24–25, 68
Beser, Rose, 66
Bethe, Hans, 70
Bevin, Ernest, 180
Bhagavad Gita (Hindu scripture), 8, 15, 134
The Big Stink (B-29), 183, 218
Blanchard, William, 156, 157, 189
Bliven, Bruce, 248–49
Bock, Frederick, 206, 240
Bock's Car (B-29), 206, 240–42, 244
Boeing, 22
Boettiger, Anna, 3
Boettiger, John, 3
Bohlen, Chip, and Potsdam Conference, 139
Bohr, Niels, 46, 70, 113
Bradley, Omar, 150
Britain/British
    and development of atomic bomb, 40, 46
    elections of 1945 in, 119, 169, 174, 180
    and Japanese peace negotiations, 148, 149
    and Potsdam Conference, 139, 148, 149, 180
    and Potsdam Declaration, 161
    and status of atomic bomb, 187–88
    and Truman tells Stalin about Manhattan Project,
        164
    Truman visit to, 187–88
    and world balance of power, 186
    See also Churchill, Winston
Brooklyn Dodgers, 197–98
Burchett, Wilfred, 250–51
Bush, Vannevar, **14**, 83
Byrnes, James
    and bombing of Hiroshima, 233
    and debate about use of atomic bomb, 84–85
    elections of 1944 and, 37
    and Groves report about testing of atomic bomb,
        160
    as head of Office of War Mobilization, 37
    and Japanese surrender, 149, 161, 246
    and Potsdam Conference, 118, 121, **122**, 136,
        139, 160
    professional background of, 37, 84
    Szilard meeting with, 84, 85
    and testing of atomic bomb, 136

Cabinet
and debate about the atomic bomb, 94–98
FDR and, 36
and FDR's death, 4–5
and Truman return from Potsdam, 238–39
Truman's first meeting with, 4–6
Truman's style with, 36
calutron machines, 59–61, **60**
Caron, George "Bob"
and bombing of Hiroshima, 226, 228
and debate about atomic bomb, 204
Dodgers ball cap of, 196, 197–98, 208, 218, 269
and *Enola Gay* departure/flight to Hiroshima,
218, 219, 221, 222–23
and Lewis relationship with enlisted men, 176
photograph of, **209**, **217**, 219
post-war life of, 269
and preparations for dropping atomic bomb,
196–98, 199, 207–8, **209**
as strike crew member, 184
Tibbets recruitment of, 25
Caron, Kay, 198
casualties
from amphibious operations, 32
from bombing of Tokyo, 163
and debate about atomic bomb, 82, 85, 86, 95,
96
of flight crew after dropping atomic bomb, 92
and German surrender, 51–52, 53
in Hiroshima, 262
on Kyushu, 192
on Luzon, 95
on Okinawa, 95, 96, 162–63
and Operation Olympic, 192
in Pacific, 163
in Philippines, 95
and U.S./allied invasion of Japan, 86, 95, 142,
168, 192
in war with Japan, 256
in World War II, 246
Cecilienhof Palace (site for Potsdam Conference),
138, 139, 165
Chiang Kai-Shek, 169
Chicago Tribune: and debate about atomic/nuclear
weapons, 248
China, 149, 161, 162, 169, 179
Churchill, Winston
and decision about use of atomic bomb, 142, 161,
162
demeanor of, 143
and development of atomic bomb, 46, 141
dream of, 169–70
and Eastern Europe, 62–63
elections of 1945 and, 119, 169, 174, 180
FDR and, 118, 121, 141
and Manhattan Project, 141
pictures of, **144**

at Potsdam Conference, 62, 117–21, 139–43, **144**,
148, 161, 162, 164, 170, 186
speeches of, 30
Stimson and, 161
and telling Stalin about atomic bomb, 142, 164
Truman and, 118, 120–21, 141–42, 143, 164, 180
at Yalta, 3, 62, 140
Clark, Mark, 18, 21
Cold War, 187, 249, 253, 275
Colorado Springs, Colorado: meeting at Second Air
Force headquarters in, 22–23
Columbia University: Manhattan Project team at, 164
communism, 108–9, 265–66, 275. *See also specific
person*
Compton, Arthur, 85
Conant, James, 83, 105, 115, 132
Congress
and debate about atomic/nuclear weapons, 82, 249
declaration of war on Japan by, 8
FDR speech about Pearl Harbor before, 8
and FDR's death, 4
and Potsdam Conference, 170
and Rayburn's "Board of Education" office, 1–2
Truman speeches before, 161
Council for a Livable World, 249
Crum, Alfred Harry, 20, 156
cyanide capsules, 214

D-Day, 53, 150
Das Kapital (Marx), 109
Davies, John, 155
Davies, Joseph, 139, 143, 170
Davis, Chelsey, 54
Dawn Over Zero (Laurence), 268
"Delivery Group," 70
Doll, Ed, 211–12
Doolittle, Jimmy, 21–22
Downey, William, 214–15, 220, 221
"Downfall". *See* Japan: U.S. invasion of
draft, armed forces, 29
DuPont, 9
Duzenbury, Wyatt, 184, 207–8, **209**, **217**, 220

Eaker, I.C., 94
Early, Steve, 2, 3
Easterly, Elliot, 215
Eastern Europe, 62–63, 118, 140, 149, 170, 186, 275
Eatherly, Claude, 184–85
Edwards, Ralph, 252
Eichelberger, Robert, 98
Einstein, Albert
and debate about atomic/nuclear weapons, 249
letter to FDR from, 44–45, **45–46**, 84, 249
personal/professional background of, 44–45
at Princeton University, 44, 265
regrets of, 249
security clearance for, 249

Eisenhower, Dwight D.
  and Allied victory in Europe, 150
  and debate about atomic/nuclear weapons, 94,
    150–51, 256
  and German surrender, 51
  and NBC show about atomic bomb, 269
  reputation of, 150
  and Stimson, 150
  and telling Stalin about atomic bomb, 150–51
  Tibbets as pilot for, 18, 21, 91
  Truman meeting with, 150–51
elections of 1944: Truman and, 36–37, 38, 39–40
elections of 1948: Truman and, 275
Emergency Committee of Atomic Scientists, 249
Enola Gay (B-29 Superfortress)
  crew of, 183–84, **217**, 219, **219**, 223–24, 237–38,
    252, 269–74
  dangers for, 214
  and debate about bombing of Hiroshima, 254
  departure of, 218–19, **219**, 220–21
  and "Enola Gay" paint job, 207, 208–10
  flight to Hiroshima of, 220–26
  honors/rewards for crew of, 238
  Lewis as pilot/copilot of, 175, 176–77, 198,
    218–19
  Lewis log about flight of, 218–19, 223, 224, 225,
    228
  loading of Little Boy on, 204, **205**, 207
  naming of, 206–7
  photograph of, **65**, **217**, 219, **219**
  and preparations for dropping atomic bomb, 204,
    205, 206
  and reactions to bombing of Hiroshima, 237–38
  recording of flight of, 224, 226, 228
  and return from Hiroshima, 227–30, 237–38
  and shock waves, 227–28
  as stored at Andrews Air Force Base, 254
  as strike plane, 177, 178, 183, 198, 200, 213
  Tanimoto check from crew of, 252
  as Tibbets airplane, 208–10
  Tibbets as pilot of, 177, 178, 183–84, 200, 218
  Tibbets tells crew about carrying the atomic
    bomb, 223–24
  triggering of bomb on, 203–4, 221–22, 224
  weight of, 220
Ent, Uzal G., 23
espionage, 107, 164–65, 172

"Fair Deal" program, 275
Farrell, Thomas
  and Besar testimony before Target Committee,
    72, 73
  and bombing of Nagasaki, 241
  and crash of B-29s, 203
  and debate about atomic bomb, 160
  and *Enola Gay* flight to/from Hiroshima, 220, 238
  Groves and, 202

  instructions for, 167
  and preparations for dropping of atomic bomb,
    202–3
  professional background of, 202
  and Target Committee, 64, 72, 73
  and testing of atomic bomb, 132
Fat Man
  and bombing of Nagasaki, 239–42, **243**, 244
  and design of B-29 airplanes, 92
  picture of, **240**
  as plutonium bomb, 71, 241
  power of, 71, 242, 256
  Russian spying on, 165
  testing of, 123, 125–35
  triggering of, 71–72
FBI (Federal Bureau of Investigation): Oppenheimer
    dossier at, 109
FDR. *See* Roosevelt, Franklin D.
Federation of Atomic Scientists, 249
Ferebee, Mary Ann (wife), 271
Ferebee, Thomas
  appearance of, 24
  and bombing of Hiroshima, 226, 228, 237–38
  death of, 271
  and debate about atomic/nuclear weapons, 271
  and departure/flight to Hiroshima, 225
  in European War, **24**
  family of, 271
  Lewis and, 89, 176
  and naming of *Enola Gay,* 206–7
  personal/professional background of, 23–24
  photographs of, **24**, **209**, **217**
  post-war life of, 271
  and preparations for dropping of atomic bomb,
    188–90, 198, 207–8, **209**, 216–17
  and return from Hiroshima, 237–38
  and rivalry about atomic bomb mission, 156
  and Rota training flight, 157
  as strike crew member, 183
  and targets for dropping of atomic bomb, 175
  Tibbets and, 23–24, **24**, 89, 271, 274
  on Tinian Island, 156, 157
  Van Kirk and, 23–24, **24**, 89, 271
  at Wendover Airfield, 23–24
Fermi, Enrico, 44, **45**, 70, 83, 113, 114, 128, 129
Finch, Bob, 197–98
First Army, U.S., 82
first1st Ordnance Squadron, 153
509th Composite Group
  and assigning atomic bomb mission to another
    group, 156–57, 189
  and B-29 production, 88, 91–92
  and bombing of Nagasaki, 239–42, **243**, 244
  and dropping of atomic bomb, 168, 175–78,
    182–85
  image of, 155
  poem about, 155

and preparations for dropping atomic bomb, 196–201, 202–17, **209**

raucous behavior among, 17, 26

secrecy about, 154–55

squadrons/groups comprising, 153

Tibbets as commander of, 17–18, 92

Tibbets briefing about Manhattan Project for, 26, 68

on Tinian Island, 26–27, 88, 91, 92, 152–58, 168, 175–78, 182–85

training of, 17, 26, 68, 92, 156–57

at Wendover Airfield, 17–18, 23–27

See also Operation Silverplate; *specific person*

Forbes, Malcolm, 270

Forrestal, James, 94, 96

Fort Pierce, Florida: Kauffman training group at, 31

Franck, James, 85, 167

Frisch, Otto, 235

frogmen, 32–35, 98, 99, 100

See also Underwater Demolition Teams; *specific person*

Fuchs, Klaus, 164–65

Fulbright, J. William, 266

Full House (B-29), 183

Furman, Robert, 171–72, 173

Gallup, George, 250

Gentry, Sue, 246

George VI (king of England): Truman visit with, 187–88

Germany

allied discussions about dealing with post-war, 143

declares war against U.S., 8

and development of atomic bomb, 44–45, **46**, 49, 84, 107–8, 172, 249

division of, 186

and Kauffman as prisoner of war, 30

and rules of engagement, 82–83

Russian nonaggression pact with, 109

surrender of, 50–52, 53, 81

U.S. invasion of, 150

See also Berlin, Germany; Potsdam Conference

Glenn L. Martin bomber plant (Omaha, Nebraska), 91–92

God's Wind at Hiroshima (Lewis), 270

Goodman, Virgil, 61

Graham, Frank, 233

Grand Island, Nebraska: B-29 training school in, 22

Great Artiste (B-29), 176, 183, 184, 213, 222, 239–40

Great Britain. *See* Britain/British

Groves, Leslie R.

and assembling of atomic bomb, 47–48

and bombing of Hiroshima, 234–35

and communism, 108, 109

death of, 267

and debate about atomic/nuclear weapons, 83, 267

and *Enola Gay* departure, 218

and espionage activities, 107

Farrell and, 202

FDR letter to Oppenheimer about, 13, **14**

Furman and, 172

as head of manufacturing phase of Manhattan Project, 42

as head of S-1 Task Force, 46

and Laurence role in Manhattan Project, 112, 114

and Oak Ridge facility, 60

Oppenheimer and, 10, 48, 109, 167, 234–35, 267

and Pentagon construction, 42

personal/professional background of, 42

personality/appearance of, 42, 48

picture of, **43**

post-war life of, 267

and preparations for dropping of atomic bomb, 202, 204

reports from, 48–49, 160–61

reputation of, 42

scientists relationship with, 13, 14, **14**, 48, 109

and secrecy of Manhattan Project, 43, 107

and security at Los Alamos, 107, 109–10

and testing of atomic bomb, 63, 101, 102, 123, 128–29, 131, 132, 134, **135**, 136, 141, 152, 160–61

Tibbets meeting with, 26–27

Truman/Stimson meeting and, 40, 48–49

and uranium supply, 47

Guam: LeMay-Tibbets-Ferebee meeting on, 188–90

Hanford, Washington, 47, 114, 249

Hannegan, Robert, 39

Harrison, George, 141

Harty, Tom, 3

Harvard University: women at, 104

Hata, Shunroku, 73

Hawkins, David, 16

Hersey, John, 251–52

high-altitude bombing, 92

"the Hill" (Los Alamos), 11

Hirohito (emperor of Japan)

American public opinion about, 161–62

bombing of palace of, 185

and graffiti on atomic bomb, 204

and Japanese surrender, 86, 142, 148, 149, 161–62, 245–46, 254

as spiritual embodiment of Japan, 245

and status of emperor, 142, 148, 149, 161–62

Hiroshima

Aioi Bridge in, 189–90, **190**, 225, 226

blackout of information about, 250

bomb shelters in, 78

casualties in, 262

destruction in, 228, **229**, 232, 236, 250–52

evacuation of children from, 74–80

filming of, 250

Hiroshima (*cont.*)
  and "final assault" plan, 78
  interviews of survivors of, 251–52
  maps of, 188–90, **190**
  Memorial Dome in, **263**
  photographs of, 188–90, **190**, **263**
  Pope John Paul visit to, 270
  post-war, 260–64
  as potential target for atomic bomb, 63, 163, 169,
    182–83
  radiation in, 262
  Truman visit to, 255
  World Peace Center in, 252
  See also Hiroshima—bombing of; Tamura, Hideko
Hiroshima—bombing of
  anniversaries of, 253–54
  backup for, 183, 206, 213, 218
  and debate about atomic/nuclear weapons, 269–70
  and *Enola Gay* departure/flight to Hiroshima,
    218–26
  explosion of bomb on, 226, 227–32, **229**, 238
  and graffiti on bomb, 204
  importance/significance of, 168
  instructions concerning, 167, 168, 182–83
  and Japanese surrender, 239, 245
  and loading of Little Boy on *Enola Gay*, 204, **205**,
    207
  navigation for, 216
  NBC TV movie about, 270
  observation planes for, 169, 183, 206, 213
  operational considerations for, 162
  photographs about, 183, 208, **209**, **217**, 220
  and power of bomb, 204, 213–14, 234
  preparations/plan for, 171–73, 175–78, 182–85,
    188–90, **190**, 196–201, **199**, 202–12, **209**,
    213–17
  press release about, 233–34
  psychological impact of, 167
  public reaction to, 246–47, 249–50, 252, 254
  recording of, 224, 226, 228
  and return from Hiroshima, 227–30
  rules for, 214
  schedule for, 181
  secrecy about, 171, 172, 181–82
  selection of planes for, 183
  strike crew for, 177, 183–85
  strike date for, 182, 190, 202–3
  strike plane for, 183–84, 213
  survivors of, 271
  takeoff for, 210
  as target for atomic bomb, 73, 188–90, **190**, 224
  Tibbets tells crew about carrying the atomic bomb
    and, 223–24
  top-secret order for, 181–82
  and triggering of bomb, 203–4, 207, 221–22, 224
  Truman decision/order about, 159, 160–61,
    162–63, 168–70, 180–81, **181**, 182–83, 255–56

Truman learns about bombing of, 232–33
Truman views/statements about, 188, 239, 245,
  254–56
and weather, 202, 213
Hitler, Adolf, 43, 44, 50, 51, 121, 138, 169
Honshu Island, 73, 95, 192
Hope, Bob, 269
Hopkins, James, 176
Hornig, Donald
  and debate about atomic/nuclear weapons, 267
  and development of atomic bomb, 102, **103**,
    104–5, 106
  post-war life of, 266–67
  reactions to bombing of Hiroshima by, 235–36
  and testing of atomic bomb, 123, 125, 126,
    127–28, 130–31
Hornig, Lilli, 102–6, **103**, 127, 235–36, 266–67
Hubbard, Jack, 129
Huddleston, Lawrence, 52, 53, 54–58, **55**, 61,
  145–46, 236, 257–60, **259**
Hull, Cordell, 246
hydrogen bomb, 265, 266

Ie Shima Island, 33, 34
India, 253
Interim Committee: and debate about atomic bomb,
  83–84, 85–87, 94
Irvine, Bill, 155
"island hopping" strategy, 32
Israel, 253
Italy, 107
Iwo Jima: backup planes at, 183, 206, 213, 218

Jabbitt III (B-29), 183
Jacobs, Randall, 191, 192–93
James, Edwin, 114
Japan
  casualties in war with, 82, 256
  and development of atomic bomb, 107
  Doolittle attack on, 21–22
  meaning of victory in, 82
  morale in, 163
  and rules of engagement, 82–83
  Russia declares war on, 62, 96, 118, 137, 140, 142,
    148, 149, 150–51, 187, 239, 254
  Spaatz as supervisor of bombing of, 177
  strategy for war against, 32, 118
  strength of military force in, 82
  Truman views/comments about, 52, 142–43
  U.S./allied invasion of, 73, 86, 94–98, 140, 142,
    163, 168, 191–92
  U.S. bombings in, 145, 152, 163, 167, 185, 194, 272
  U.S. declaration of war against, 8
  U.S. dropping of leaflets over, 239
  war crimes of, 82
  and warning Japan about atomic bombs, 97, 102,
    239

See also Japan—surrender of; *specific person, location, or topic*
Japan—surrender of
allied negotiations with, 142–43, 148–51
and bombings of Hiroshima and Nagasaki, 239, 245
and China, 161, 162, 169
and debate about atomic/nuclear weapons, 254
and dropping of leaflets on Japan, 180
FDR and, 149, 247
and formal surrender of Japan, 246–47
Hirohito and, 86, 142, 148–49, 161–62, 245–46, 254
last chance for, 160
Potsdam Declaration and, 161, 169, 174, 179–80
public reaction to, 246–47, 249–50
and Russia-Japan peace deal, 148
and Truman decision about use of atomic bomb, 159, 160–61, 162, 169, 180
Truman views/statements about, 148, 245, 255
ultimatum for, 148, 161, 162, 169, 179–80
and "unconditional surrender," 94, 96, 149, 161, 162, 174, 179–80, 245, 246, 254
and warning about use of atomic bomb, 160, 169
Jeppson, Morris, 184, 198, 207, **217**, 220–21, 223
John Paul (pope), 270
Johnson, Lyndon B., **103**, 266
Joint Chiefs of Staff, 94, 96, 162
Jones, Thomas O., 12, 13, 15, 130, 132

Kaltenborn, H.V., 66
Kamikaze attacks, 180
Kauffman, Draper
appearance of, 193
and bombing of Hiroshima, 237
concerns/fears of, 99–100
and European war, 30
father's relationship with, 30, 98–99
and FDR death, 34
Jacobs meeting with, 192–93
and Jacobs-Turner letter, 191, 192–93
and Los Alamos, 35
in Oceanside, California, 98–100, 192–93
at Okinawa, 28, 29–30, 33–35, 98
and Operation Olympic, 191–92
and Pearl Harbor, 30–31
picture of, **31**
premonition of death of, 193
as prisoner of war, 30
professional background of, 30–32, **31**, 98–99
Pyle and, 34
and training of frogmen, 28, 29, 99, 100
two weeks leave for, 192–93
Kauffman, James "Reggie," 30, 98–99
Kauffman, Peggy, 192, 237
Keitel, Wilhelm, 51
Kerama Retto Island, 33

Kimita, Japan: and evacuation of children from Hiroshima, 74–80
King, Ernest, 94
Kirschenbaum, David, 270
Kirtland Air Force Base: Beser-Tibbets flight to, 69
Kistiakowsky, George, 105–6, 126, 132, 167
Kokura, Japan, 64, 169, 182–83, 239–40
Korea, and China, 149
Korean War, 253, 275
Koriyama, 175, 177
Kyle, William, **41**
Kyoto, Japan, 63, 162
Kyushu, 95, 96, 191–92

Lansdale, John, 22–23, 69–70
Laurence, Florence, 114
Laurence, William
appearance of, 111
Beser and, 211, 218
and bombing of Nagasaki, 240, 241, 242, 268
Conant and, 115
death of, 268
and *Enola Gay* departure/flight to Hiroshima, 218, 220
Groves and, 113, 114
Lewis and, 218–19, 223, 228
at Los Alamos, 111–16
and Manhattan Project, 114–16
as *New York Times* reporter, 112, **112**, 113, 114
Oppenheimer and, 113
personal/professional background of, 112–13
photograph of, **112**
post-war life of, 268
Pulitzer Prize for, 112, 268
reputation of, 112
Saturday Evening Post stories of, 113–14
and testing of atomic bomb, 129–30, 134
on Titian Island, **112**
War Department and, 211, 268
Lawrence Berkeley National Laboratory (California): espionage agents at, 107
Lawrence, Ernest O., 60
Leahy, William
and debate about atomic/nuclear weapons, 94–95, 96, 119, 188, 254
and formal surrender of Japan, 248
and George VI-Truman discussion, 188
Japanese peace negotiations and, 149
Potsdam Conference and, 119, 121, **122**, 139, 140, 186–87
and world balance of power, 186–87
Ledien, Harold, 33
LeMay, Curtis, 82, 88–89, 153, 156–57, 189–90, 239, 244
Lewis, Robert A.
AWOL Christmas flight of, 176
and B-29 planes, 88, 89, 92

Lewis, Robert A. (*cont.*)
  and bomb accident on runway, 176–77
  and bombing of Hiroshima, 228, 252, 269–70
  and bull story, 178
  death of, 270
  and debate about atomic/nuclear weapons,
    269–70
  Edwards interview of, 252
  and "82" (B-29 Superfortress), 175, 176
  and *Enola Gay* departure/flight to Hiroshima,
    218–19, 221, 223–24, 225
  and "Enola Gay" paint job, 208–10
  family of, 270
  Ferebee relationship with, 89
  flight log of, 269, 270
  and Hiroshima survivors, 270
  Laurence and, 218–19, 223, 228
  LeMay praise for, 88–89
  log of, 218–19, 223, 224, 225, 228
  and NBC show about atomic bomb, 269
  Newark flight of, 90–91
  in Omaha, 88, 90–91, 92
  personal/professional background of, 88–89
  personality of, 88, 89
  photograph of, **90**, **209**, **217**
  as pilot/copilot for dropping of atomic bomb,
    177, 178, 185, 198, 218–19
  and preparations for dropping atomic bomb, 198,
    207–10, **209**
  reputation of, 25, 88–89, 91
  and return from Hiroshima, 229–30
  and secrecy about Manhattan Project, 90
  and targets for dropping of atomic bomb, 175–78
  Tibbets and, 25, 89, 91, 176, 177–78, 185, 208–9,
    270
  and Tibbets-Blanchard Rota training flight, 157
Limited Test Ban Treaty (1963), 253
Lindbergh, Charles, 88, 89
Little Boy
  bomb-making materials for, 171–73
  and design of B-29s, 92
  firing mechanism for, 71
  instability of, 71
  power of, 204, 213–14, 234, 242, 256
  testing of, 125
  triggering of, 71
  as type of atomic bomb, 71
  uranium core of, 71, 125
  weight of, 71, 220
  See also atomic bomb—target for; atomic
    bomb—testing of; atomic/nuclear weapons;
    Hiroshima—bombing of
Little White House: at Potsdam Conference, 119–
    21, **120**, 136, 140, 159, 160, 162, 168, 179, 187
London *Daily Express*, Burchett story in, 250–51
London, England, bombing of, 30
LORAN (Long Range Navigation) beam, 72–73

Los Alamos, New Mexico
  Beser visit to, 69–71
  and debate about atomic/nuclear weapons,
    166–67, 249
  description of, 11
  and Groves-Oppenheimer relationship, 48
  Kauffman knowledge about, 35
  as place for assembling atomic bomb, 47–48
  post-war activities at, 264–65
  and proximity fuse development, 67
  reactions to bombing of Hiroshima at, 234–36
  reactions to testing of atomic bomb at, 166–67
  research at, 114
  restrictions on employees at, 107
  Russian spy at, 164–65
  scientists at, 69, 70–71, 166–67, 234–36
  secrecy about, 48
  security at, 107–8, **108**, 110
  as Site Y (Weapons and Design Lab), 48
  See also Manhattan Project; *specific person*
Luzon: casualties on, 95

MacArthur, Douglas
  as allied supreme commander over Japan, 246
  and debate about use of atomic bomb, 94
  and dropping of atomic bomb, 168
  and formal surrender of Japan, 246
  orders blackout of information, 250, 251
  in Philippines, 95
  and U.S. invasion of Japan, 192
Manhattan Project
  authorization of, 8–9, 256
  beginning of, 41
  cost of, 152, 256
  doubts about, 13
  and doubts about Truman, 9
  espionage at, 107, 164–65
  FDR and, 8–9, 13, **14**, 256
  and FDR's death, 8–9, 12–16
  Groves report about, 48–49
  Laurence stories about, 111–16
  military domination of, 84
  Oppenheimer as director of, 7–16, 109
  purpose of, 7, 23
  recruitment of scientists for, 10
  and restrictions on scientists, 13, **14**, 48
  as "S-1," 41
  scientists involved in, 13, **14**, 17–18, 48, 70
  secrecy about, 6, 35, 36, 41, 43, 48, 49, 68–69, 90,
    97, 105, 107, 114, 130, 132–34
  security for, 107–10
  Truman concerns about, 93–94
  Truman informs Stalin about, 163–64, 165
  Truman-Stimson briefing/discussion about, 6,
    36, 40
  uncertainty about future of, 8–9, 16
  See also specific person

Manley, John, 234
Marines, U.S.: on Okinawa, 34
Marshall, George, 94, 95, 136, 162–63, 168, 202
Marshall Plan, 276
Maruki, Ira, 250
Maruki, Toshi, 250
Marx, Karl, 109
Massachusetts Institute of Technology:
    Oppenheimer lecture at, 113
McCarthy, Joseph, 275
McCloy, John J., 94, 96–97
McKibbin, Dorothy, 11
McVay, Charles II, 172
military
    control of atomic/nuclear technology by,
        249
    domination of Manhattan Project by, 84
    See also specific person or branch
Miyoshi (Hideko's friend), 74, 78, 194, 195–96,
    261–62
Molotov, Vyacheslav, 165
Monsanto, 9
Morrison, Philip, 9, 13, 15, 102
Moynahan, John, 167
Mutual Assured Destruction (MAD), 253

Nagasaki
    blackout of information about, 250
    bombing of, 239–42, 243, 244, 249–50, 268
    casualties at, 242
    debriefing about, 244
    devastation of, 250
    explosion of bomb at, 242, 243, 244
    filming of, 250
    as target for atomic bomb, 163, 169, 242, 244
    Truman statement about, 245
National Air and Space Museum (Smithsonian):
    fiftieth anniversary exhibit at, 253–54
National Aviation Hall of Fame, 273
National Review: and debate about atomic/nuclear
    weapons, 252
Navy Department, U.S.: and bombing of Hiroshima,
    232
Navy, U.S.: bomb disposal school for, 30–31, 31
NBC
    The Story of the Atomic Bomb on, 269
    TV movie about bombing of Hiroshima by, 270
Necessary Evil (B-29), 183, 213, 222
Nelson, Richard H. "Junior," 184, 207–8, 209, 217,
    224, 228, 230
New Republic: Bliven story in, 248–49
New York Times
    and debate about atomic/nuclear weapons,
        248
    Laurence stories in, 268
    and Laurence's Pulitzer Prize, 268
    and Lewis log, 219

Truman interview with, 255
    See also Laurence, William
New Yorker magazine: cartoons from, 251
Newark, New Jersey: Lewis flight to, 90–91
Niigata, 64, 169, 182–83
Nimitz, Chester, 30, 154, 168
97th Bombardment Group: Tibbets as commander
    of, 21
Nolan, James, 171–72, 238
Norden bomb sight, 216–17
North Atlantic Treaty Organization (NATO), 276
North Korea, 253
nuclear bombs. See atomic/nuclear weapons

Oak Ridge, Tennessee
    creation of uranium enrichment facility at, 47, 56
    and debate about atomic/nuclear weapons, 249
    life in, 145–47
    secrecy at, 53, 58–59
    as site of world's first nuclear reactor, 47
    uranium separation plants at, 114
    workers at, 58–61, 60
    See also Sisson, Ruth
observation planes
    and bombing of Hiroshima, 169, 183, 206, 213,
        242
    and bombing of Nagasaki, 242
Oceanside, California: Kauffman in, 98–100, 192–93
Okinawa, Japan
    Bock's Car return to, 244
    casualties on, 34, 95, 96, 162–63
    Draper at, 98
    frogmen on, 28–29, 33–35
    Japanese attacks on, 28
    logistical proximity to Japan of, 33
    Marshall description of battle for, 162–63
    Pyle story about, 34
    U.S. base/forces on, 34, 99
Omaha, Nebraska: B-29 production in, 88–89,
    91–92
Operation Coronet, 192
Operation Olympic. See Kyushu
Operation Silverplate, 23–27. See also 509th
    Composite Group; Tibbets, Paul Jr.
Oppenheimer, J. Robert
    appearance of, 9, 102
    and Atomic Energy Commission, 265
    awards/honors for, 266
    and bombing of Hiroshima, 234–35
    and communism, 108–9, 265–66
    death of, 266
    and debate about atomic/nuclear weapons, 83, 85,
        86, 103, 254–55, 264–65, 266
    and development of atomic bomb, 204
    dinner parties of, 11, 11
    as director of Manhattan Project, 7–16, 109
    family of, 11

Oppenheimer, J. Robert (*cont.*)
  FBI dossier on, 109
  FDR and, 12–13, **14**
  and FDR eulogy/memorial service, 7, 8, 12–16
  Groves and, 10, 48, 109, 167, 234–35, 267
  and instructions for dropping atomic bomb,
    167
  as Interim Committee member, 83
  and Los Alamos as place for assembling atomic
    bomb, 47–48
  as martyr, 266
  MIT lecture by, 113
  personal/professional background of, 9–10
  personality/talents of, 7–8, 9–10, 11
  picture of, **11**
  post-war life of, 264–66
  public image of, 266
  and reactions to testing of atomic bomb, 166,
    167
  reputation of, 166, 264, 266
  resignation of, 264–65
  and scientists, 102, 110
  as security risk, 265–66
  and Target Committee, 63
  and Teller petition, 102
  and testing of atomic bomb, 63, 101, 102, 123,
    125–26, **127**, 128–30, 134, 135, **135**
  Tibbets meeting with, 70
  Truman and, 16, 254–55
  See also specific person
Oppenheimer, Kitty, 11, 109, 126
Osaka, Japan: firebombing raids on, 82

Pacific: casualties in, 163
Pacific Fleet, 154
Pakistan, 253
Papalia, Joseph, 270
Parsons, Martha, 203
Parsons, William "Deak"
  and bombing of Hiroshima, 210, 227–28, 230,
    234, 238
  dangers facing, 214
  and *Enola Gay* departure/flight to Hiroshima,
    220–21, 223
  as explosives expert, 22, 203
  family of, 203
  Oppenheimer and, 203
  and overloading of B-29s, 203
  photograph of, **217**
  and preparations for dropping atomic bomb, 198,
    199, 200, 201, 203–4, 207
  professional background of, 184, 203
  and return from Hiroshima, 238
  as strike crew member, 184
  and suicide, 214
  and Tibbet meeting in Colorado Springs, 22
Pasco, Washington: defense project in, 41

Pearl Harbor
  Beser and, 66
  Japanese attack on, 8, 25, 66, 149, 162, 241, 245
  Kauffman and, 30–31
Pendergast, Jim, 37
Pendergast, Tom, 37, 38, 143
Pentagon: construction of, 42
Perry, Charles, 184, 210
Philippines, 95, 98, 193
Pika-don ("Flash-bang") (Maruki), 250
plutonium
  and backup bombs, 169
  firing unit for detonating, 106
  and Hanford facility, 114
  and Hornig research, 106
  and Oak Ridge facility, 47
  research about, 84
  shortage of, 86
  and testing of atomic bomb, 123–35
  uranium as source of, 47
  See also Fat Man
Porter, John, **217**
Potsdam Conference (1945)
  agenda for, 139–40
  atomic bomb as topic at, 119, 122–23, 136–37,
    141, 142, 181
  Berlin tour during, 121–23, **122**
  Cecilienhof Palace as site for, **138**, 139, 165
  Congress and, 170
  differences/disagreements at, 140, 170, 186
  and Eastern Europe, 118, 140, 149, 170, 186, 275
  and Japanese negotiations, 142–43
  Little White House at, 119–21, **120**, 136, 140,
    159, 160, 162, 168, 179, 187
  opening of, 138–39
  pictures at, **144**, 170
  Russia as host for, 139
  and telling Stalin about atomic bomb, 142,
    150–51, 163–64, 165
  and testing of atomic bomb, 62, 117, 122–23,
    136–37, 140, 141
  Truman as chairman of, 139
  Truman at, 117–23, **120**, 136–40, 141–44,
    148–51, 159–65, 168–70, 186–87
  and Truman decision about use of atomic bomb,
    159, 160–61, 162–63, 168–70
  Truman return from, 187–88, 238–39
  Truman statements/views about, 117–18,
    179–81, 186, 245
  and world balance of power, 186
  See also specific person or nation
Potsdam Declaration, 161, 169, 174, 179–80,
    246–47
Princeton University: scientists at, 44, 265, 266
prisoners of war, Americans as, 94, 161, 245
Project X. *See* Oak Ridge, Tennessee
proximity fuse, 67

pumpkin bombs, 152, 157, 215
Pyle, Ernie, 34

radar, 25, 66–68, 70, 152–53. *See also* Beser, Jacob
radiation/radioactivity, 106, 125–26, 172, 200, 210, 238, 262, 268
Ramsey, Norman, 22, 69, 70
Rayburn, Sam: "Board of Education" office of, 1–2
Raymond (Soviet courier), 164–65
Red Gremlin (Tibbets B-17 airplane), 21, 23, **24**, 206, 274
rice paper, 211–12
Rickey, Branch, 197
Roosevelt, Eleanor, 3–4, 247
Roosevelt, Franklin D.
    accomplishments of, 8
    authorization/approval of Manhattan Project by, 8–9, 13, **14**, 256
    Churchill and, 118, 121, 141
    death of, 3–6, 8–9, 34
    Einstein letter to, 44–45, **45–46**, 84, 249
    elections of 1944 and, 36–37, 38
    faith of, 15–16
    and German surrender, 51
    health decline of, 37
    and Japanese attack on Pearl Harbor, 8
    and Japanese surrender, 149, 247
    memorial service for, 7, 8
    mobilization of armed forces by, 29
    Oppenheimer and, 12–13, **14**
    reputation of, 276
    Stalin and, 118, 137
    style of, 36
    Szilard letter to, 84
    Truman relationship with, 3, 38, 39–40
    Truman to pursue agenda of, 5–6
    in Warm Springs, Georgia, 3
    at Yalta, 3, 62, 140
Rota: and Tibbets-Blanchard Rota training flight, 157
Royal Naval Volunteer Reserve: Kauffman in, 30
Russia
    and Berlin Blockage, 253
    and China, 149
    and debate about atomic/nuclear weapons, 96, 249, 252
    and declaring war on Japan, 62, 96, 118, 137, 140, 142, 148, 149, 150–51, 187, 239, 254
    deterioration in U.S. relations with, 275
    and development of atomic/nuclear weapons, 40, 48, 49, 84–85, 107, 164, 165, 253, 265
    and Eastern Europe, 118, 140, 149, 170, 186, 275
    German nonaggression pact with, 109
    as host for Potsdam Conference, 139
    Japan peace deal with, 148
    and Potsdam Conference, 62–63, 117–20, 137–40, 142–43, **144**, 148, 150–51, 163–64, 165, 169, 170, 181, 186

and security about atomic bomb, 107–8, **108**
    as spying on Manhattan Project, 164–65
    and testing of atomic bomb, 101
    Truman response to, 276
    U.S. arms treaties with, 253
    and world balance of power, 186
    See also Cold War; Stalin, Joseph

"S-1". *See* Manhattan Project
S-1 Task Force, 46–47
The Sacred Cow (Truman presidential plane), 187
Sato, Naotake (Japanese ambassador to Russia), 148
Saturday Evening Post: Laurence article in, 112–14
Schiffler, Hubert, 270
Schwenk, Lilli. *See* Hornig, Lilli
scientists
    age of, 69, 106
    background checks on, 108
    and bombing of Hiroshima, 235
    and bombing of Nagasaki, 240
    communism and, 107, 108, 109
    and debate about atomic/nuclear weapons, 84–85, 102, 106, 166–67, 249, 267
    and development of atomic bomb, 204, 237
    Groves relationship with, 13, 14, **14**, 48, 109
    influence of, 102
    Laurence interviews of, 115
    at Los Alamos, 69, 70–71
    Oppenheimer and, 102, 110
    and preparations for dropping the atomic bomb, 198, 210
    recruitment of, 10
    restrictions on, 13, **14**, 48
    screening and monitoring of, 109
    and security, 110
    and testing of atomic bomb, 125, 126, 128–29, 130, 166
    Tibbets discussions with, 17–18
    See also specific person or organization
Seabees: on Tinian Island, 153
Second General Army, Japanese, 73
2nd Armored Division, U.S., 121
security: for Manhattan Project, 107–10
Senate, U.S.
    Special Committee to Investigate the National Defense Program of, 38
    Truman as president of, 1
    Truman (Bess) on payroll of, 38, 39
Shawn, William, 251
shock waves, 92, 200, 227–28
Shumard, Robert H., 184, 207–8, **209**, **217**, 228, 269
Sisson, Beulah Marie (mother), 56–57, 145, 236
Sisson, Ruth, 52–61, **55**, **60**, 145–47, **147**, 236–37, 257–60, **259**
Sisson, W.D. (brother), 57, 58
Sisson, William (father), 145, 146
Site W. *See* Hanford, Washington

Site X. *See* Oak Ridge, Tennessee
Site Y. *See* Los Alamos, New Mexico
603rd Air Engineering Squadron, 153
Smith, Merriman, 188
Smithsonian
    National Air and Space Museum at, 253–54
    Udvar-Hazy Center of, 254
Snider, Hideko Tamura. *See* Tamura, Hideko
Soviet Union. *See* Russia
Spaatz, Carl, 168, 177, 238
Special Committee to Investigate the National
        Defense Program, Senate: Truman as chairman
        of, 38
St. Louis Post Dispatch: Truman comments in, 38
Stalin, Joseph
    appearance of, 137
    atomic bomb views of, 164
    Attlee and, 170
    and declaring war on Japan, 137, 140, 187
    demeanor of, 143
    and development of atomic bomb, 169
    and dropping of atomic bomb, 181
    and Eastern Europe, 62–63, 170, 186
    FDR and, 118, 137
    and Hitler's death, 138
    Japanese negotiations and, 142–43
    pictures of, **144**
    and Potsdam Conference, 62–63, 117–18, 120,
        137–40, 142–43, **144**, 148, 150–51, 163–64,
        165, 169, 170, 181, 186
    Truman and, 118, 138, 143, 186
    Truman informs Stalin about atomic bomb, 142,
        150–51, 163–64, 165
    at Yalta, 3, 62, 118, 137, 140
    See also Russia
Standard Oil, 9
State Department, U.S., and Potsdam Conference,
        118
Stiborik, Joseph "Joe," 184, 207–8, **209**, **217**, 218
Stilwell, Joseph, 29
Stimson, Henry
    appearance of, 42
    and bombing of Hiroshima, 233
    as in charge of Manhattan Project, 41
    Churchill and, 161
    and debate about atomic bomb, 81, 82–83, 86–87,
        94, 95–96, 159, 160–61, 162
    Eisenhower and, 150
    and Groves report, 48, 49
    health of, 136
    and Japanese surrender, 149, 161
    McCloy and, 97
    personal/professional background of, 40–41, 42
    picture of, **41**
    and potential targets for atomic bomb, 64
    and Potsdam Conference, 136, 141, 142, 159,
        160–61, 162, 168

    reputation of, 42
    and testing of atomic bomb, 136, 141, 142
    Truman briefing/discussion with, 6, 36, 40, 48, 49
    and Truman decision to drop atomic bomb, 168
    views about war of, 82–83
    War Department appointment of, 41
Stone, Harlan, 4, 5
Straight Flush (B-29), 183, 184–85, 206, 224
Strange Cargo (B-29), 176
Strategic Air Forces, U.S., 177
Strategic Bombing Survey, U.S., 262
Subic Bay (Philippines): Kauffman at, 98
Suzuki, Kantaro, 180
Sweeney, Charles, 176, 184, 239–40, 241, 242, 244
Szilard, Leo
    atomic theories of, 43–44, **45**
    Byrnes meeting with, 84
    and debate about atomic/nuclear weapons, 13,
        84–85, 102, 106, 167, 249
    Einstein and, 44, **45**, 84
    and Einstein letter to FDR, **45**, 84
    letter to FDR from, 84
    petition of, 13, 267
    Truman meeting with, 84

Tamura, Fumiko (aunt), 231
Tamura, Hideko, 74–80, **76**, 194–96, **195**, 230–32,
        260–64, **263**
Tamura, Hisao (uncle), 260
Tamura, Jiro (father), 74, 75–76, 77, 78, 79, 194, 230,
        260, 261, 262
Tamura, Kimiko (mother), 74, 75–77, **76**,
        78–79, 194, 195–96, 230, 231, 232, 260, 261,
        262
Tanimoto, Kiyoshi, 252
Target Committee, 62, 63–65, 72–73, 102
Teller, Edward, 102, 128, 132, 266
Tennessee Valley Authority, 56
1027th Air Materiel Squadron, 153
Thirty Seconds Over Tokyo (movie), 22
This Is Your Life show, 252
313th Bombardment Wing, 155
320th Troop Carrier Squadron, 153
390th Air Service Group, 153
393rd Bomb Squadron, 153
Tibbets, Enola Gay (mother), 20, 206–7, 209, 210
Tibbets, Lucy Wingate (wife), 18, 21
Tibbets, Paul Jr.
    appearance of, 18
    arrest of, 23
    awards/honors for, 238, 273
    B-29s and, 18–19, 22, 91–92, 271
    and bombing of Hiroshima, 204, 218, 219, **219**,
        220–21, 222–23, 224, 225, 226, 228–30, 237,
        238
    and bombing of Nagasaki, 239, 241, 244
    and bull story, 178

at Colorado Springs meeting, 22–23
concerns of, 215
and crew for dropping of atomic bomb, 177,
183–84
crew relationship with, 175, 182
cyanide capsules and, 214
death of, 273, 274
and debate about atomic/nuclear weapons, 255,
273–74
early interest in flying of, 19–20
in European war, 18–19, 21
family of, 18, 19, 20
favorite food of, 184, 210
first learns about Manhattan Project, 23
as "first strike" pilot, 91, 157, 177, 179, 182–83,
198, 200, 218
and 509th Composite Group briefing, 26
as 509th Composite Group commander, 17–18,
91–92
and 509th Composite Group secrecy, 154–55
good luck ritual of, 184
Groves meeting with, 26–27
and Hiroshima as target for atomic bomb, 73
and LeMay rivalry about atomic bomb mission,
156–57
Los Alamos visit by Beser and, 69–71
and naming of *Enola Gay,* 206–7
Oppenheimer meeting with, 70
personal/professional background of, 18–20,
21–22, 177, 220
personality of, 89, 220
photographs of, **21, 24, 209, 217**
post-war life of, 273–74
and potential targets for atomic bomb, 64,
175
and preparations for dropping atomic bomb,
182–85, 188–90, 198, **199,** 201, 203, 204,
206–8, **209,** 210, 213–16
and *Red Gremlin,* 21, 23, **24,** 206, 274
reputation/talents of, 18, 19, 91, 273
responsibilities of, 18
Rota training flight and, 157
scientists and, 17–18
Target Committee and, 62, 63, 64, 72, 73
and testing of atomic bomb, 63, 152, 156
and Tinian Island, 26–27, 152–58, 182–85
and training of airmen, 152
Truman meeting with, 255
See also Operation Silverplate; *specific person*
Tibbets, Paul Sr. (father), 19, 20, 206
Tinian Island
aerial views of, **154**
Bock's Car return to, 244
bomb accident on runway on, 176–77
and bombing of Nagasaki, 239–42, **243,** 244
"Destination" as code name for, 153
Enola Gay return to, 237–38

509th Composite Group on, 26–27, 88, 91, 92,
152–58, 168, 175–78, 182–85
Indianapolis voyage to, 171–73
as launching point for Japanese invasion, 153
Laurence at, **112**
layout of streets on, 153
as major U.S. military base, 153, 171–74
and preparations for dropping of atomic bomb,
202–18, **209**
rivalries on, 154–57
Seabees on, 153
uranium-235 transported to, 171–73
Tokyo, Japan, 162, 163, 192, 231
Trinity explosion. *See* atomic bomb—testing of
Truman, Elizabeth "Bess"
death of, 276
and Gentry, 246
and Japanese surrender, 247
on Senate payroll, 38, 39
Truman relationship with, 4, 38, 93, 117, 140, 148,
168, 179, 181, 238, 276
Truman, Harry S
achievements of, 275, 276
appearance of, 37
approval ratings for, 274–75
atomic/nuclear bomb views/concerns of, 93–94,
117–18, 149, 150–51, 161, 162, 168, 169, 187,
188
Bess relationship with, 4, 38, 39, 93, 117, 140, 148,
168, 179, 181, 276
death of, 276
and debate about atomic/nuclear weapons, 81,
82, 84, 87
elections of 1944 and, 36–37, 38–40
elections of 1948 and, 275
family of, 1, 4, 5, 179, 247
and FDR agenda, 5–6
FDR and, 3, 38, 39–40
fears of, 49
and German surrender, 50–52
health of, 168
and Japanese surrender, 246–47
personality/demeanor of, 36, 37, 143
pictures of, **144**
post-war challenges facing, 274–75
post-war/presidency life of, 274–76
professional background of, 37–38
and Rayburn's "Board of Education" office, 1–2
reputation of, 276
as Senate president, 1
as Senator, 37–39, 41
Stimson briefing/discussion with, 6, 36, 40, 48–49
swearing in as president of, 4–5, **5**
as vice president, 1–4
See also specific person or topic
Truman, Margaret, 4, 39, 93, 168, 180, 181
Truman, Mary, 255

Truman Committee, 38, 41
Tuckerman, Peggy, 31
Turner, Richmond, 31–32, 191, 192–93
20th Air Force, U.S., 153, 168

U-235 isotope, 47
Uanna, William, 224
Underwater Demolition Flotilla, 100
Underwater Demolition Teams, U.S, 31, 99. *See also*
    frogmen; *specific person*
Union Carbide, 9
United Kingdom. *See* British; Churchill, Winston
University of Chicago
    Hideko at, 264
    Metallurgical Laboratory at, 84, 114, 249
uranium
    and backup bombs, 169
    calutron machines for enrichment of, 59–61, **60**
    and Einstein letter to FDR, 44, 45, **45–46**
    FDR forms advisory committee on, 45–46
    German research with, 44–45, **45–46**
    as key to atomic energy, 115
    Laurence stories about, 114, 115
    and Oak Ridge facility, 47, 114
    and preparations for dropping atomic bomb, 182
    sources of, 47
    stealing of, 172
    transport to Tinian of, 171–73
    See also Little Boy
USS *Augusta*: Truman on, 118, 187, 188, 232–33
USS *Callaghan*: kamikaze attack on, 180
USS *Gilmer*, 29, 98
USS *Indianapolis*, 171–73, **173**, 204, 238

Van Kirk, Theodore "Dutch"
    and B-29s, 271
    and bombing of Hiroshima, 228, 253–54
    and debate about atomic/nuclear weapons,
        253–54, 272
    and *Enola Gay* departure/flight to Hiroshima,
        219, 221, 223, 225
    in European War, **24**, 89
    family of, 200, 271
    Ferebee and, 23–24, **24**, 89, 271
    Lewis and, 89, 176
    log of, 221
    and naming of *Enola Gay*, 206–7
    personal/professional background of, 23–24
    photographs of, **24**, **209**, **217**, 219

post-war life of, 271–72
and preparations for dropping atomic bomb, 198,
    200–201, 207–8, **209**, 216, 217
recruitment of, 23–24
and Rota flight of Tibbets and Blanchard, 157
as strike crew member, 183
and targets for dropping of atomic bomb, 175
Tibbets and, 23–24, **24**, 89, 274
at Wendover Airfield, 23–24

Wallace, Henry, 36, 37
Wallace, Madge, 4
War Department, U.S, 83, 94, 169, 211, 268. *See also*
    specific person
Warm Springs, Georgia: FDR in, 3
weather
    and bombing of Hirohito's palace, 185
    and bombing of Nagasaki, 239–40
    and dropping of atomic bomb, 70, 169, 182–83,
        202, 213, 218, 224, 239–40, 246
    and testing of atomic bomb, 123, 125, 134
Weisskopf, Victor, **11**
Wells, H.G., 44
Wendover Airfield (Utah), 509th Composite Group
    at, 17–18, 23–27, 68
Whitman, Alden, 255
Wilson, Anne, 167
Wilson, Robert, 167
women
    as "Calutron Girls," 60–61
    at Harvard University, 104
    as workers at Oak Ridge facility, 60–61
    See also specific person
Woods Hole Oceanographic Institution: Underwater
    Explosives Research Laboratory at, 105
World Peace Center (Hiroshima), 252
The World Set Free (Wells), 44
World War II
    casualties in, 246
    cost of, 82, 246
    debate about how to end, 94–98
    post-war life after, 257–76

Yalta Summit, 3, 62, 118, 137, 140
Yokohama, Japan: as potential target for atomic
    bomb, 64
Young, Don, 214

Zensho Temple (Japan), 74, 80

IMAGE CREDITS

PAGE/CREDIT

5   Harry S. Truman Presidential Library

11   Los Alamos National Laboratory

14   National Archives and Records Administration

21   National Archives and Records Administration

24   National Archives and Records Administration

31   National Archives and Records Administration

41   U.S. Department of Energy

43   U.S. Department of Energy

45   National Archives and Records Administration

55   Courtesy of Ruth Huddleston

60   Courtesy of Ruth Huddleston

65   Courtesy of Jacob Beser's family

76   Courtesy of Hideko Tamura Snider

90   National Archives and Records Administration

103   Lilli Hornig photo: Los Alamos National Laboratory
Donald Hornig photo: Lyndon Baines Johnson Presidential Library

108   National Archives and Records Administration

112   National Archives and Records Administration

120   United States Army Signal Corps, Harry S. Truman Presidential Library

122   United States Army Signal Corps, Harry S. Truman Presidential Library

124   Top: Los Alamos National Laboratory
Bottom: Los Alamos National Laboratory

127   Los Alamos National Laboratory

131   Los Alamos National Laboratory

133   National Archives and Record Administration

135   Los Alamos National Laboratory

138   United States Army Signal Corps, Harry S. Truman Presidential Library

144 Top: Harry S. Truman Presidential Library
    Bottom: Harry S. Truman Presidential Library
147 Courtesy of Ruth Huddleston
154 Atomic Heritage
173 Atomic Heritage
181 Harry S. Truman Presidential Library
190 National Archives and Records Administration
195 Courtesy of Hideko Tamura Snider
199 National Archives and Records Administration
205 Top: National Archives and Records Administration
    Bottom: Courtesy of the 509th Composite Group
209 National Archives and Records Administration
217 National Archives and Records Administration
219 National Archives and Records Administration
229 National Archives and Records Administration
240 National Archives and Records Administration
243 National Archives and Records Administration
259 Courtesy of Ruth Huddleston
261 National Archives and Records Administration
263 Courtesy of Hideko Tamura Snider

ABOUT THE AUTHORS

CHRIS WALLACE is the anchor of *Fox News Sunday*, Fox Broadcasting's Sunday morning public affairs program. He joined Fox News in 2003. In his seventeen years at Fox, Wallace has covered almost every key political event, and he has interviewed U.S. and world leaders, including seven American presidents. Wallace was the first journalist from Fox News to moderate a general election presidential debate in October 2016. Throughout his fifty-plus years in broadcasting, Wallace has won every major broadcast news award for his reporting, including three Emmy Awards, the duPont-Columbia Silver Baton, and the Peabody Award.

MITCH WEISS is a Pulitzer Prize–winning investigative journalist for the Associated Press, covering subjects ranging from military misconduct, government corruption, and white collar crimes to the housing meltdown and unsafe medical devices. He is also the critically acclaimed author or coauthor of seven books.